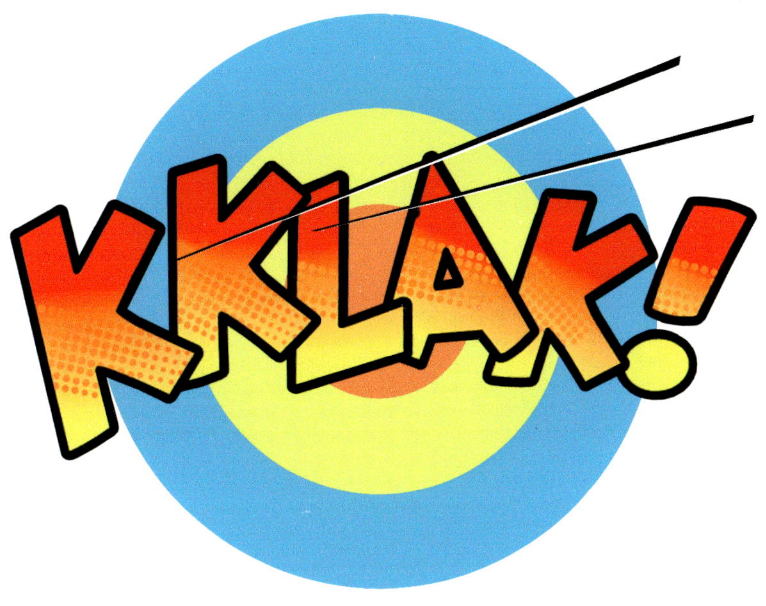

I would like to dedicate this book to all the fans who have followed and loved my Doctor Who *art from childhood to the present day.*

Chris Achilléos 1947-2021

THE DOCTOR WHO ART OF CHRIS ACHILLÉOS

The right of Chris Achilléos to be identified as the Author of the Work has been asserted by him in accordance with the Copyright, Designs and Patents Act 1988.

Copyright © Chris Achilléos 2021/24
Artwork © Chris Achilléos 2021/24
Text © Candy Jar 2021/24

An Unofficial Doctor Who Book.
Please check out the bibliography at the back of this title if you wish to purchase any of the available BBC books or CDs.

Many thanks to Craig Robins for his digital experience.

Published by
Candy Jar Books, Mackintosh House,
136 Newport Road, Cardiff, CF24 1DJ
www.candyjarbooks.co.uk
www.chrisachilleos.co.uk

Printed and bound in the UK by
ESP Colour, Millbuck Close, Swindon, SN2 8XU
on responsibly sourced paper

Book design by Shaun Russell & Chris Achilléos
Editor: Shaun Russell
Edited by Rachael Russell, Karen North & Will Rees
Doctor Who is © British Broadcasting Corporation 1963, 2024

*"Chris Achilléos' artwork perfectly captures the
action packed spirit of 1970s* Doctor Who.
It's like he invented it himself."
Peter Capaldi

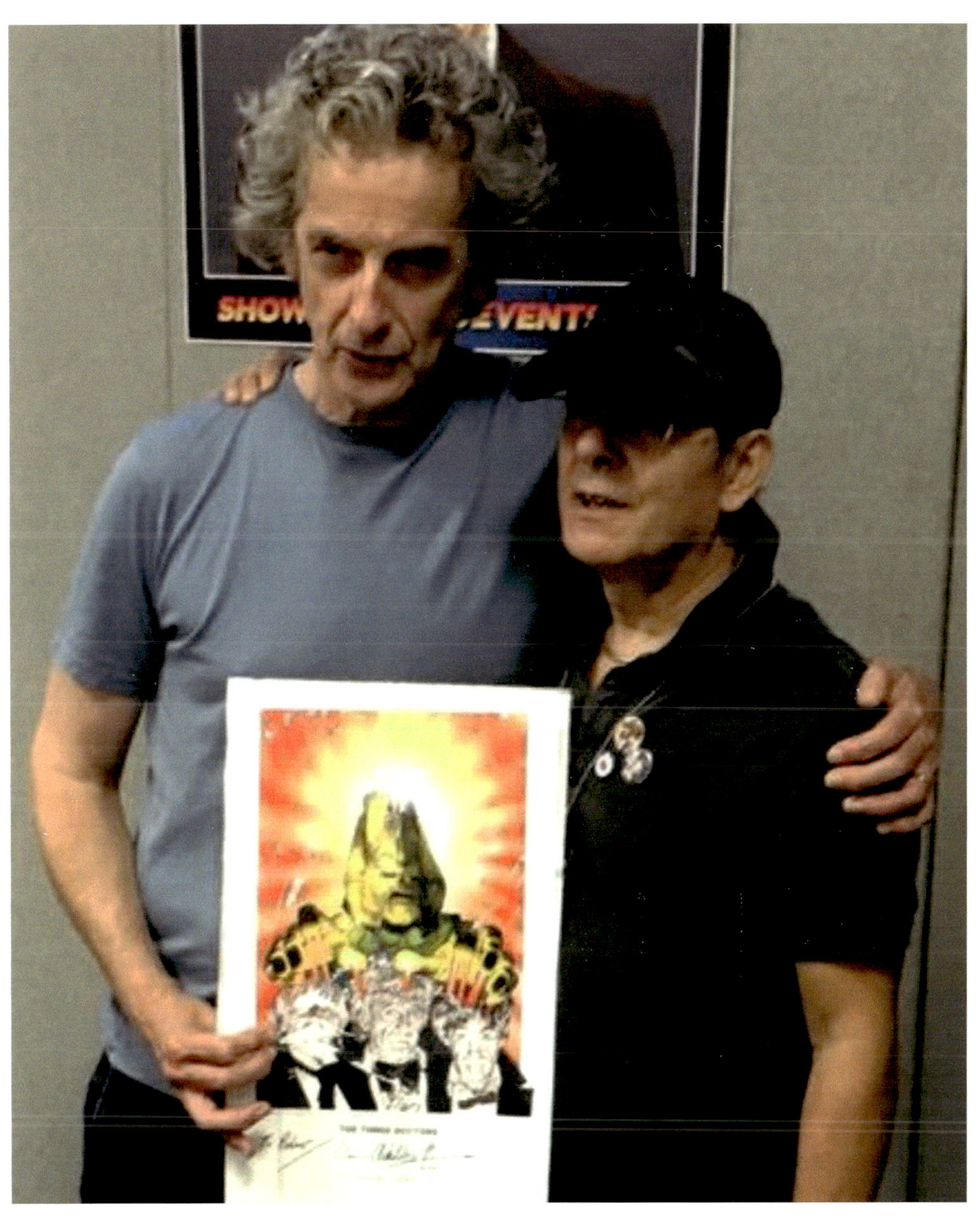

Tom Baker signing copies of the 1970s novel
Doctor Who and the Genesis of the Daleks.

CONTENTS

FOREWORD BY TERRANCE DICKS

Some years ago when I was still working on *Doctor Who* I saw a poster for an exhibition of book covers in a Piccadilly gallery. I went in to have a look. There were vast numbers of different book covers. They were shown without book titles or authors' names and it struck me what beautiful paintings many of them were. How galling it must be to do a lovely painting and then have some fool of an author write his name and book title all over it.

The names of the artists were listed, but most were strange to me – with one exception: Chris Achilléos! This is because when it came to the question of choosing an artist for the cover of the Target Books novelisations, Chris Achilléos' name was always the first to be mentioned. He was the go-to artist for *Doctor Who* novelisations, which I was then writing at a great rate.

His name is known and respected in the art world of book illustration and at least one writer knows it too!

Terrance Dicks, 2019

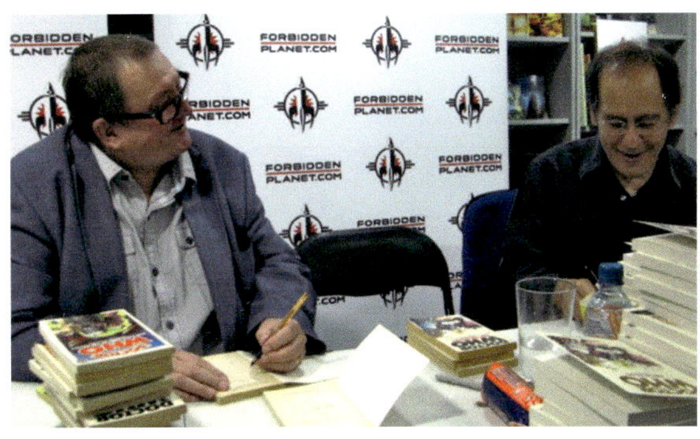

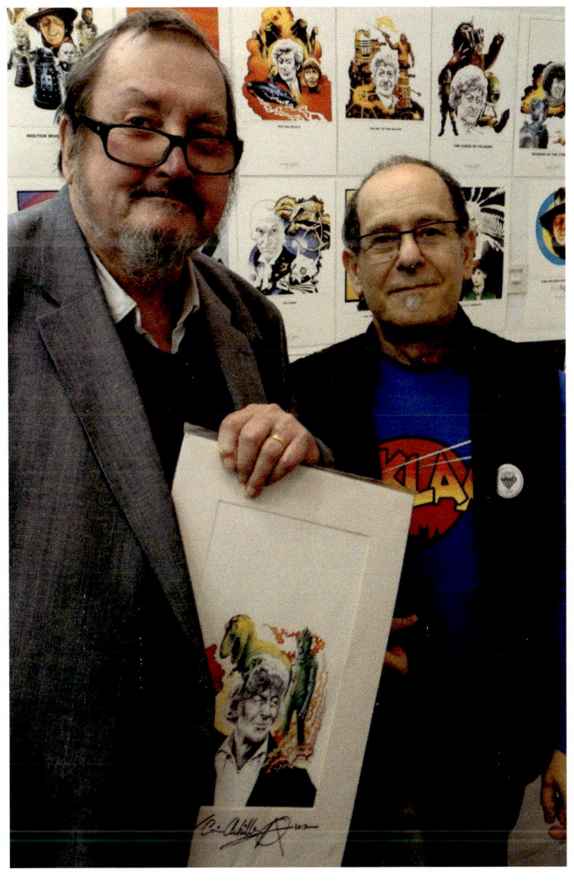

(above) Terrance Dicks and Chris signing at Forbidden Planet 2012.

THE LIFE OF CHRIS ACHILLÉOS

Chris Achilléos was a revered British-Cypriot fantasy artist. His art has been displayed on hundreds of fantasy book covers, including the work of Robert E Howard, Edgar Rice Burroughs and Michael Moorcock. He was a conceptual artist for George Lucas' *Willow*, amongst other movies. His artwork can also be found on various album covers, film posters, private commissions and in his best selling books, *Beauty and the Beast*, *Sirens*, *Medusa* and *Amazona*.

From the early 1970s, Achilléos produced over thirty covers for official *Doctor Who* novelisations, crafting a signature style which became indelibly associated with the show's classic era. With the 2013 commission of work to celebrate its fiftieth anniversary, Achilléos' contributions to *Doctor Who* entered a fifth decade.

Achilléos was born in Cyprus in 1947. His early childhood was characterised by tragedy, tumult and the indefatigable spirit of his mother:

'My mother was an adopted child. When she became of age, she had an arranged marriage to my father, who was in his fifties. They had four children: three girls and me. He died of lung cancer when I was very young. My mum was widowed in her late twenties and left with four children to care for.

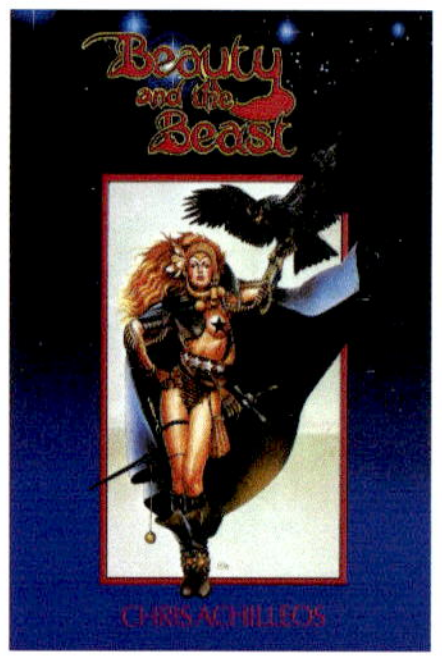
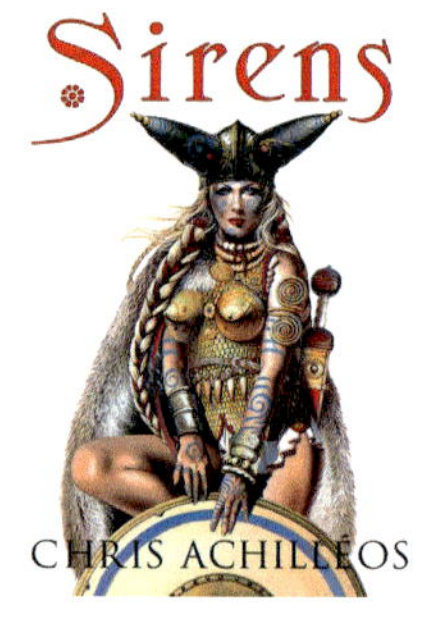
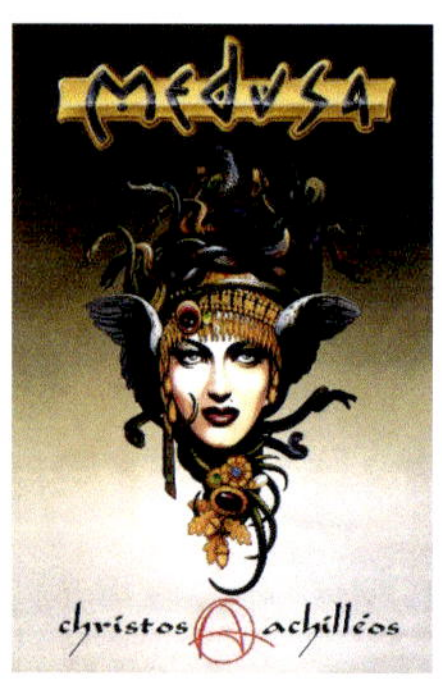
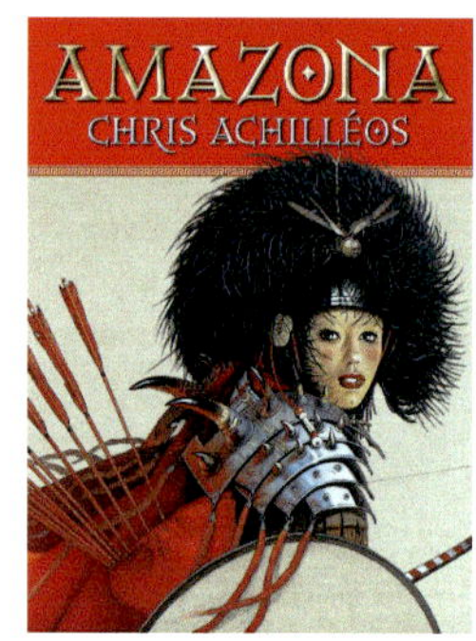
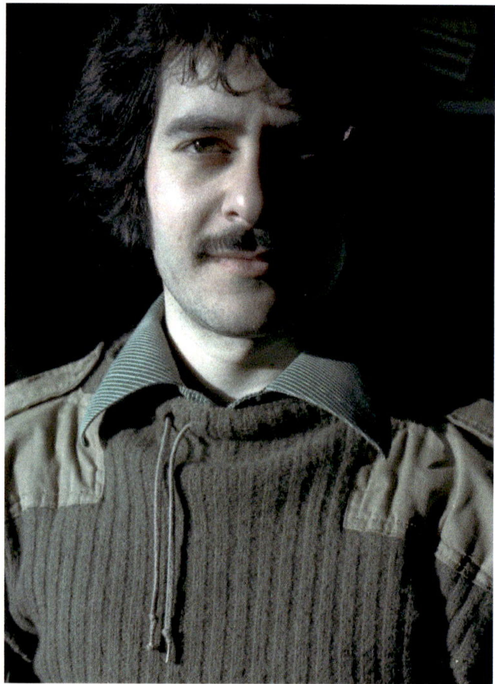

(above) covers of Beauty and the Beast *(1978),* Sirens
(1986), Medusa *(2002) and* Amazona *(2004).*
(above right) Chris in 1975 wearing his
favourite WW2 jumper.

'As we grew, so did the insurrection against British rule. I got caught up in this from a young age, and it was very worrying for my poor mother. She could see the way things were going; she had nobody around to protect us, and my sisters were coming of age.'

In 1960, Achilléos' mother moved her young family to London, leaving behind the proprietorship of her self-built dressmaking business for work in a factory. They were met with an unwelcoming reception.

'On the first day at school, I was attacked by another kid. I didn't speak a word of English. I asked another Cypriot kid why this boy wanted to hit me. He replied, "You don't need to do anything; they just hate us."'

The young Achilléos' first years in Britain were isolating, but he took solace in his developing eye for art.

'I would go to the library and take out as many books as I could carry – anything which had exciting pictures. World War Two aircraft, designs of yachts – anything. But my true love was always comics. *Lion* and *Eagle* were the best. They were my motivation to learn to read and write English; I wanted to know what was said in the speech bubbles!'

At sixteen, Achilléos was still developing his English, but his artistic talents were becoming clear. With the encouragement of an inspirational art teacher, he studied Technical and Scientific Illustration at Hornsey Art College.

'I got in on the strength of the drawings I did at home. My room walls were covered in all sorts of drawings, from barbarians and Spartans to aeroplanes and guns. I could not afford to buy proper drawing paper, so I would draw on the back of wallpaper. I remember the butcher gave me some white paper to draw on. At my interview, I unrolled my wallpaper drawings and I was in.'

Achilléos' association with the book trade began early. His first professional project was helping one of his college tutors illustrate *the Moon Flight Atlas*, by Patrick Moore.

'We worked all weekend, without a break, as everything had to be ready by Monday morning. In the same room Patrick Moore was typing away like a machine! I was eighteen at the time. I was amazed when they used one of my works for the cover of the book. I included the work in my finals exhibition and got top marks.'

After graduation, and a brief employment producing technical drawings, Achilléos began working on fantasy novels. With the sixties in full swing, he also made a name for himself fusing fantasy with erotica.

Achilléos' covers for *Doctor Who* defined a generation's image of the Doctor and his adventures. Lavishly detailed, with psychedelic overtones and an unapologetically pulpy sensibility, his work both reproduced and reinterpreted the eccentric energy of the show's classic era.

To this day, *Doctor Who* luminaries tip their hat to the influence of Achilléos' work. The opening of a 2016 exhibition of his cover art attracted the series' then-showrunner Steven Moffat, as well as twelfth Doctor Peter Capaldi.

'I recently discovered that Peter was a fan of the series before he was the Doctor. It brings me a lot of pleasure to join Peter and the list of luminaries that have contributed so much to this iconic series. It's wonderful to think that my artwork from fifty years ago is still relevant to fans today.'

Until his death in 2021, Achilléos continued to draw and paint for publishers and on private commission, and he was a regular at conventions, meeting his many fans and exhibiting his decades of artwork.

'It means a lot to me that my work has become a source of escapism for many *Doctor Who* fans, and it's their support over the years that has kept the flame alive. Meeting these fans is always a pleasure. I hope they enjoy seeing all my *Doctor Who* artwork collected together for the first time.'

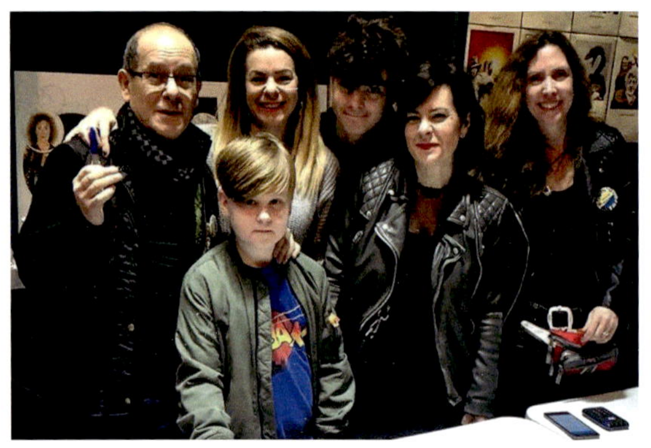

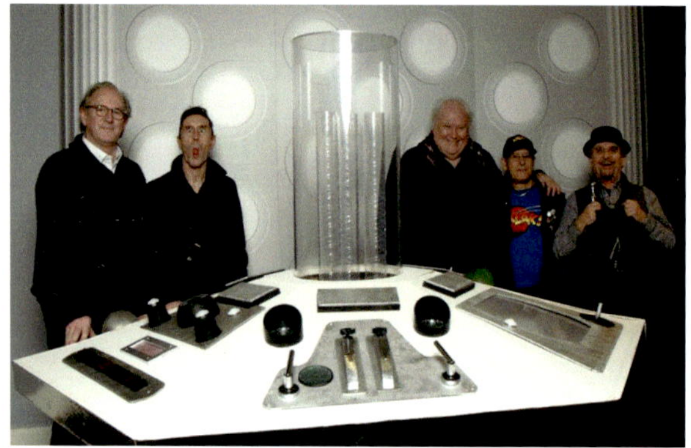

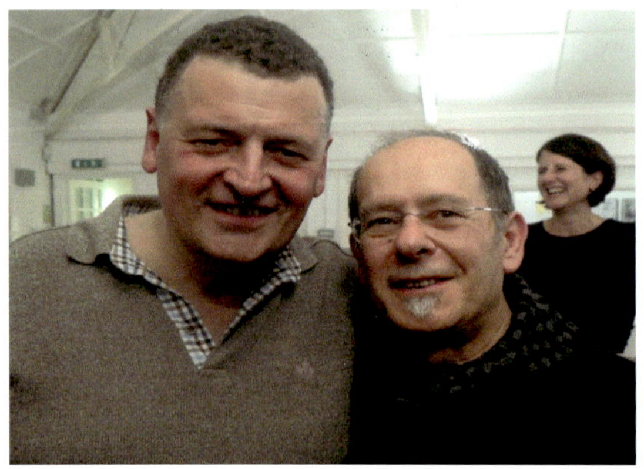

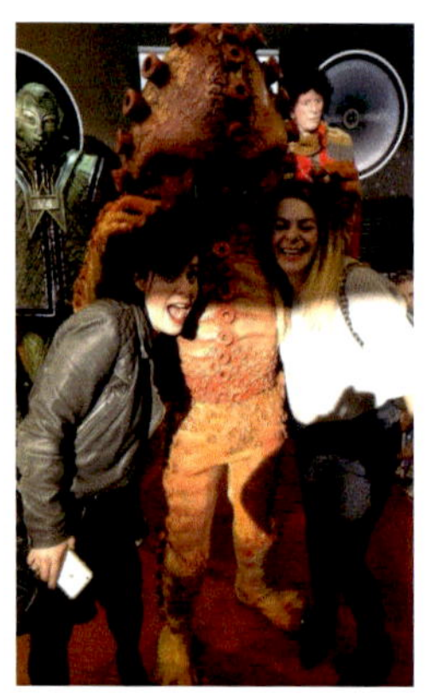

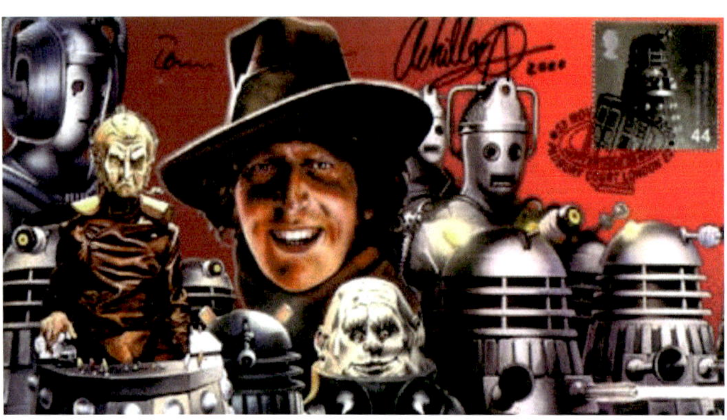

(top left) Chris with his wife, Natasha; grandson, Tyler; daughter, Anna; grandson, Joshua; and daughter, Esther.
(top right) Peter Davison, Paul McGann, Colin Baker, Chris and Sylvester McCoy.
(middle left) Steven Moffat and Chris.
(middle right) Esther, Zygon, Anna.
(bottom) First day cover featuring Chris' work from the Stamp Centre, 2000.

THE DOCTOR AND ME BY CHRIS ACHILLÉOS

" I'd been in the country for three years by the time *Doctor Who* started. I was in my own little world: introverted, in my room, drawing away. My mum rented a tiny little TV for us. We used to be glued to it; we had nothing like that back in little Cyprus. *Doctor Who* seemed really alien to me. I was still learning the language, the culture, and here was this show that was literally out of this world. It was very strange, very hard to understand, but it was interesting, especially on a tiny, round TV full of interference. It did almost seem like a signal from outer space!

Since then I have met many of the Doctors, companions and fans – and witnessing their love for the programme takes me back to the times in my bedroom.

Actually the things I liked about it as a child still resonate with me today: the original theme music and title sequence (and all its variations throughout the years), the possibilities opened up by the concept of time travel, the living TARDIS, and the idea of the regenerating Doctor. "

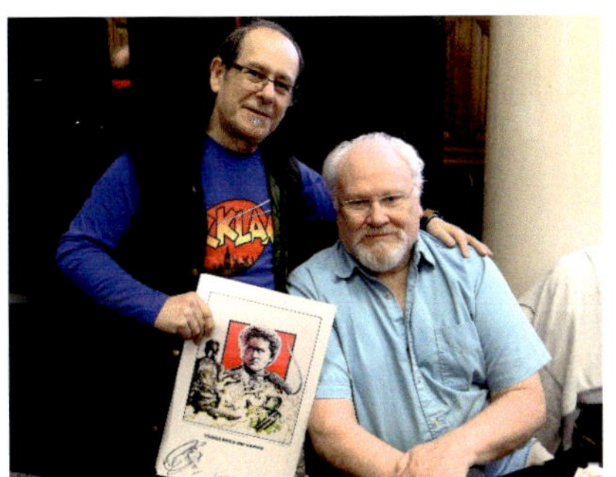

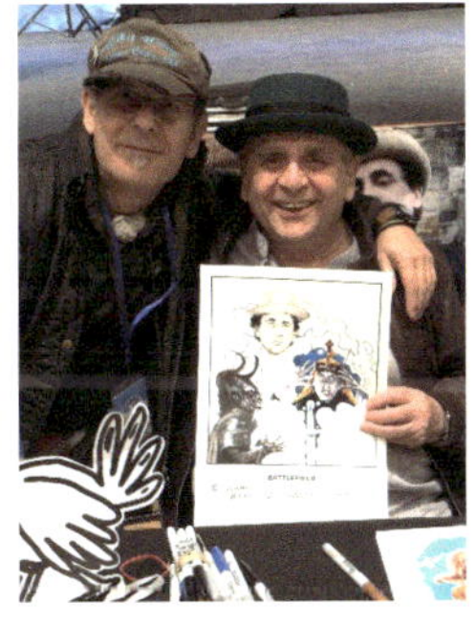

*(far left) Chris and Colin Baker
(left) Chris and Sylvester McCoy
(below) Chris, Elisabeth Sladen
& Tom Baker signing
ut the Stamp Centre, 2000.*

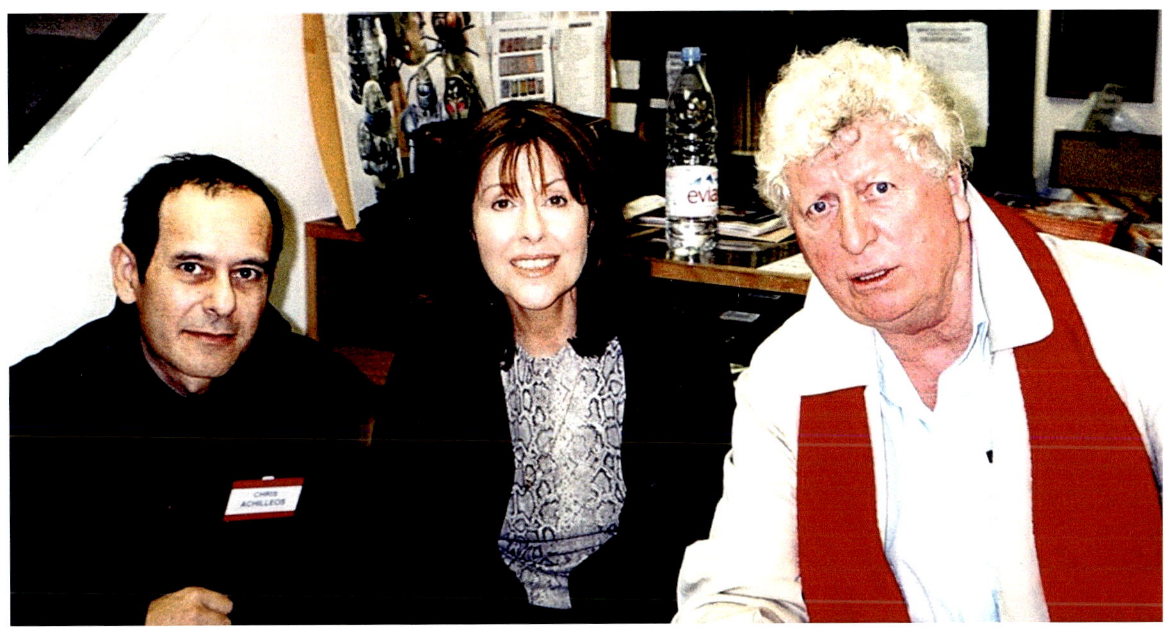

DOCTOR WHO AND THE DALEKS

Writer: David Whitaker **Doctor:** First **Release date:** 2 May 1973 **Release order:** 1

The Doctor Who and the Daleks *BBC CD and book are available from retailers. See bibliography for details.*

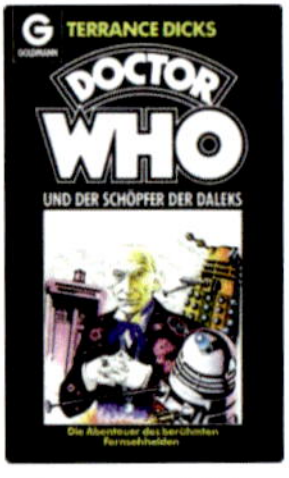
German Edition

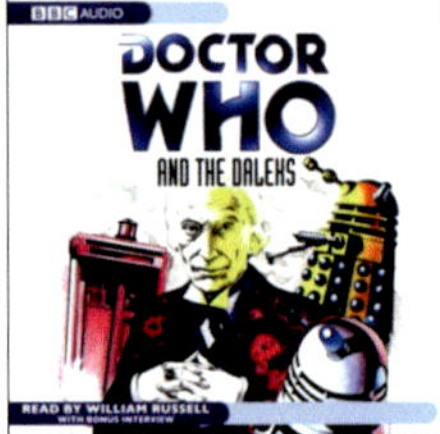
BBC Audiobook CD

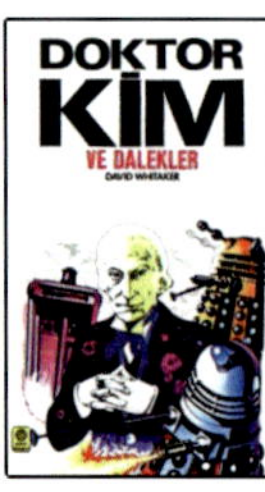
Turkish Edition

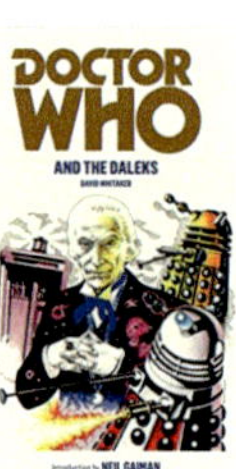
BBC Reissue

"The Doctor stood up slowly and looked down at me, fingering his glasses thoughtfully.

'We're wanderers, Chesterton, Susan and I. Cut off from our own planet and separated from it by a million, million years of your time.'"

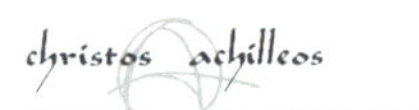

66 The first cover I did was *The Daleks*, although commissions came together in three, with all three to be done at the same time.

On TV the Daleks were in black and white, and I really didn't have any reference for their colours, other than the comic *TV 21*, which had some Daleks on the back cover. So I looked at those and put together these crazy colours.

But I didn't stop to think that the police box was blue! That's when the publishers started sending me a few photos to copy from: the monsters, the doctors – templates to follow.

The first three covers, of which *The Daleks* was the first, really set out the approach I would take for all the covers to come. **99**

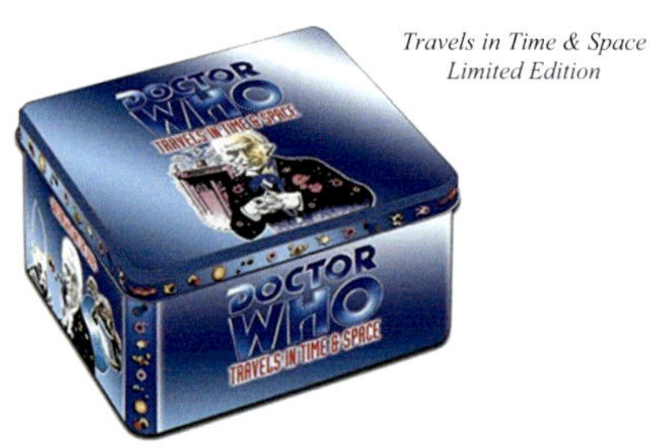
Travels in Time & Space Limited Edition

This is Doctor Who's first exciting adventure – with the Daleks!

Ian Chesterton and Barbara Wright travel with the mysterious Doctor Who and his granddaughter, Susan, to the planet of Skaro in the space-time machine, Tardis.

There they strive to save the peace-loving Thals from the evil intentions of the hideous Daleks. Can they succeed? And what is more important, will they ever again see their native Earth?

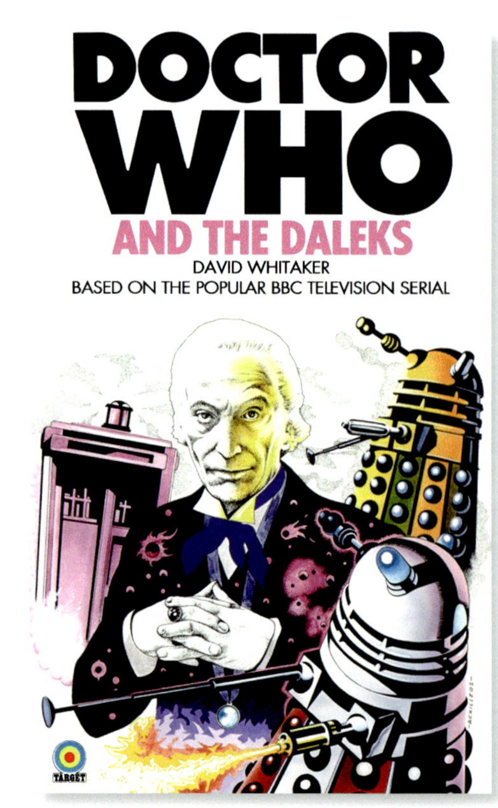

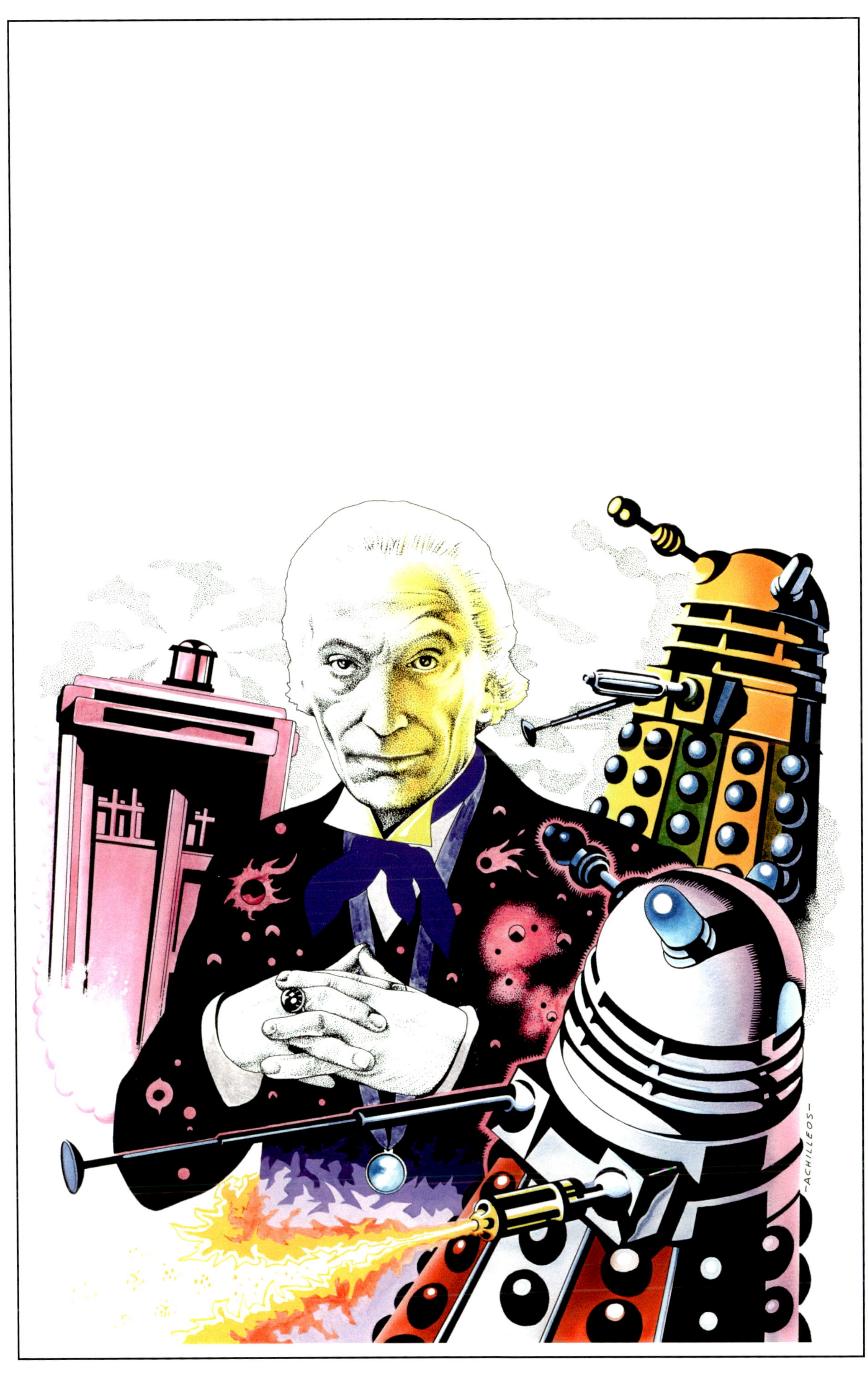

DOCTOR WHO AND THE ZARBI

Writer: Bill Strutton **Doctor:** First **Release date:** 2 May 1973 **Release order:** 2

The Doctor Who and the Zarbi *BBC CD and book is available from retailers. See bibliography for details.*

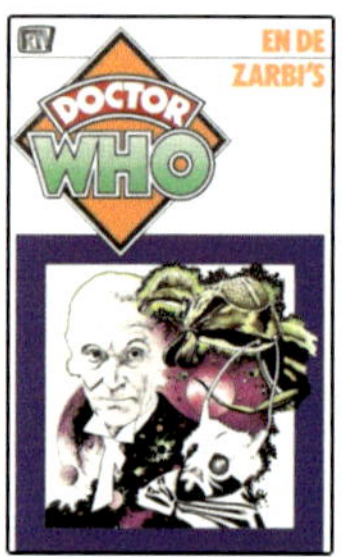

Dutch Edition

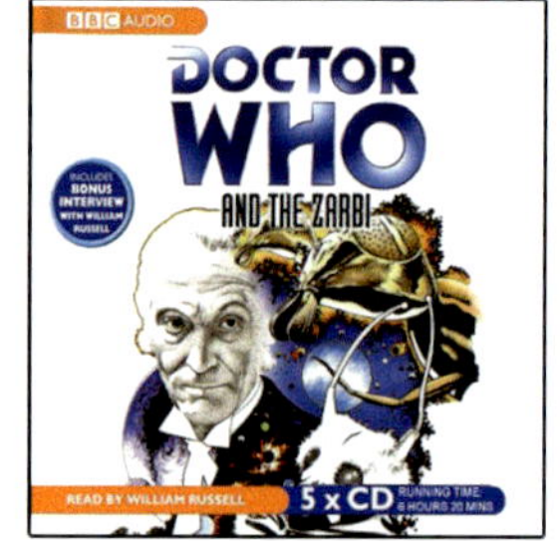

BBC Audiobook CD

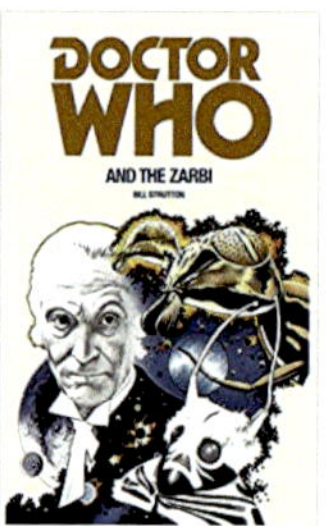

BBC Reissue

"Two things are infinite: the universe and human stupidity; and I'm not sure about the universe."

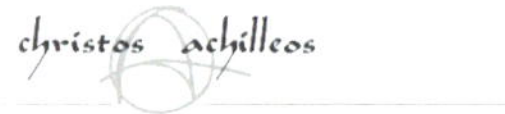

Doctor Who lands his space-time machine Tardis on the cold, craggy planet of Vortis. The Doctor and his companions, Ian and Vicki, are soon captured by the Zarbi, huge ant-like creatures with metallic bodies and pincer claws; meanwhile Barbara falls into the hands of the friendly Menoptera who have come to rid Vortis of the malevolent power of the Zarbi...

❝ *The Zarbi* has more of the special effects that I started to do with *The Daleks*, on the coat of the Doctor. I was a big fan and collector of British and American comics. The little round things with the energy bars around them were inspired by Jack Kirby, who I regard as a genius. ❞

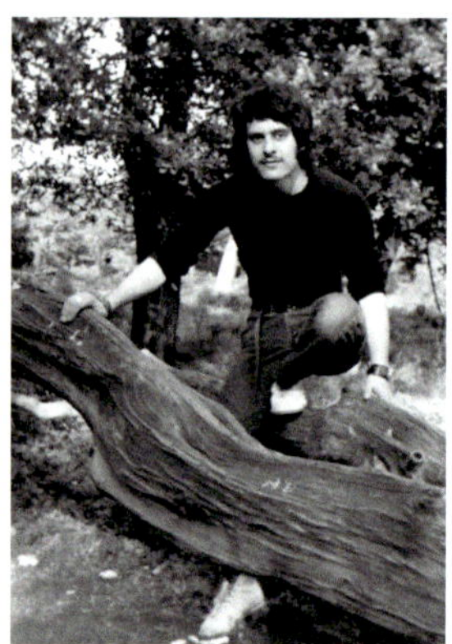

(left) Chris in the early 1970s.

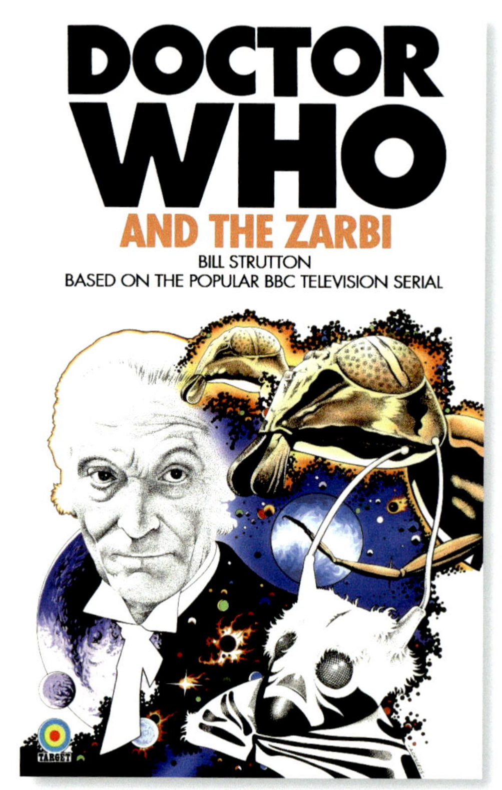

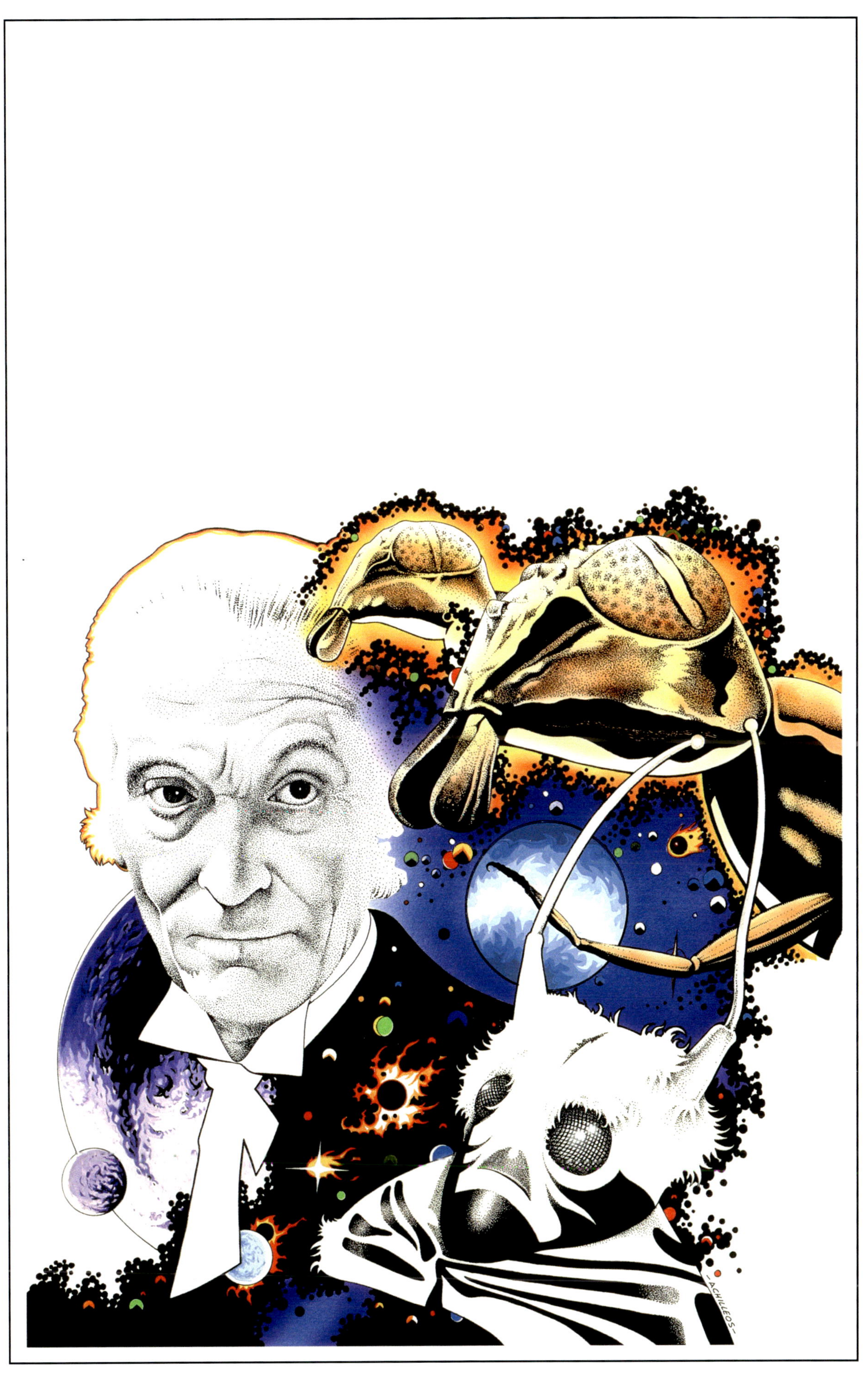

DOCTOR WHO AND THE CRUSADERS

Writer: David Whitaker **Doctor:** First **Release date:** 2 May 1973 **Release order:** 3

The Doctor Who and the Crusaders *BBC book is available from retailers. See bibliography for details.*

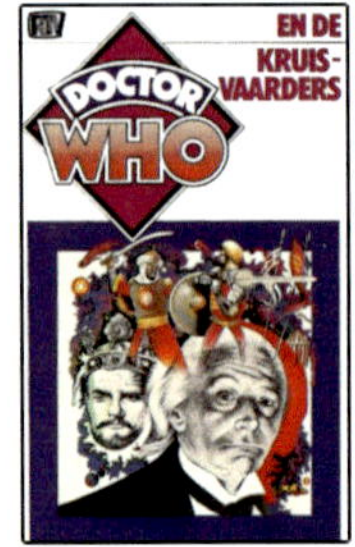

Dutch Edition

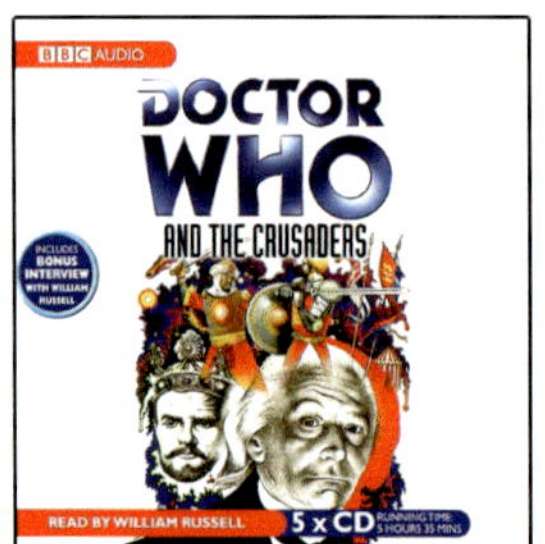

BBC Audiobook CD

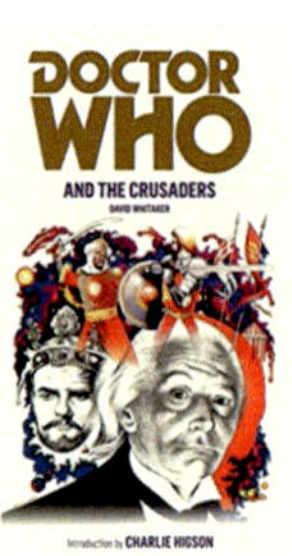

BBC Reissue

"The fascination your planet has for me is that its Time pattern, that is, past, present, future, is all one – like a long, winding mountain path. When the four of us land at any given point on that path, we are still only climbers."

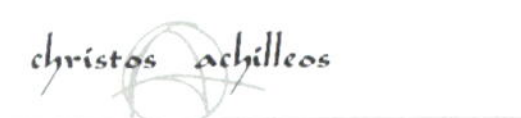

“ On *The Crusaders* I remember I made the mistake of using a repidograph pen that was too fine, so all the dots are really tiny and it took me forever to do them! You can see how there are much more dots and closer together.

I made up the appearances of King Richard and Saladin, as I didn't have any reference material to work from. ”

Back on Earth again, Tardis lands into the midst of the harsh, cruel world of the twelfth-century Crusades. Soon the adventurers are embroiled in the conflict between Richard the Lionheart and the Sultan Saladin, ruler of the warlike Saracens...

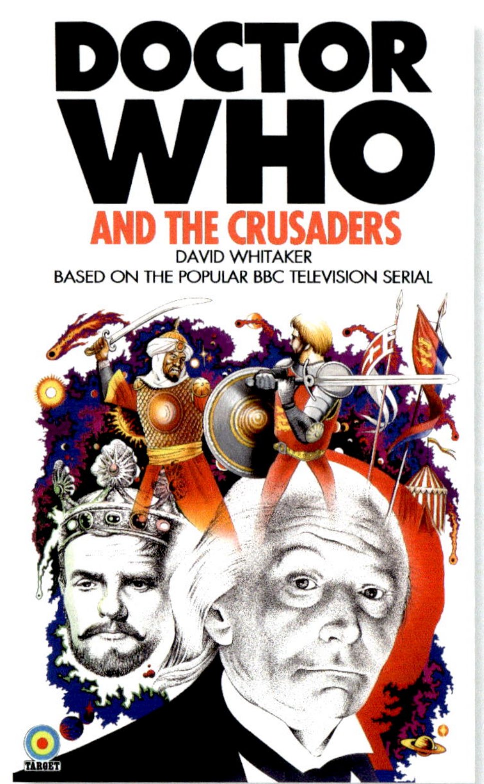

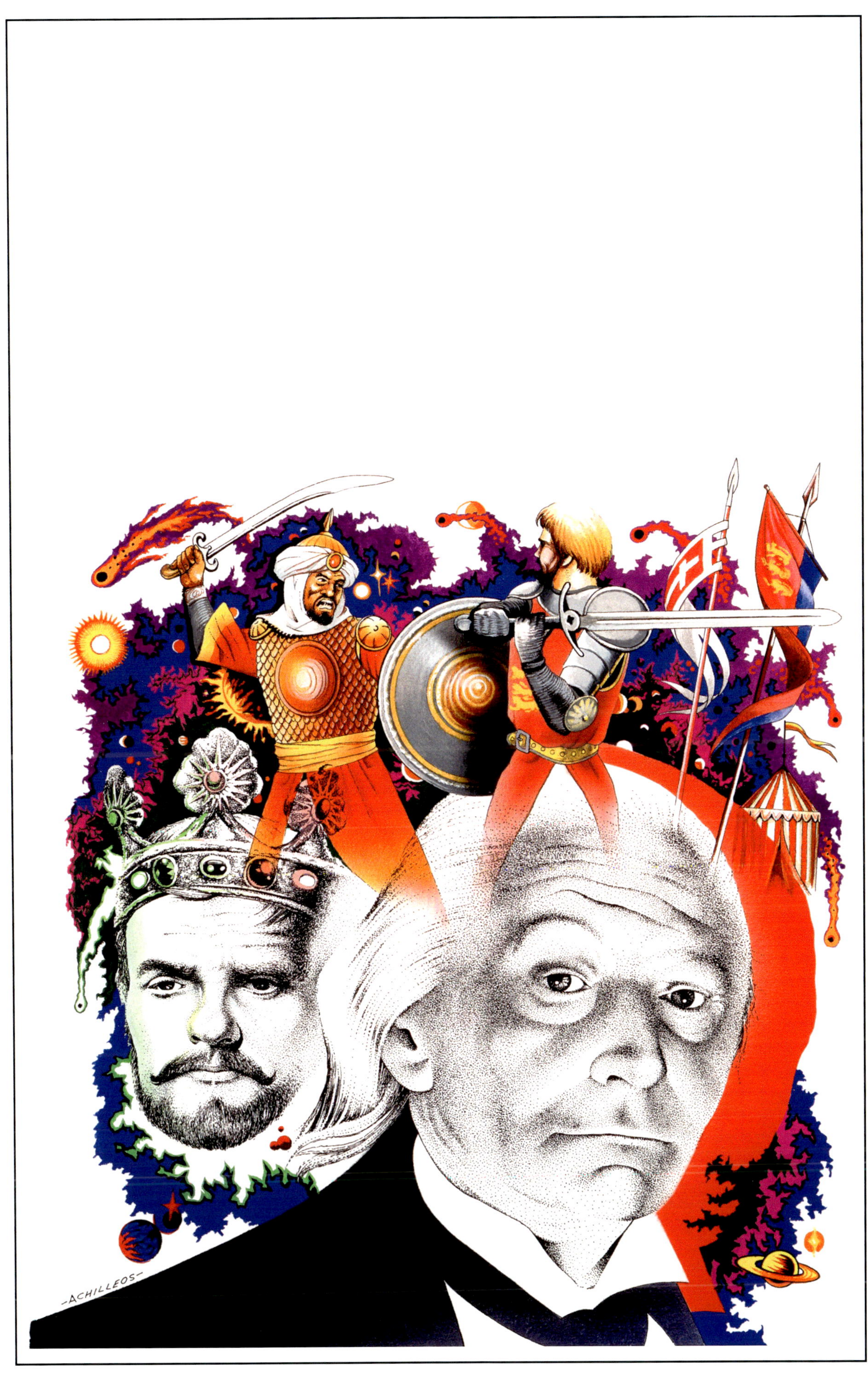

DOCTOR WHO AND THE AUTON INVASION

Writer: Terrance Dicks **Doctor:** Third **Release date:** 17 January 1974 **Release order:** 4

The Doctor Who and the
Auton Invasion *BBC CD and
book are available from retailers.
See bibliography for details.*

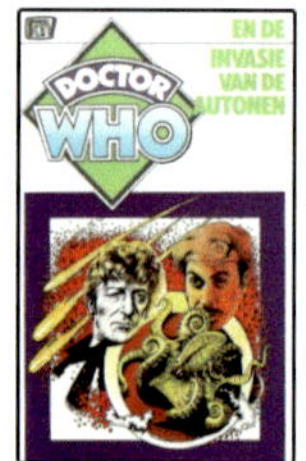
Dutch Edition

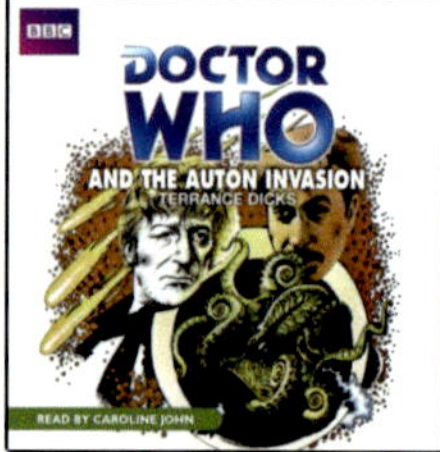
BBC Audiobook CD

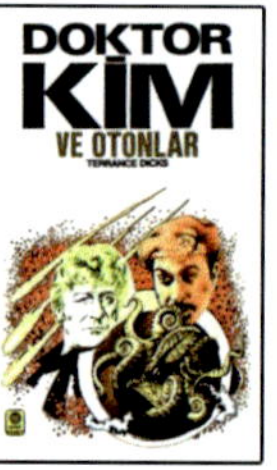
Turkish Edition

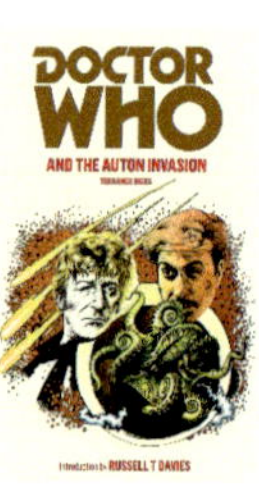
BBC Reissue

"The Brigadier paused for a moment, obviously choosing his words with great care. 'We deal with the odd – the unexplained. We're prepared to tackle anything on Earth. Or beyond the Earth, if necessary.'

Liz looked at him in amazement. To her astonishment he seemed quite serious."

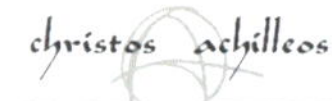

❝ *The Auton Invasion* and the other previous ones set the style I would ultimately become associated with.

Again, I wasn't provided with any reference of what the Nestene looked like, so I made it into this kind of octopus thing.

I always tried to keep in mind that I was doing these covers for kids, and children were thrilled by these creatures and monsters in vibrant colour.

Looking at it now I wish didn't have the Nestene tentacle overlapping the Brigadier's face. **❞**

In this, the first adventure of his third 'incarnation', Doctor Who, Liz Shaw, and the Brigadier grapple with the nightmarish invasion of the Autons – living, giant-sized, plastic-modelled 'humans' with no hair and sightless eyes; waxwork replicas and tailor's dummies whose murderous behaviour is directed by the Nestene Consciousness – a malignant, squid-like monster of cosmic proportions and indescribably hideous appearance.

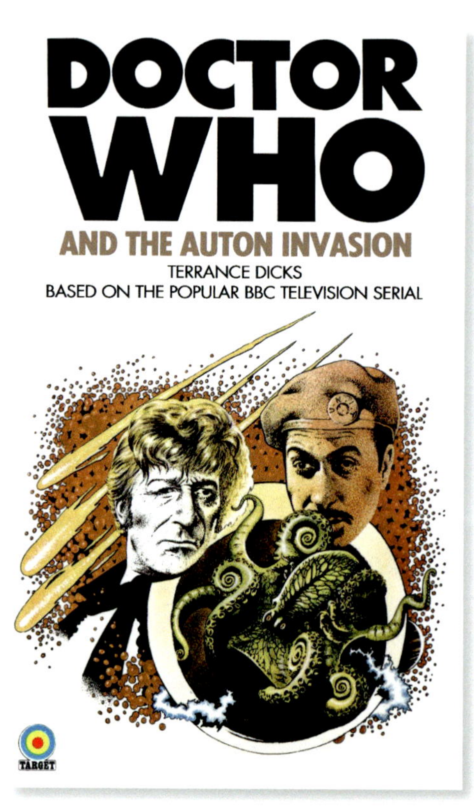

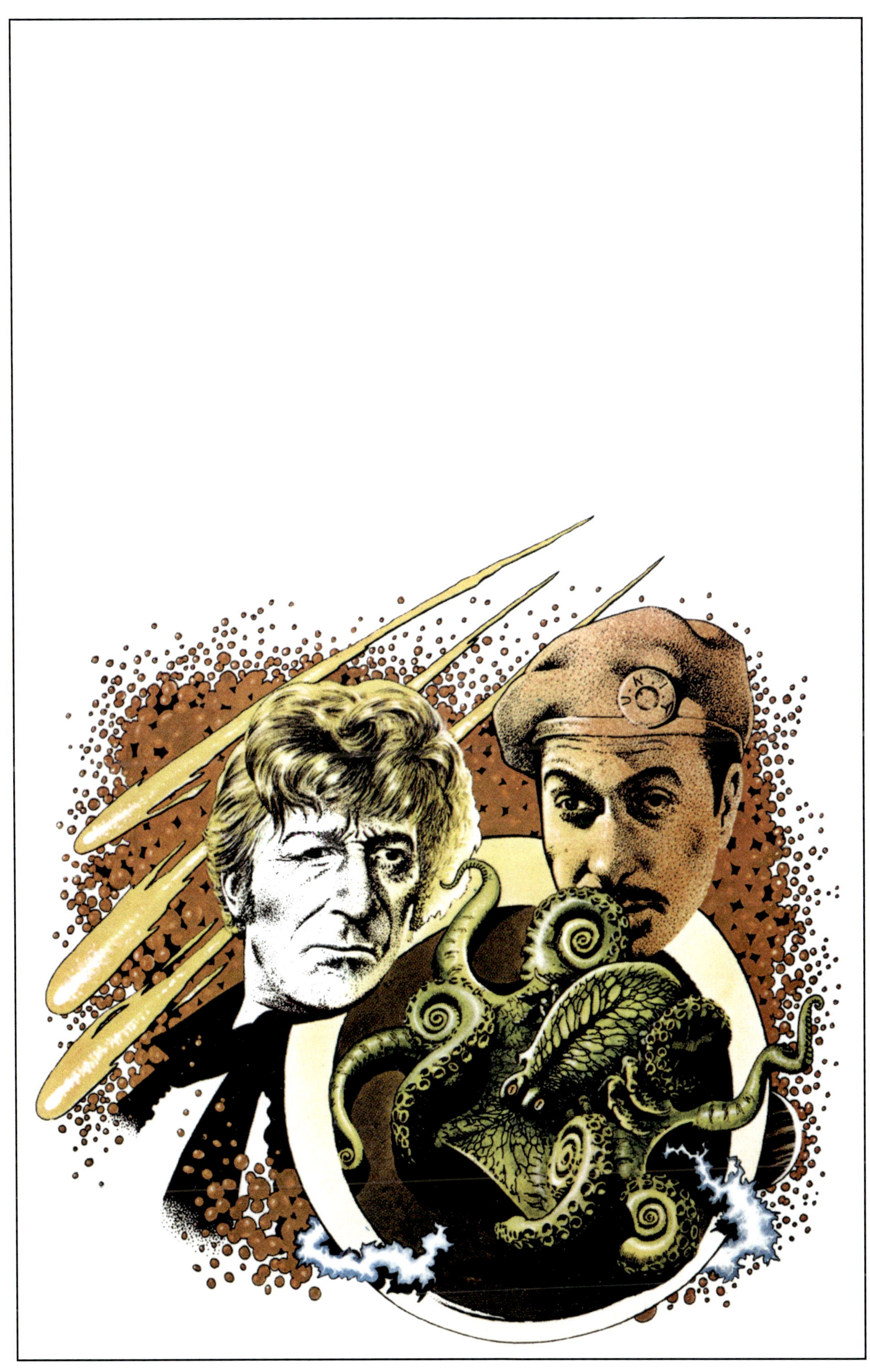

DOCTOR WHO AND THE CAVE-MONSTERS

Writer: Malcolm Hulke **Doctor:** Third **Release date:** 17 January 1974 **Release order:** 5

The Doctor Who and the Cave Monsters *BBC CD and book are available from retailers. See bibliography for details.*

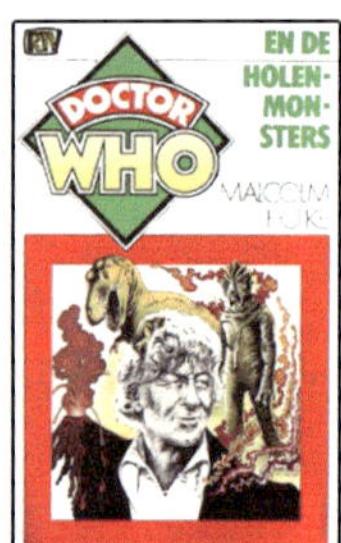

Dutch Edition

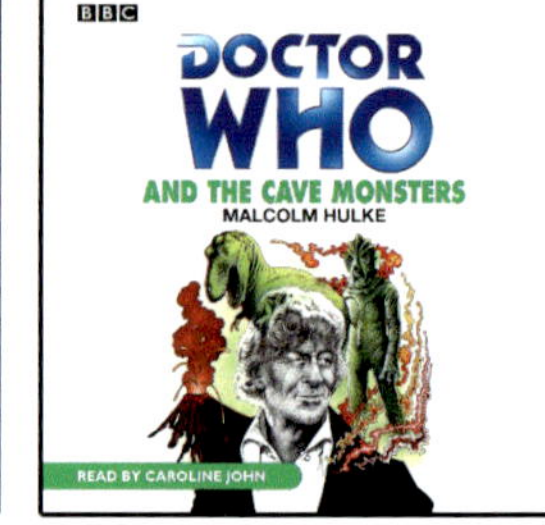

BBC Audiobook CD

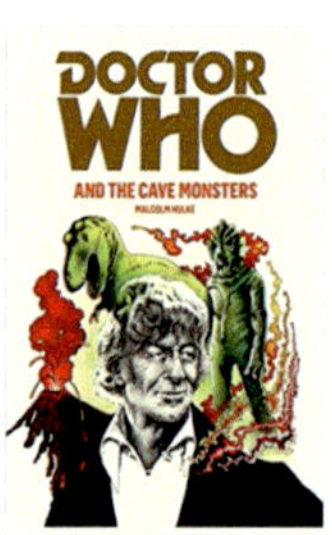

BBC Reissue

"Then there was another explosion, and the entrance to the cave collapsed in a deluge of huge rocks.

'He's sealed them in,' the Doctor said quietly.

Liz nodded. 'He had to. They'd never have accepted sharing this world.'

The Doctor felt anger rising in him. 'We've lost the chance to find out now,' he said. 'We shall never know.'"

christos achilléos

❝ For this one, I was given a few useful photos to work with, including a very good reference photograph of Jon Pertwee, and a decent picture for the Silurian, but that was it. I drew those two, but then I realised it wasn't enough. So I drew a T. rex, thinking the kids would love a good dinosaur. I then added the erupting volcano and more effects, which made it all work quite well. ❞

All is not well at the Wenley Moor underground atomic research station: there are unaccountable losses of power-output; nervous breakdowns amongst the staff; and then – a death! UNIT is called in and the Brigadier is soon joined by Doctor Who and Liz Shaw in a tense and exciting adventure with subterranean reptile men – Silurians – and a 40ft. high Tyrannosaurus rex, the biggest, most savage mammal which ever trod the earth!

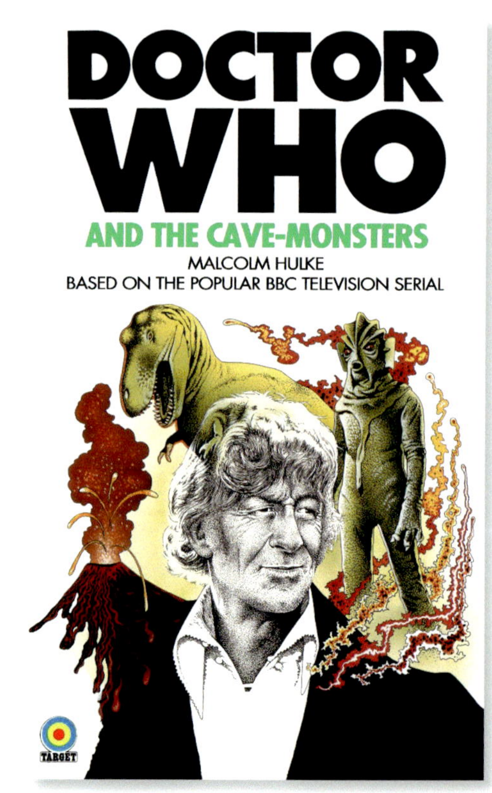

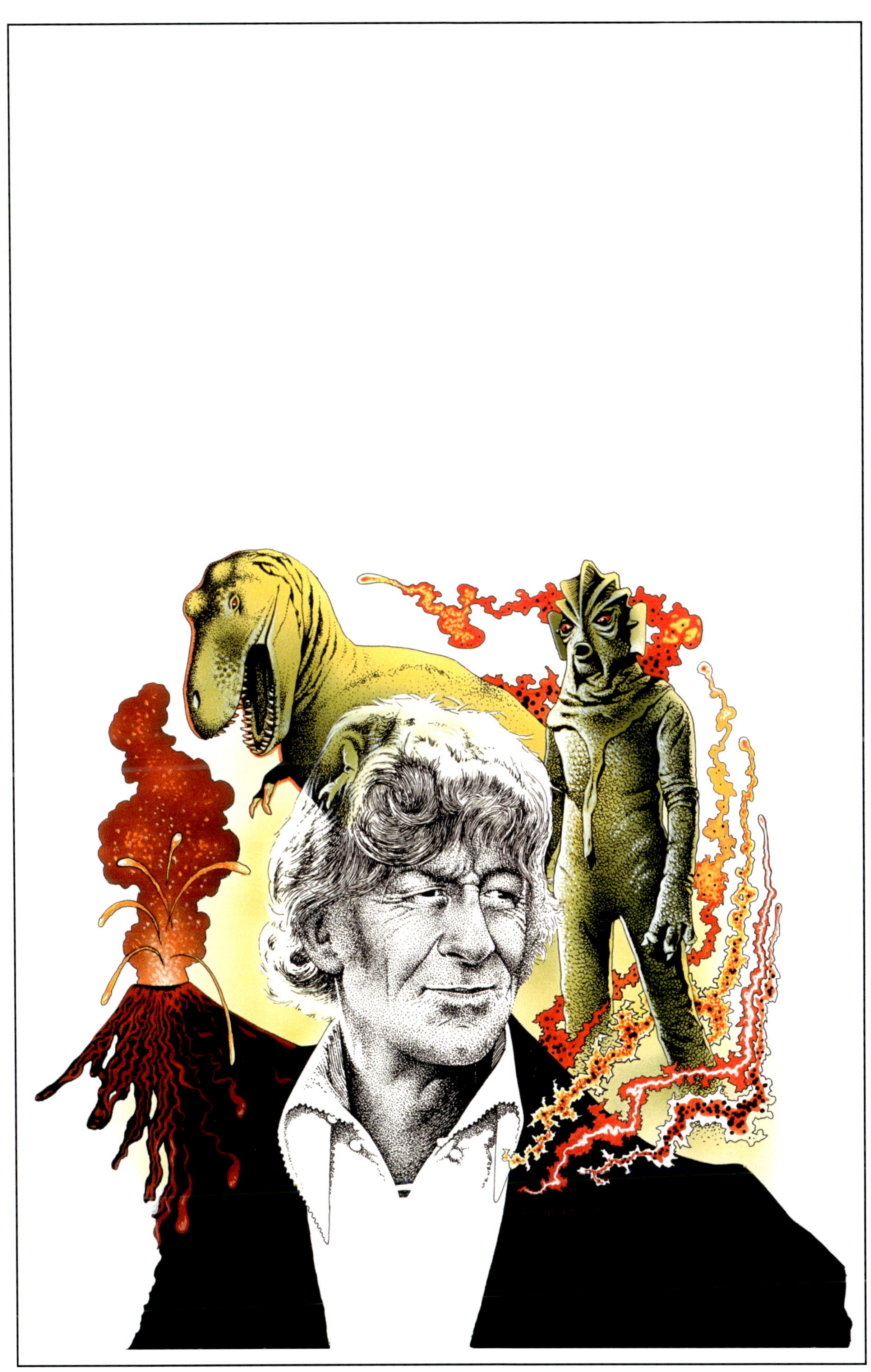

DOCTOR WHO AND THE DAY OF THE DALEKS

Writer: Terrance Dicks **Doctor:** Third **Release date:** 18 March 1974 **Release order:** 6

The Doctor Who and the Day of the Daleks *BBC book is available from retailers. See bibliography for details.*

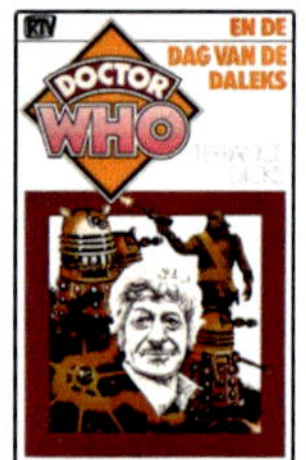
Dutch Edition

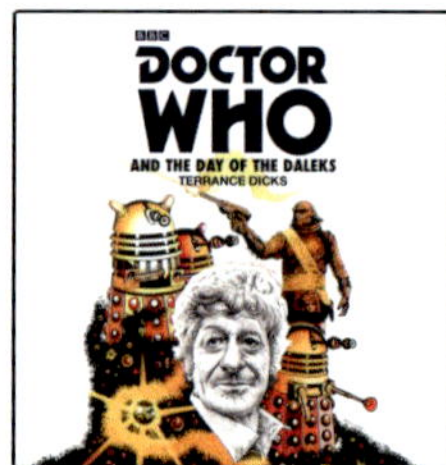
BBC Audiobook CD

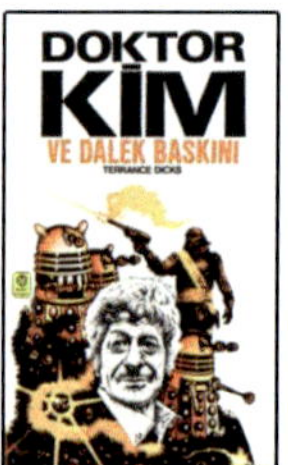
Turkish Edition

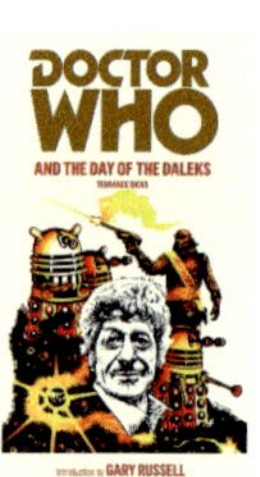
BBC Reissue

"Leaping up, the Doctor dashed back inside the TARDIS. Through its open doors Jo could see that he was bent over the central control column, making careful adjustments to the instruments. As he did so the laboratory door opened. Jo looked up and to her utter astonishment she saw the Doctor standing in the doorway.

Amazed, she looked back inside the TARDIS. There was the Doctor still bending over the console."

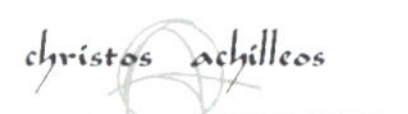

66 By *The Day of the Daleks*, I had some pictures for reference. I combined the Daleks with space and other effects. I think it's a good design, with a simple colour scheme.

People always tell me that I put the Daleks' stalk the wrong way round. But why aren't there any left-handed Daleks? I think there should be! ☺

The real reason is that, if an image didn't fit my design one way, I'd make it fit the other way. I didn't think it would matter – and it didn't to the kids at the time. 99

Mysterious humans from 22nd-century Earth 'time-jump' back into the 20th century so as to assassinate a high-ranking diplomat on whom the peace of the world depends. Doctor Who, Jo Grant and the Brigadier are soon called in to investigate. Jo is accidentally transported forward to the 22nd century; the Doctor follows, eventually to be captured by his oldest and deadliest enemy – the DALEKS! Having submitted the Doctor to the fearful Mind Analysis Machine, the DALEKS plan a 'time-jump' attack on Earth in the 20th century! ...

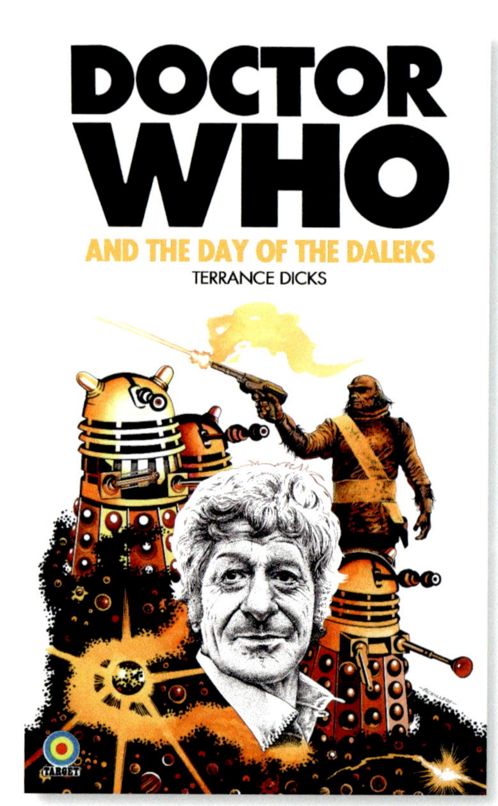

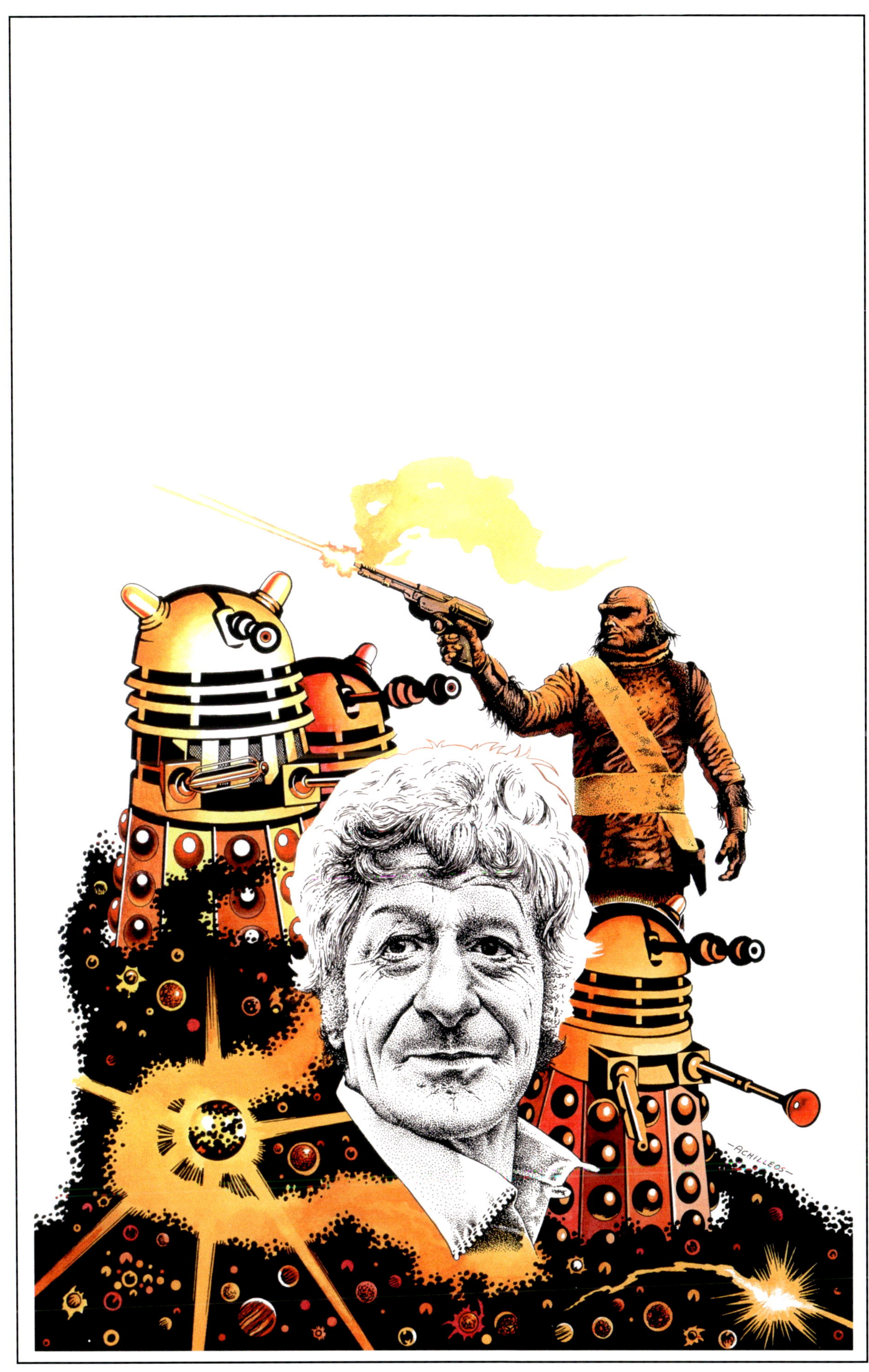

DOCTOR WHO AND THE DOOMSDAY WEAPON

Writer: Malcolm Hulke **Doctor:** Third **Release date:** 18 March 1974 **Release order:** 7

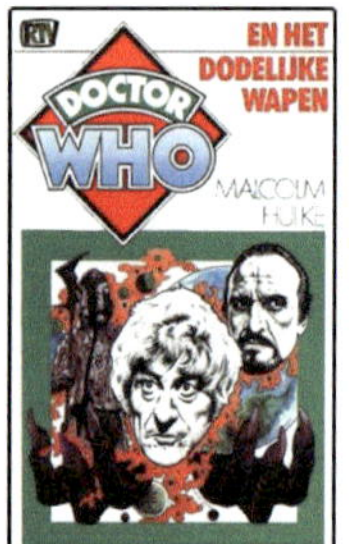

Dutch Edition

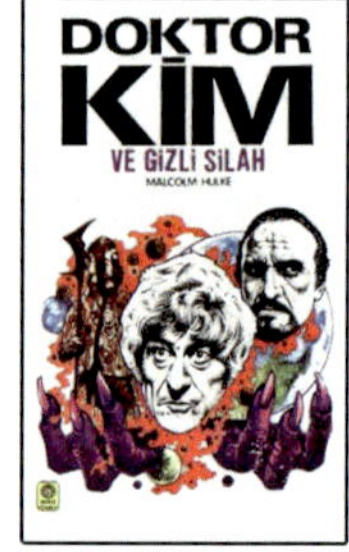

Turkish Edition

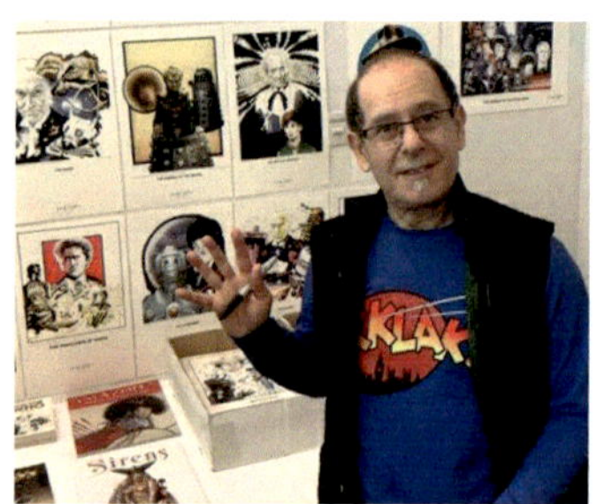

Chris with Sharpie at the ready

"Cautiously, Jo entered the TARDIS. It was at least twenty times bigger inside than outside. She stood just inside, unable to speak. The Doctor, however, followed her in and immediately went to the central console in the middle of the vast, highly polished floor."

christos achilleos

❝ This is my least favourite, next to *Seeds of Doom*.

One thing I can't fault is Jon Pertwee's face. I drew his face quite a lot in those days. Around this time my publisher received a letter informing them that Jon Pertwee thought that I drew his nose too big! I laughed out loud when I read it.

I did meet Jon a few times over the years at conventions, but he never gave me the time of day, not like Tom Baker, who was always a laugh.

I quite like the composition, but I feel I that I made quite a mess with colouring. **❞**

The evil Master has stolen the Time Lords' file on the horrifying Doomsday Weapon with which, when he finds it, he can blast whole planets out of existence and make himself ruler of the Galaxy!

The Time Lords direct Doctor Who and Jo Grant in TARDIS to a bleak planet in the year 2471 where they find colonists from Earth under threat from mysterious, savage, monster lizards with frightful claws! And hidden upon this planet is the Doomsday Weapon for which the Master is intently searching...

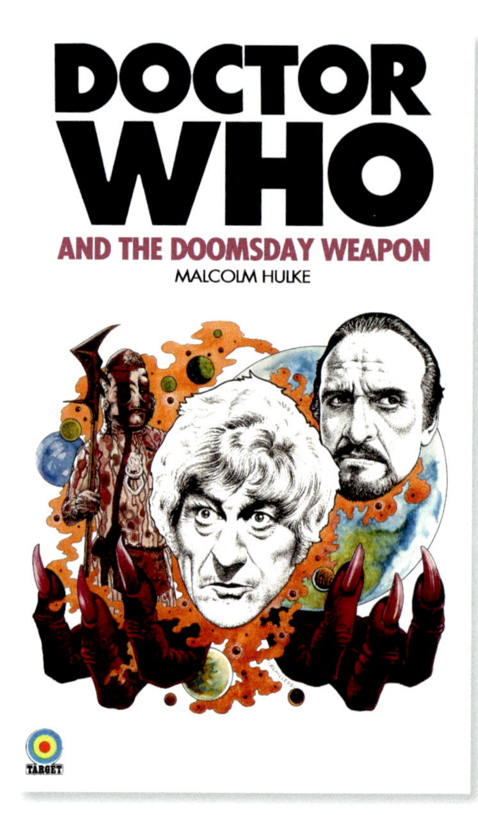

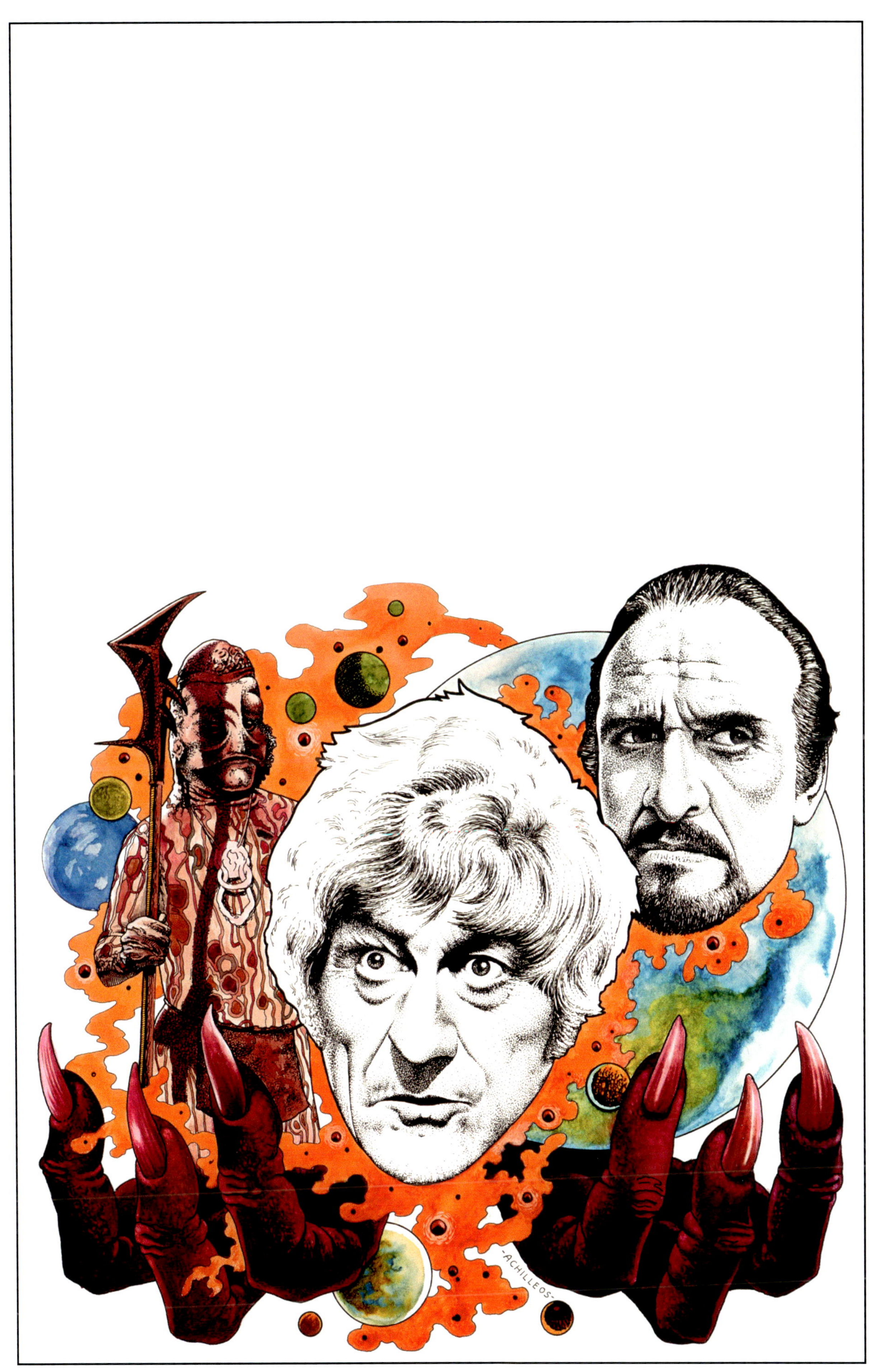

DOCTOR WHO AND THE DÆMONS

Writer: Barry Letts **Doctor:** Third **Release date:** 17 October 1974 **Release order:** 8

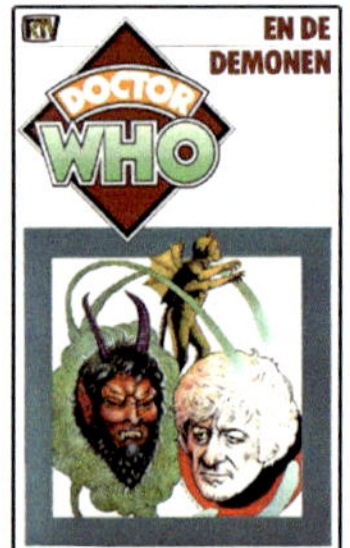

Dutch Edition

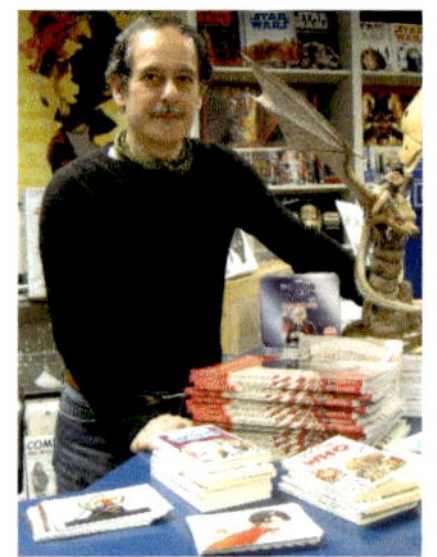

Chris signing his books

"The Brigadier looked at the stone imp once more sitting on the wall, its head malevolently swinging from side to side.

'Never mind,' said the Brigadier. 'We'll soon fix him. Corporal!'

Corporal Nevin, the crack shot of UNIT, twice runner up at Bisley, came over to his Commanding Officer at the double. 'Sir?' he said.

'That fellow over there,' said the Brigadier. 'The chap with wings. Five rounds rapid.'"

christos achilléos

" I doubt *The Dæmons* made Mr Pertwee feel much better. Unintentionally I've got the tip of his nose glowing on this one! ☺

I like Azal and Bok, but again it's a poor cover. It goes well with *The Dæmons* and *The Doomsday Weapon* because it's almost the same design, just shuffled about.

I was almost running out of ideas for the square format, so I put in this green stuff attacking the Doctor. **"**

Doctor Who is strangely concerned about Professor Horner's plan to cut open an ancient barrow near the peaceful English village of Devil's End; equally worried is Miss Hawthorne, the local white witch, who foretells a terrible disaster if he goes ahead; determined that the Professor should is Mr Magister, the new vicar (in truth the Master) whose secret ceremonies are designed to conjure up from out of the barrow a horribly powerful being from a far-off planet ... The Brigadier and Jo Grant assist Doctor Who in this exciting confrontation with the forces of black magic!

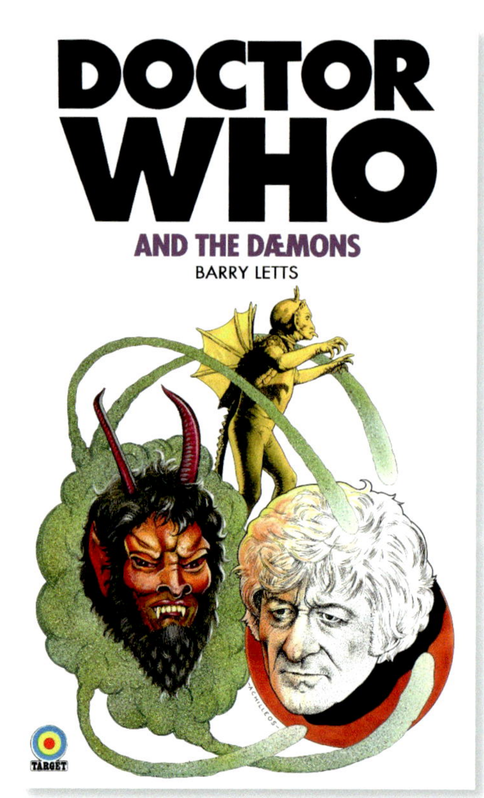

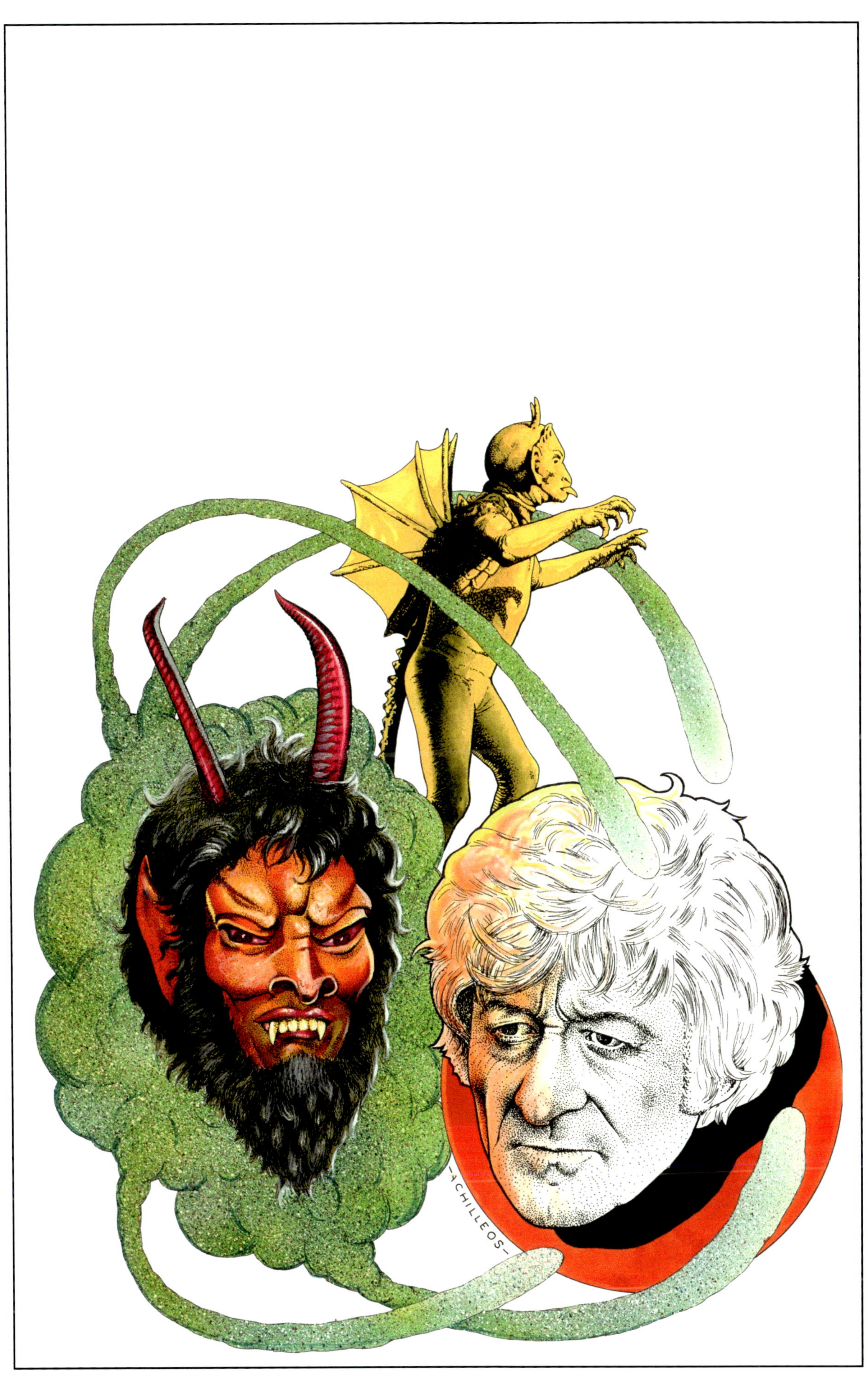

DOCTOR WHO AND THE SEA-DEVILS

Writer: Malcolm Hulke **Doctor:** Third **Release date:** 17 October 1974 **Release order:** 9

"'You know the Golden Rule of the Time Lords – just to sit and watch, but never actually do anything? He and I are different. We wanted to get out into the Universe, to meet other species, to explore.'

'One for good and the other for evil?' said Jo.

'Yes, you could say that.'"

christos achilleos

❝ The water on this one is pure Frank Bellamy.

Frank did things I can't explain to this day. He worked on *The Eagle*, *Dan Dare*, *Thunderbirds*, but my favourite was the centre spread of *Heros the Spartan*; that just did it all for me. I mean, the hero was a Spartan! That meant a lot to a young Greek Cypriot kid in a foreign land like me.

I never really got involved with comic books myself. I tried my hand at two samples at college. One was about the Persian Wars and the 300; the other one was a future version of *War of the Worlds*.

Inside some of the early *Doctor Who* books, there were small black and white drawings, and a little drawing on the back cover. I was made to do those, but eventually they got someone else to do them. **❞**

Whilst visiting the Master, who has been exiled to a luxurious castle prison on a small island, Doctor Who and Jo Grant learn that a number of ships have vanished in the area. Whilst investigating these mysterious disappearances, Jo and the Doctor are attacked by a Sea-Devil, one of a submarine colony distantly related to the Silurians. Soon they discover that the Sea-Devils plan to conquer the Earth and enslave humanity, aided and abetted by the Master. What can Doctor Who do to stop them?

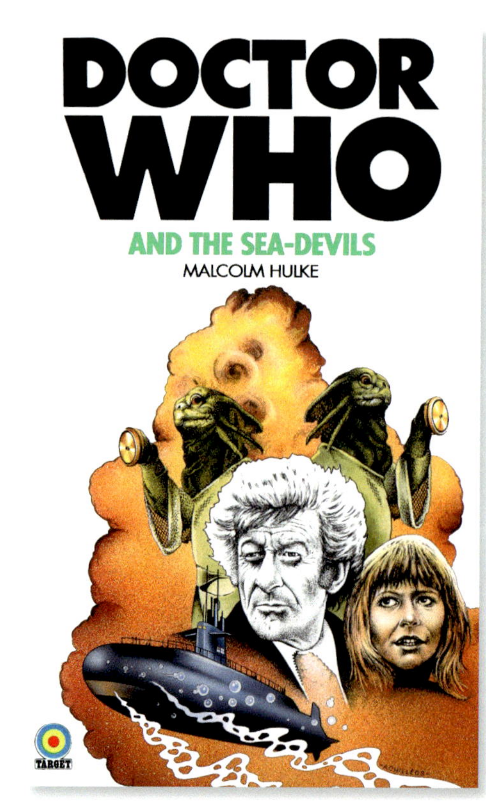

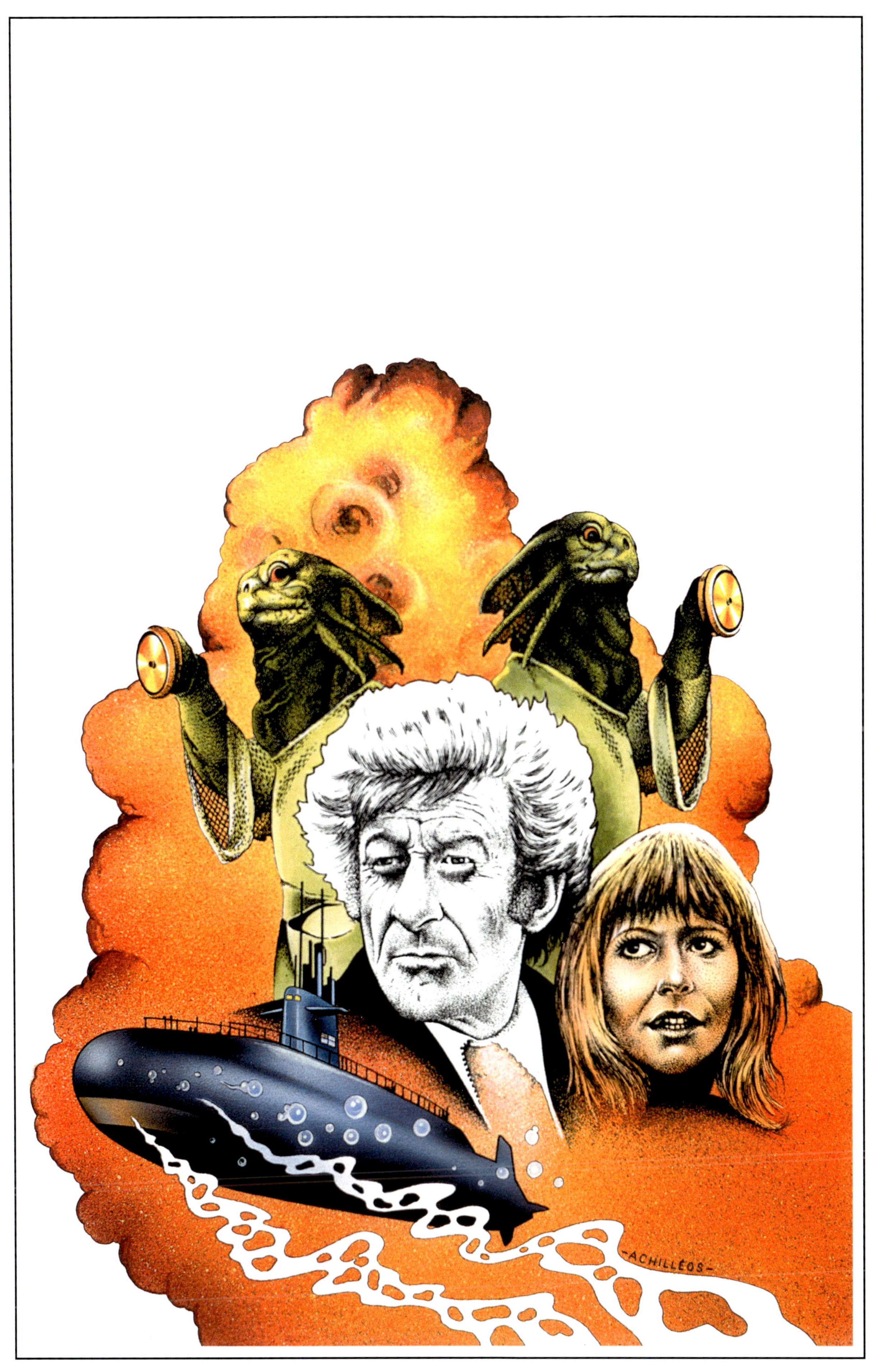

DOCTOR WHO AND THE ABOMINABLE SNOWMEN

Writer: Terrance Dicks **Doctor:** Second **Release date:** 21 November 1974 **Release order:** 10

The Doctor Who and the Abominable Snowmen *BBC CD and book are available from retailers. See bibliography for details.*

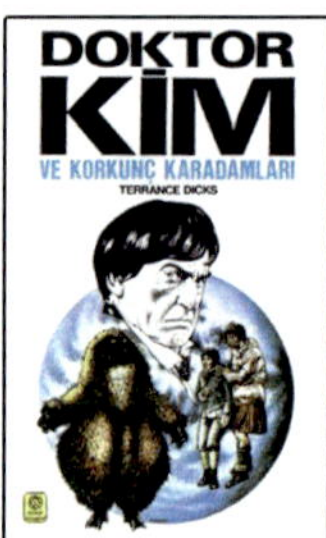

Turkish Edition

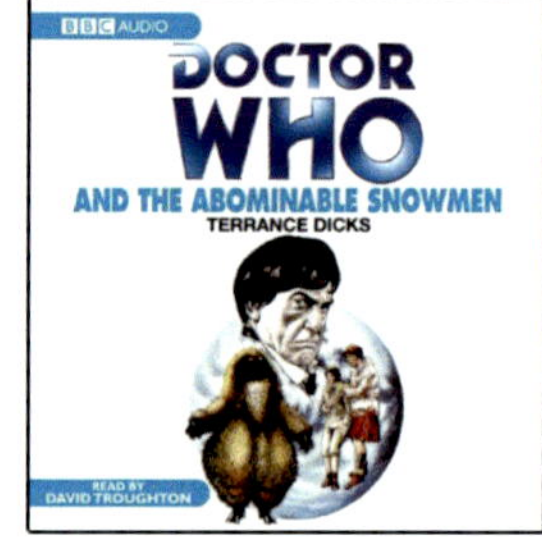

BBC Audiobook CD

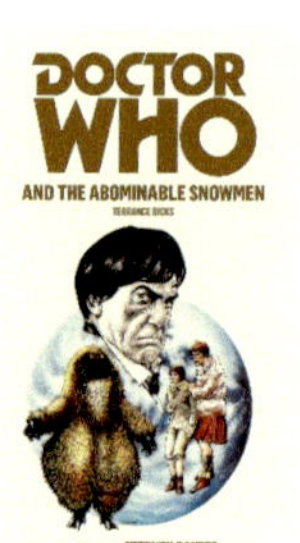

BBC Reissue

"Jamie studied the creature cautiously, fascinated by his first clear look at a Yeti. It was massive, about seven or eight feet tall, Jamie guessed, and covered in shaggy, brown fur."

christos achilleos

66 This is one of my favourite covers. I feel that I have captured the mystery of Patrick Troughton's Doctor. Using the Earth in the background is simple but effective. I always try to encapsulate the story on the cover. Here all the elements come together. The photo of Troughton I used was the perfect reference point, particularly the way he looks at you. I feel that eye contact on covers is very important. Troughton seems very angry, with the companions looking terrified. 99

A single blow from the giant, hairy paw smashes the explorer to the ground. Terrified, he flees from the monster's glowing eyes and savage fangs...

Why are the peaceful Yeti now spreading death and destruction? And what is the secret behind the glowing cave on the mountain?

When Doctor Who discovers that a long-dead friend is still alive, he knows why his visit to the lonely Himalayan monastery has led to a struggle to save the Earth!

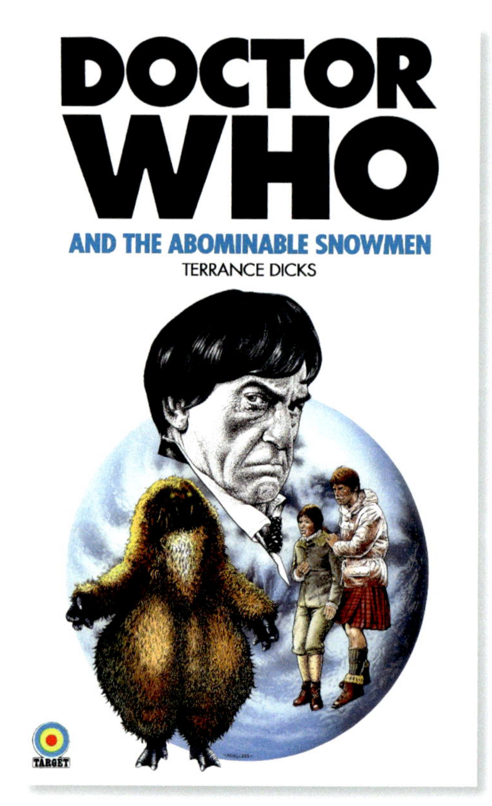

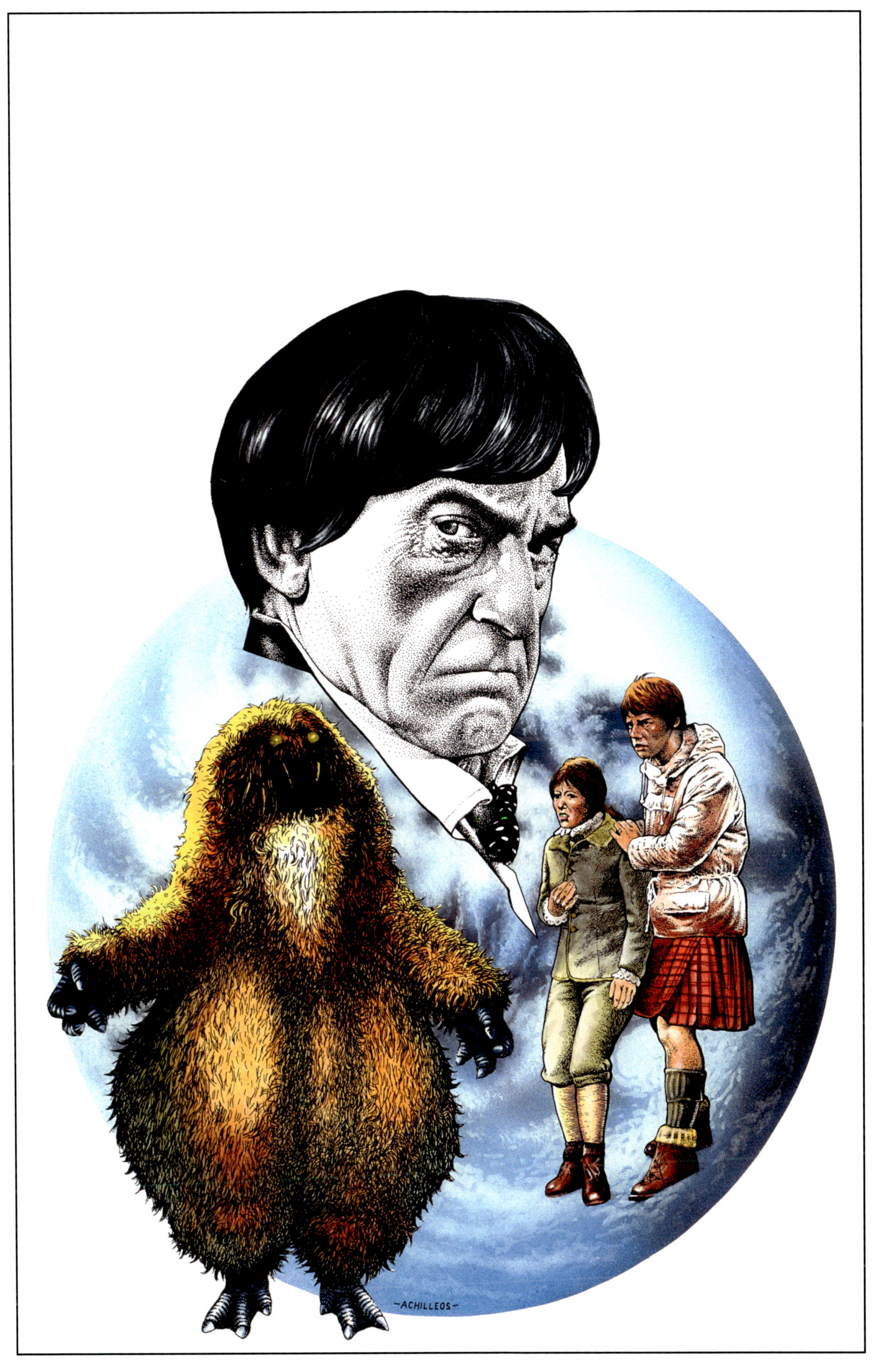

DOCTOR WHO AND THE CURSE OF PELADON

Writer: Brian Hayles **Doctor:** Third **Release date:** 16 January 1975 **Release order:** 11

The Doctor Who and the Curse of Peladon *BBC CD is available from retailers. See bibliography for details.*

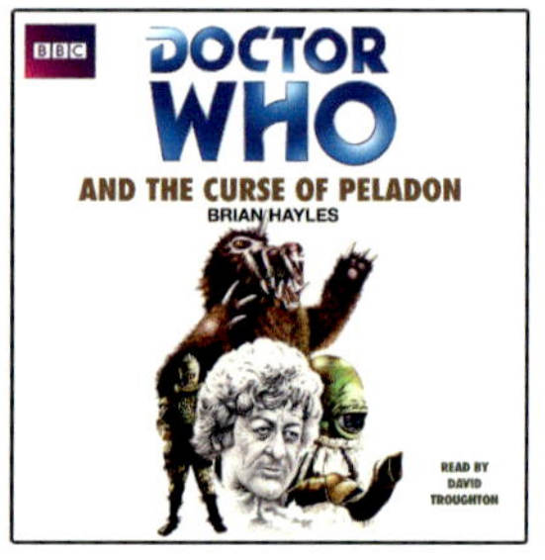

BBC Audiobook CD

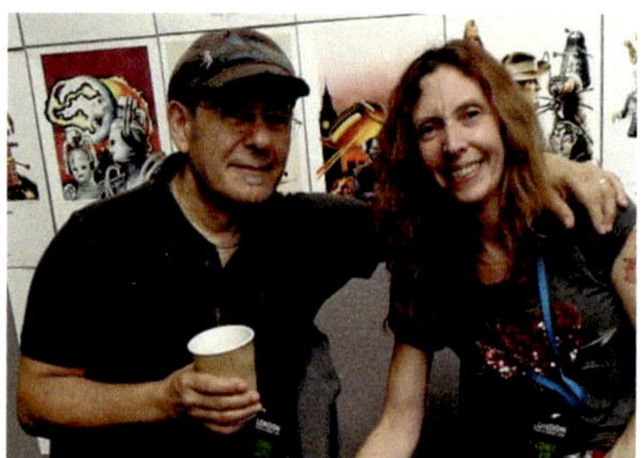

Chris with his wife, Natasha, at the London Film and ComicCon, 2018

"Jo edged closer to the Doctor, and tried not to shudder at the threatening Martians, then something that looked like an operatic octopus – she lost track counting the tentacles – and, finally, a travelling goldfish bowl with a nasty-looking creepy-crawly swimming about inside. It was all too much!"

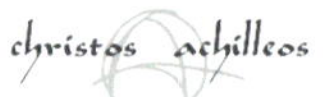

66 I like the pyramid design of this one and the way all the elements fit together. I remember liking all three of the monsters, so I tried to fit them all in. One thing I don't like is the dots fading away by Jon Pertwee's chin. I would never do that now. It looks like he's just sort of floating there. But the rest is OK. 99

Again, the terrifying cry rang out. The Doctor quickened his pace along the gloomy tunnels of the castle. Suddenly, from the darkness lumbered the mighty Aggedor, Royal Beast and Protector of the Kingdom of Peladon!

The Doctor fumbled in his pocket. Would the device work? As he trained the spinning mirror on the eyes of Aggedor, the terrible claws came closer and closer...

What is the secret behind the killings on the planet of Peladon? Is Aggedor seeking revenge because the King of Peladon wants the kingdom to become a member of the Galactic Federation? Will the Doctor escape the claws of Aggedor and discover the truth?

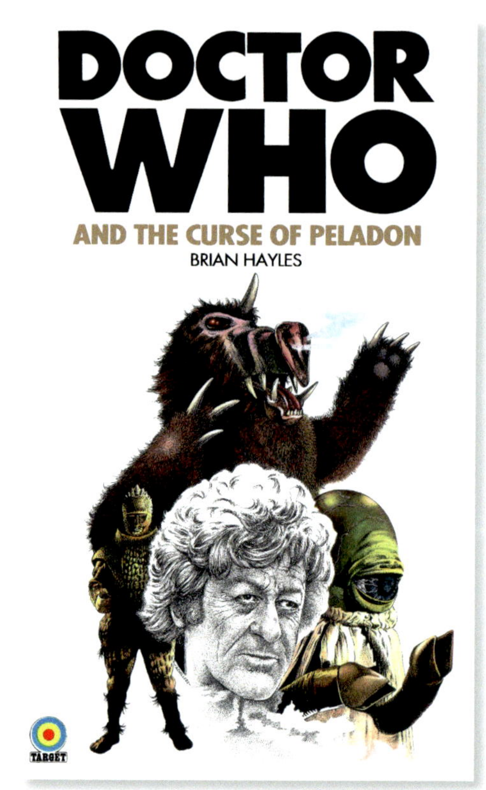

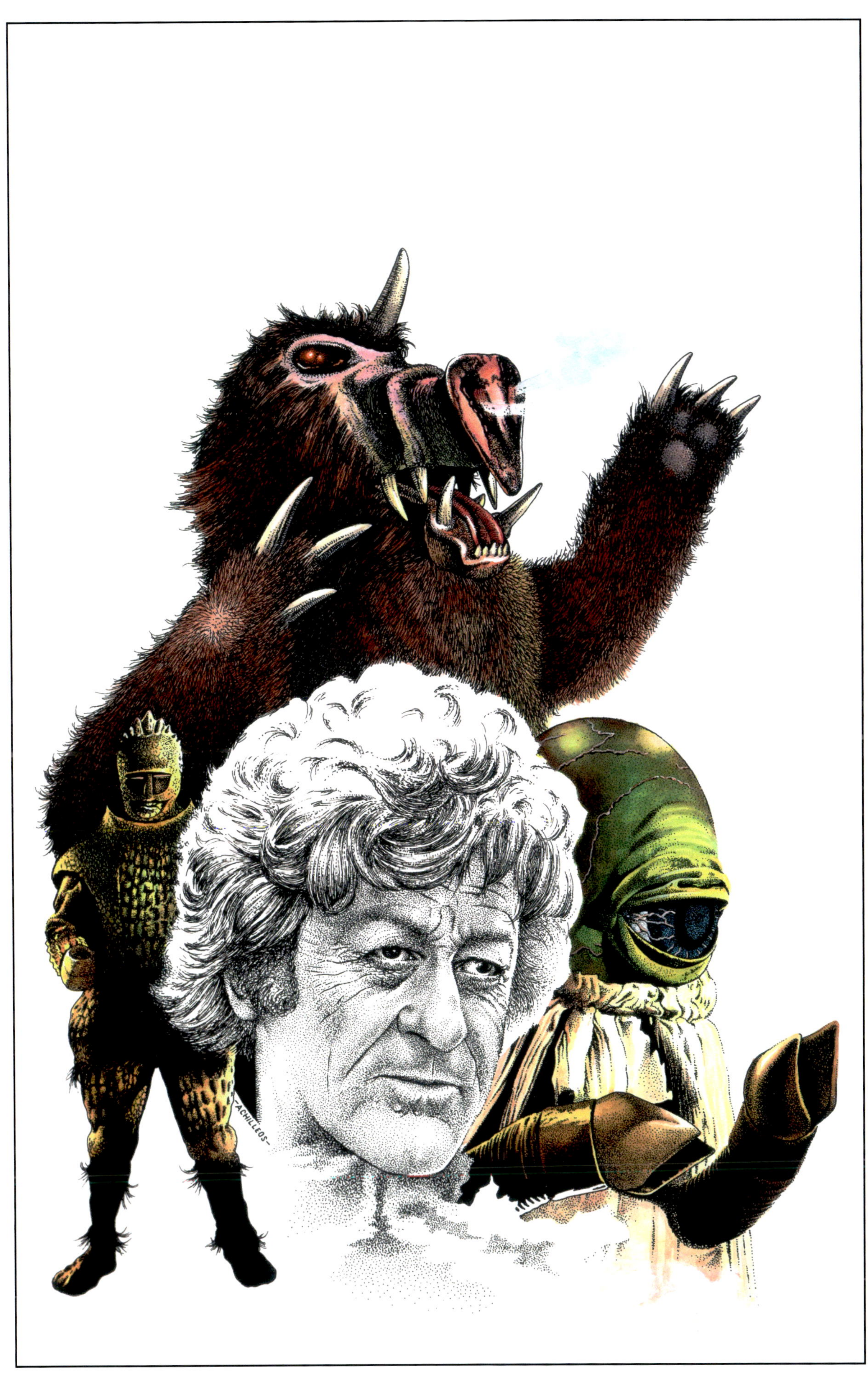

DOCTOR WHO AND THE CYBERMEN

Writer: Gerry Davis **Doctor:** Second **Release date:** 20 February 1975 **Release order:** 12

The Doctor Who and the Cybermen *BBC CD and book are available from retailers. See bibliography for details.*

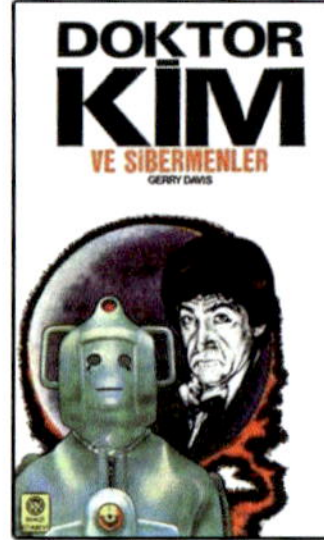

Turkish Edition

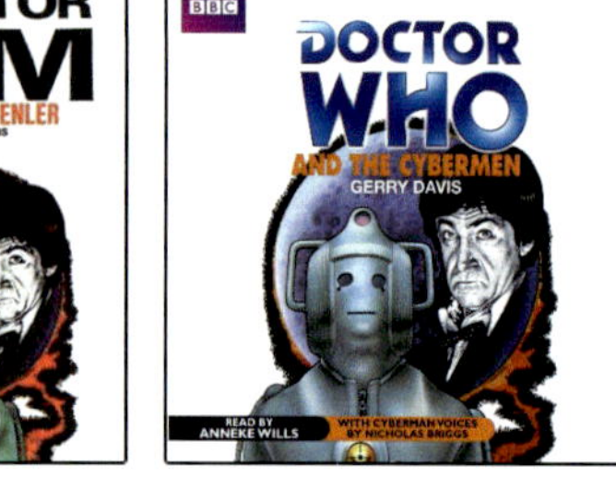

BBC Audiobook CD

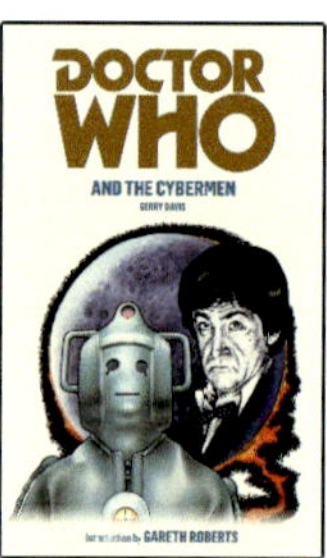

BBC Reissue

"The Doctor stopped about two feet from the bed, turned round and waved the others back. He leant forward to pull off the blanket but, before he could do so, the bedclothes were flung off and a Cyberman, gleaming dully in the red glow, swung massively to his feet, holding a Cyber-weapon."

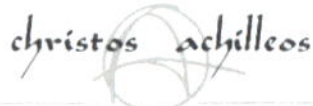

❝ I loved using backgrounds like this one. Here you've got the moon engulfed in Cyberman energy. Nobody mentioned it to me until recently, but apparently that's the wrong Cyberman. The publishers gave me that photo to work with. Patrick Troughton was wonderful to draw if you had a good photo of him. **❞**

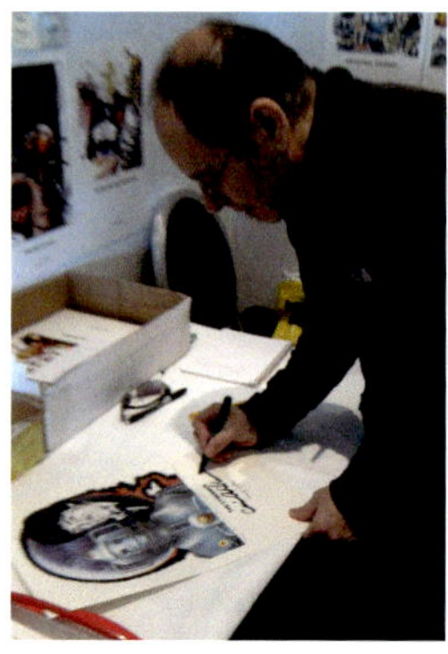

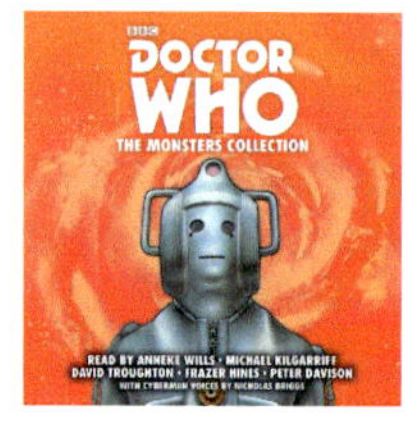

BBC Monsters Collection CD

(left) Chris signing a print of Doctor Who and the Cybermen. *Thanks to Patrick White for photo.*

One by one, their limbs became diseased – they were replaced by plastic and steel!

Little by little, their brains tired – computers worked just as well!

With metal limbs, they had the strength of ten men. They could live in the airless vacuum of space. They had no heart, no feelings, no emotions and only one goal – power!

In the year 2070, a small blue planet caught their attention. They would land on its satellite and, from there, attack, ransack, destroy and finally abandon...

THE SATELLITE WAS THE MOON
THE HELPLESS PLANET – EARTH
THEIR NAMES? THE CYBERMEN!

Can the Doctor defeat an enemy whose threat is almost as great as that of the mighty Daleks?

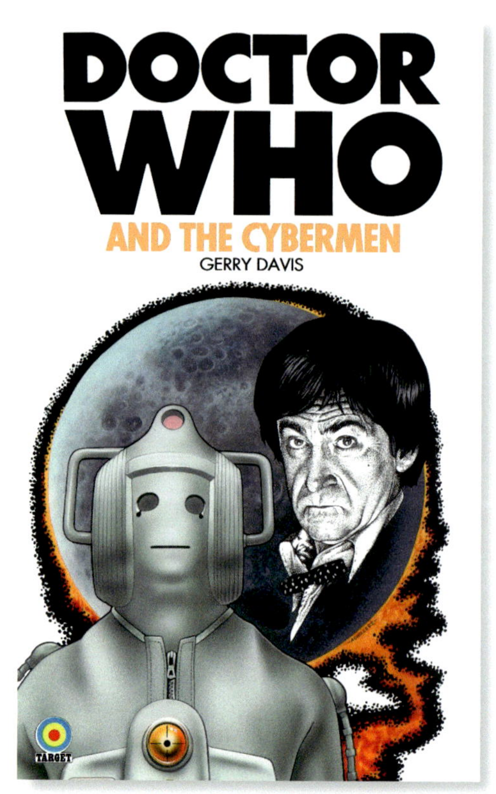

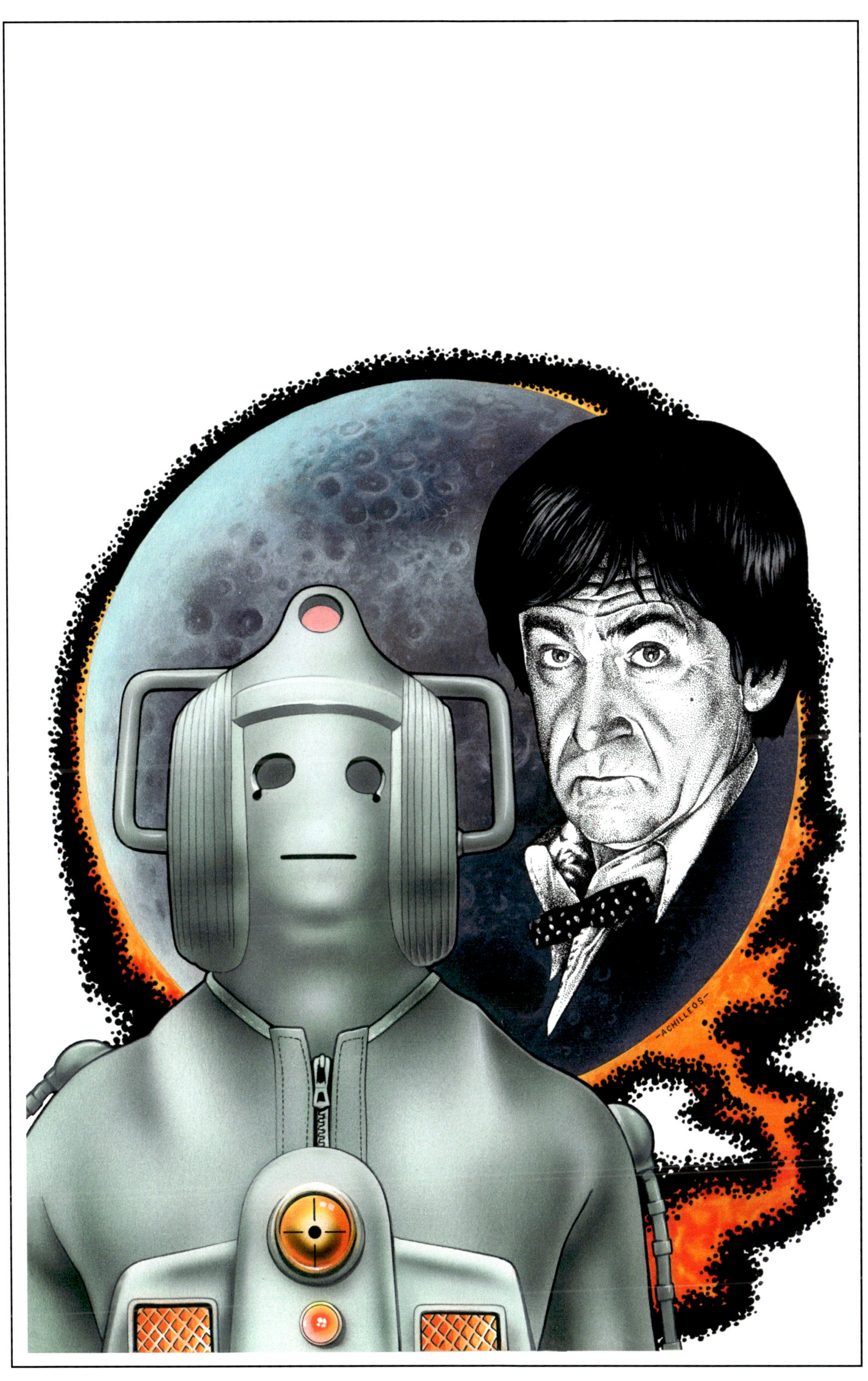

DOCTOR WHO: THE THREE DOCTORS

Writer: Terrance Dicks **Doctor:** 1, 2, 3 **Release date:** 20 November 1975 **Release order:** 17

The Doctor Who: The Three Doctors *BBC CD and book are available from retailers. See bibliography for details.*

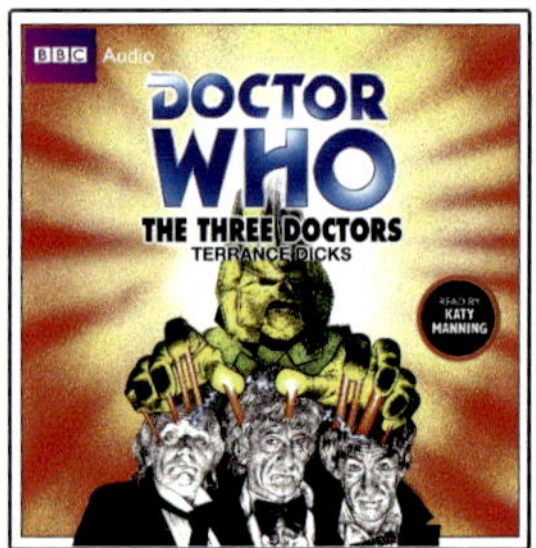

BBC Audiobook CD

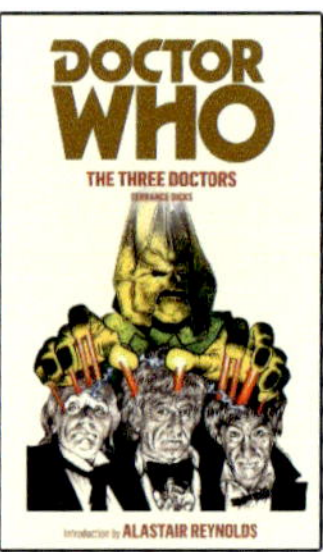

BBC Reissue

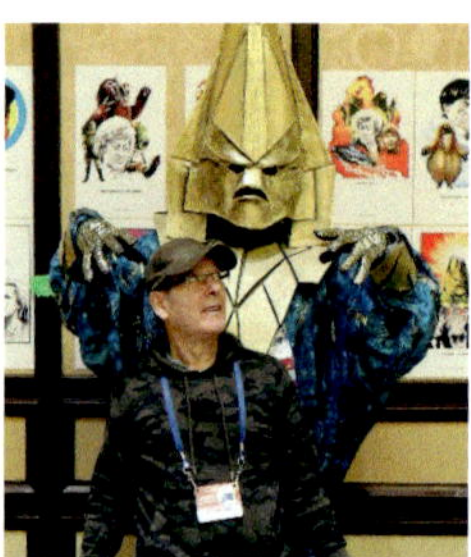

Omega and Chris at Gallifrey Convention, USA

"The Brigadier was staring around him with an air of polite interest. 'Do you know, Doctor,' he said suddenly, 'this thing seems to be bigger on the inside than on the outside.'"

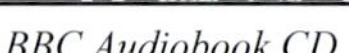

❝ This is by far one of my most popular covers, and it signals a change of approach. That actually came from Brian Boyle, the art director, who decided the illustration should fill the whole cover, even behind the huge logo on the top which took almost half the space. So I decided to use the very bright colours for the background, and it worked very well.

The concept design was inspired by the great Jack Kirby, a cover he did for the *Fantastic Four* comic. I'm not sure if it's entirely accurate to the episode itself, but I thought it would look menacing for the kids. You see this creature exerting this God-like power over the three Doctors, brainwashing them. ❞

Jo glanced up at the Doctor. 'Things must be pretty serious then.'

'They are, Jo. Very serious indeed. The whole of the Universe is in danger!'

The most amazing Who adventure, in which Doctors One, Two and Three cross time and space and come together to fight a ruthlessly dangerous enemy – Omega. Once a Time Lord, now exiled to a black hole in space, Omega is seeking a bitter and deadly revenge against the whole Universe...

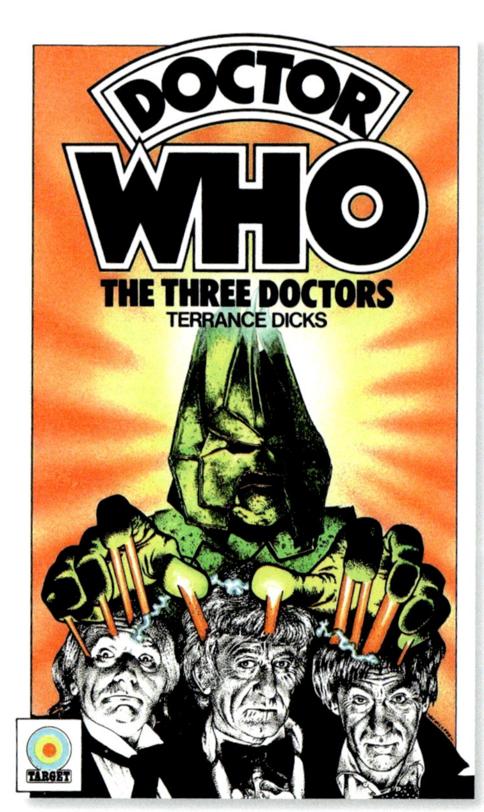

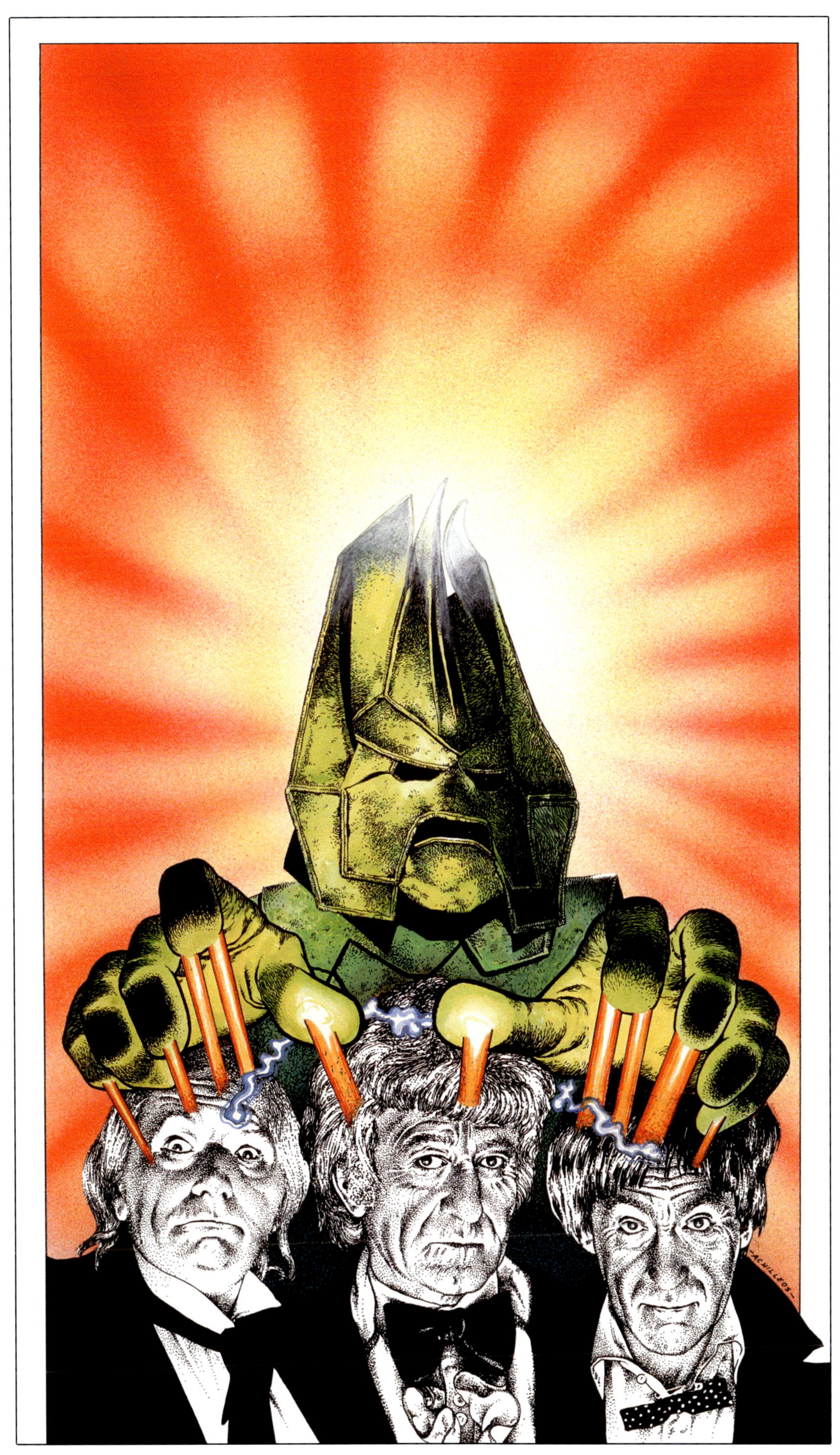

DOCTOR WHO AND THE LOCH NESS MONSTER

Writer: Terrance Dicks **Doctor:** Fourth **Release date:** 15 January 1976 **Release order:** 18

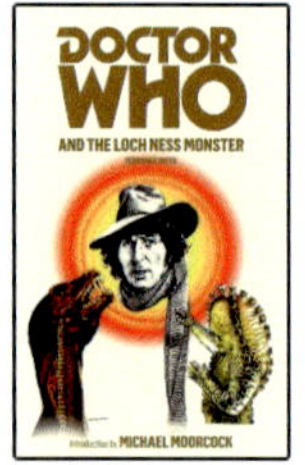

BBC Reissue

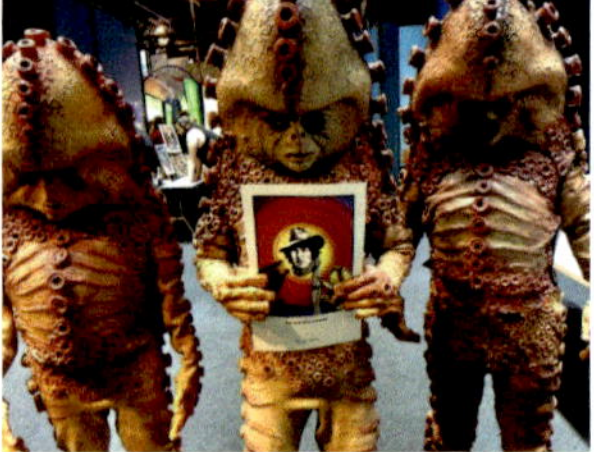

Zygons admiring Chris' work

The Doctor Who and the Loch Ness Monster *BBC book are available from retailers. See bibliography for details.*

"The Doctor, who had no inhibitions about showing his feelings, slapped the Brigadier on the back, shook him warmly by the hand and said, 'Hello, Brigadier, hello. I say, I do like the local garb. Suits you, you know, suits you very well.' He gazed admiringly at the Brigadier's kilt."

christos achilleos

Why is Doctor Who suddenly summoned to the shores of Loch Ness? Terror and panic spread as the third oil rig is smashed into the sea by a mysterious force... the monster?

The controlling power must be the Zygons – alien creatures who have lived hidden on Earth for thousands of years, and now feel strong enough to take over the planet... The Doctor, Sarah and UNIT have different ideas – but can they outwit the supreme cunning of the ruthless Zygons?

❝ Again, *The Loch Ness Monster* is about colour, big colourful backgrounds. It has that sort of, 'Hey, hey hey! That's all folks!' kind of look. I didn't think of it at the time; I was just trying to do something punchy.

And of course, this was the first Tom Baker cover I did.

I had no reference for the monster, so I phoned the publishers and said, "Look, it's the Loch Ness Monster, but you haven't given me anything to work from, so what do I do? You'll have to get me something or I'll make it up."

So they went to the BBC, who finally came up with a tiny Polaroid photo, which I might still have somewhere: a Polaroid of this figurine but just from the neck up.

All in all, I think it's a smart bit of airbrushing: the little creature on the right, and the Doctor's scarf coming down, that sort of worried look on his face and all the energy bars and colours. Not bad! **❞**

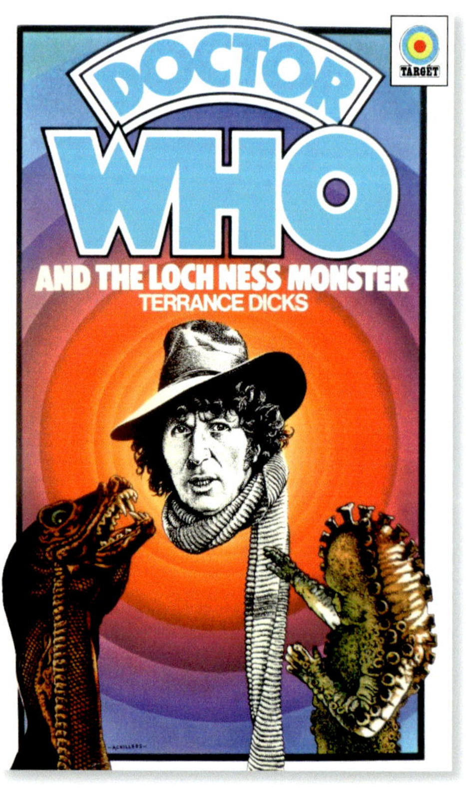

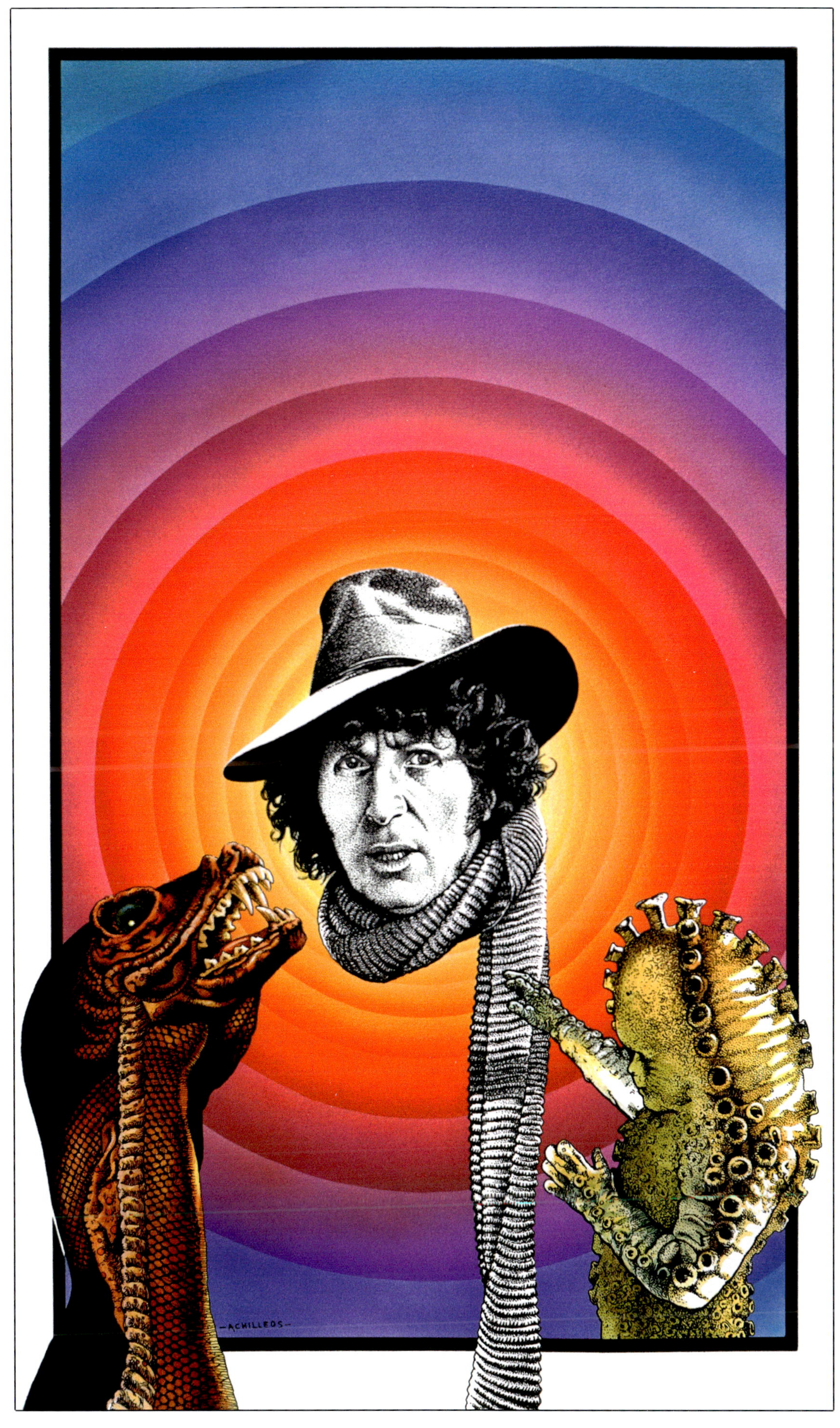

DOCTOR WHO AND THE DINOSAUR INVASION

Writer: Malcolm Hulke **Doctor:** Third **Release date:** 15 January 1976 **Release order:** 19

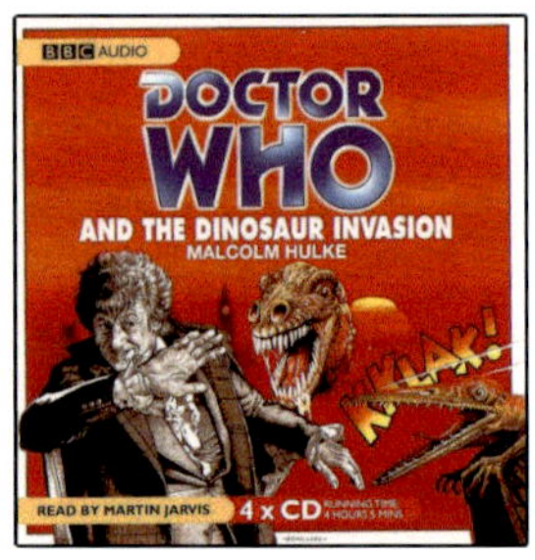

BBC Audiobook CD

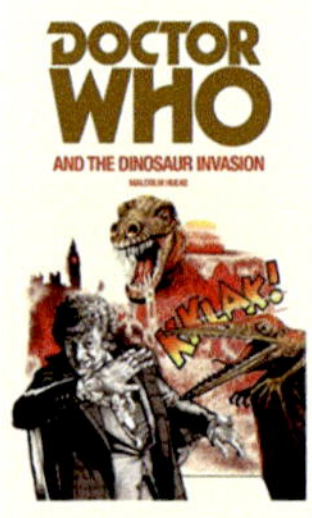

BBC Reissue

The Doctor Who and the Dinosaur Invasion *BBC CD and book are available from retailers. See bibliography for details.*

"The stegosaurus, thirty feet long and weighing two tons, stood bewildered in a narrow Hampstead side street. In the distance it could see the green of Hampstead Heath, and the prospect of so much lush foliage made its salivic juices run. But immediately ahead was a little group of mammalian midgets coloured brown, and they were frightening because they carried sticks that made big bangs."

christos achilleos

❝ By '76 I was really busy doing adult fantasy and science fiction covers. The '*Kklak!*' came from my love of American comics. Once I thought of it, I just had to put it on there. By this time, I had been doing *Doctor Who* work for a while, and I had got in a good rhythm.

When I unveiled it to the publishers, they said, 'Oh my God, what's this? This, this "*Kklak!*", you've got to get rid of it, Chris.'

'Why?' I said.

'Well, this is a book cover, not a comic.'

I said, 'Well obviously it's not a comic, it's a cover. But you know, it puts another dimension in it; it puts sound in it, to bring it to life. Trust me,' I said, 'the kids will love it.'

I knew it was the right thing to do, and I refused to take it out or do it again. When it was published, it became one of their best-selling covers ever. I understood their market better than them. **❞**

The Doctor walked slowly forward into the cul-de-sac. The giant dinosaur turned its head to focus on the midget now approaching... the Doctor aimed his gun to fire... suddenly from behind came a great roar of anger. He spun round – blocking the exit from the narrow street towered a Tyrannosaurus rex, its savage jaws dripping with blood...

The Doctor and Sarah arrive back in the TARDIS to find London completely deserted – except for the dinosaurs. Has the return of these prehistoric creatures been deliberately planned and, if so, who can be behind it all?

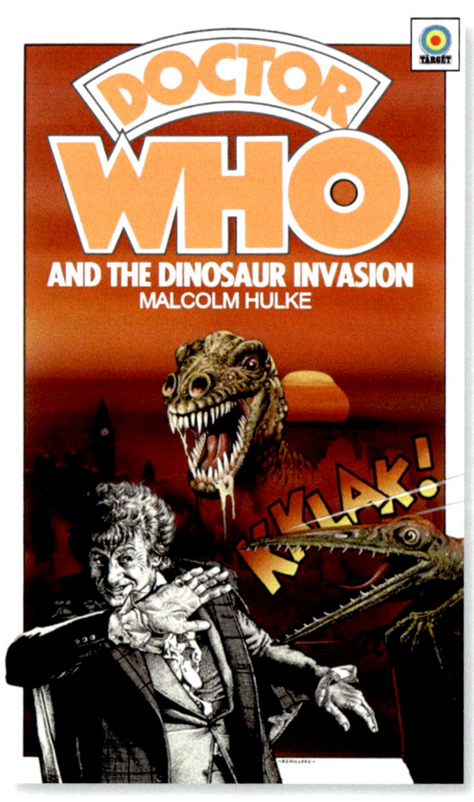

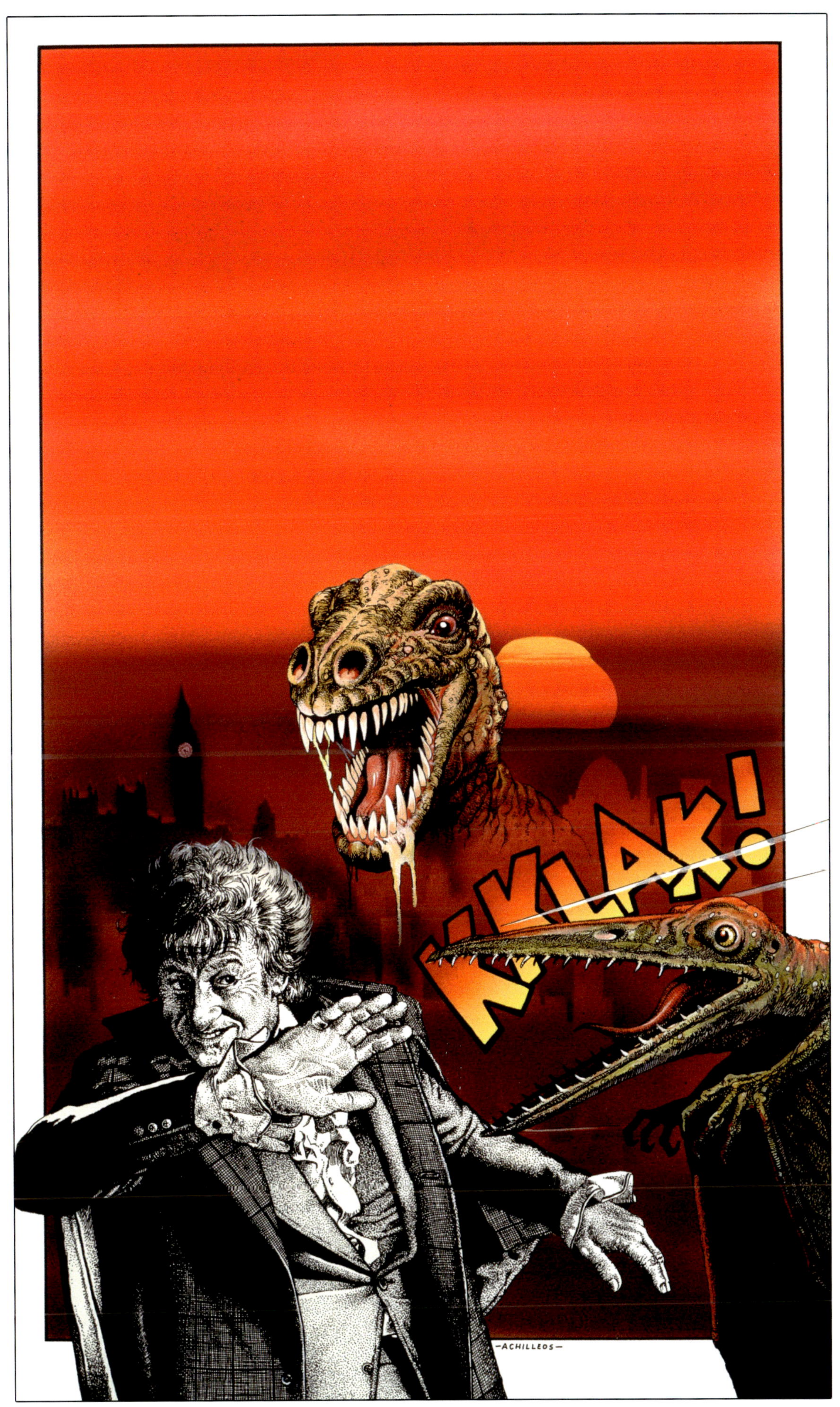

K KLAK!
ACHILLEOS

DOCTOR WHO AND THE TENTH PLANET

Writer: Gerry Davis **Doctor:** First **Release date:** 19 February 1976 **Release order:** 20

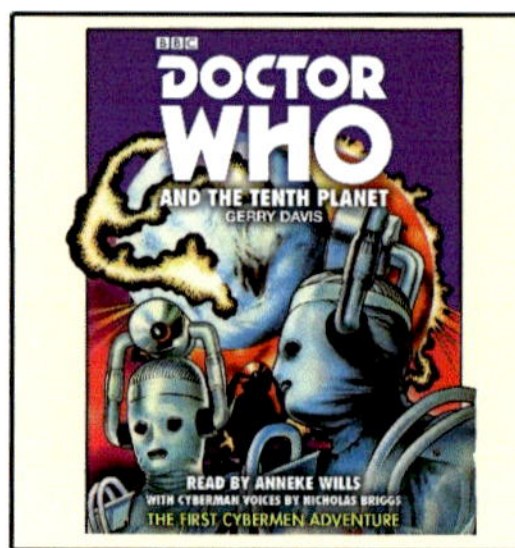

BBC Audiobook CD

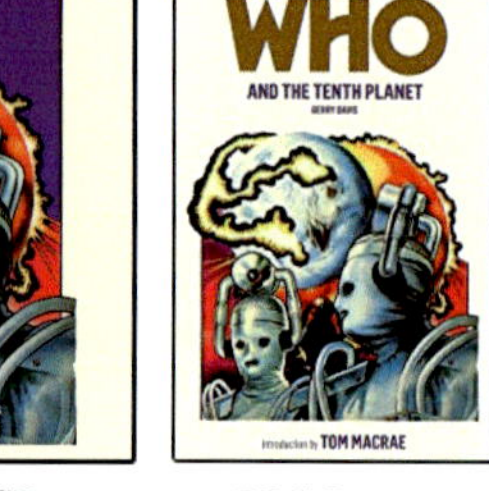

BBC Reissue

The Doctor Who and the Tenth Planet *BBC CD and book are available from retailers. See bibliography for details.*

"[Ben] reached forward gingerly and pulled back the edge of the cloak. The face under the cloak was not the Doctor's. It was the face of a much younger man — a man in his early forties. The Doctor's long, silver locks had been replaced with short, dark hair, and the newcomer had a swarthy, almost gypsy, appearance."

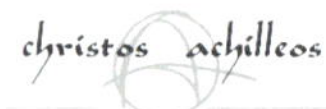

The Sergeant blinked again. Three lights were moving towards him through the murk of the blizzard. Even as he looked, the lights changed into three tall, straight figures, clad in silver-armoured suits, advancing across the ice with a slow deliberate step. Horror-struck, the Sergeant reached for his gun, and a stream of bullets sprayed across the marching figures. BUT THEY CONTINUED MARCHING...

The Cybermen have arrived. The first invasion of Earth by this invincible, fearless race — and the last thrilling adventure of the first Doctor Who.

❝ The right Cybermen this time! ☺

I have very few memories of doing the cover for *The Tenth Planet*. I do remember, however, that my reference material was limited… again. This, of course, makes my work so much harder. This is the first of my covers that doesn't feature the Doctor, and because I got away with it, I did it again for the next one, *The Ice Warriors*. This one's a bit messy, and the colours aren't quite right. Despite this, I tried to encapsulate the Cybermen's envelopment of Earth behind them. To be honest, I could have done a lot better. I guess it did the job though, and I'm told lots of people still like it. ❞

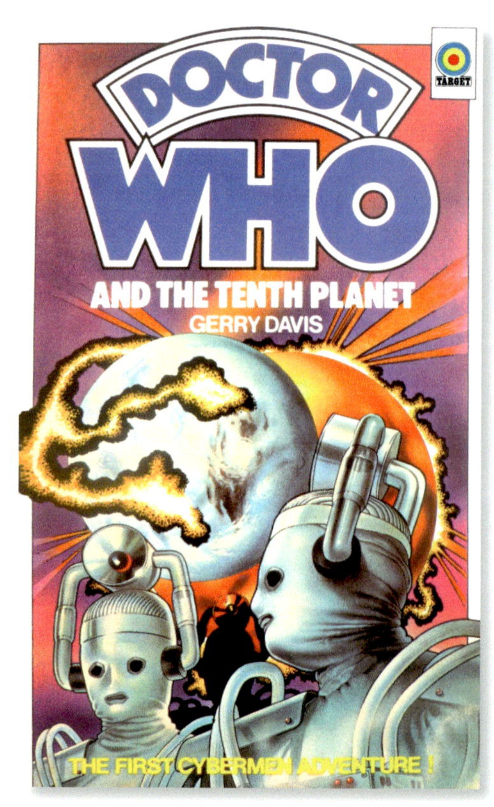

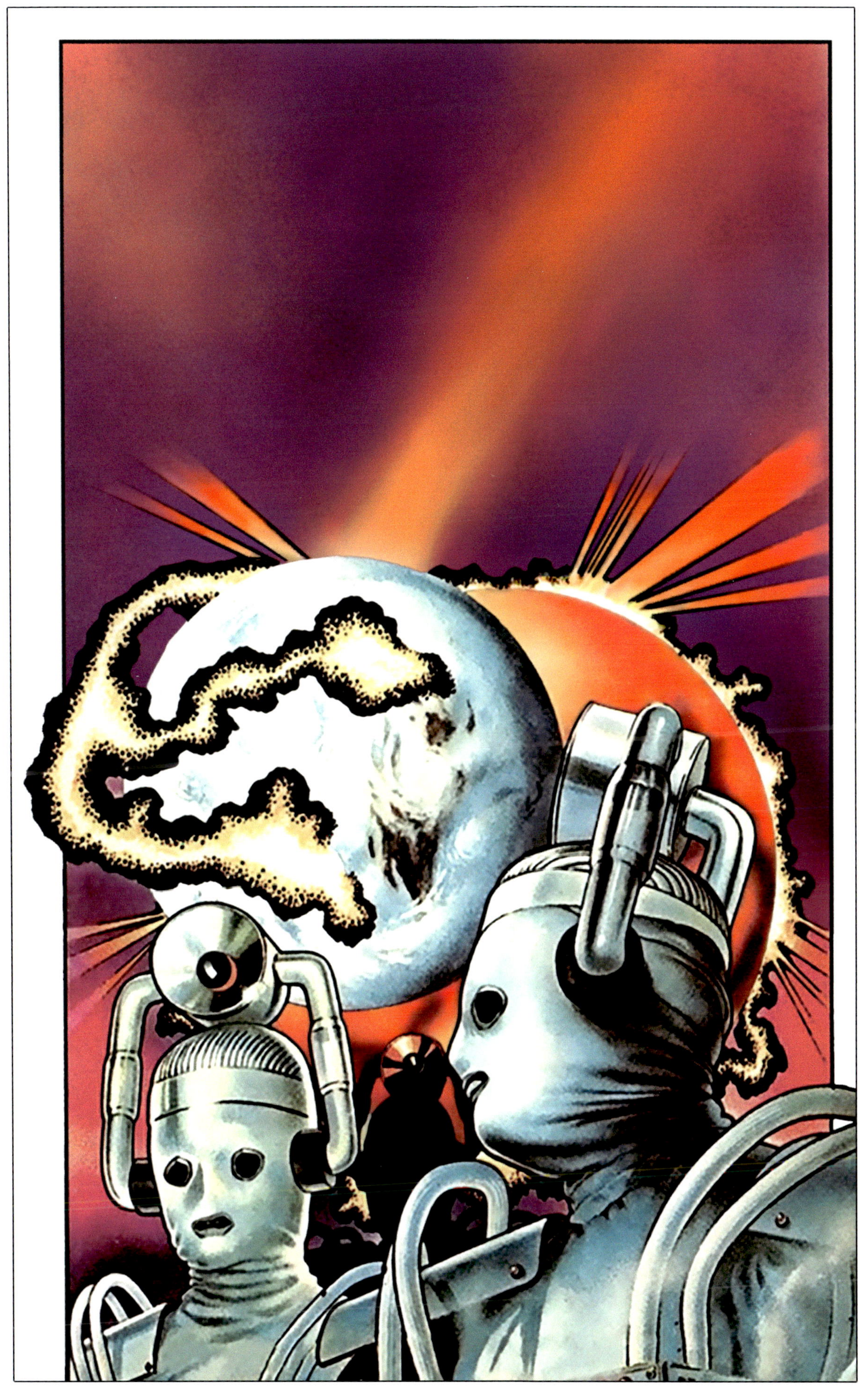

DOCTOR WHO AND THE ICE WARRIORS

Writer: Brian Hayles **Doctor:** Second **Release date:** 18 March 1976 **Release order:** 21

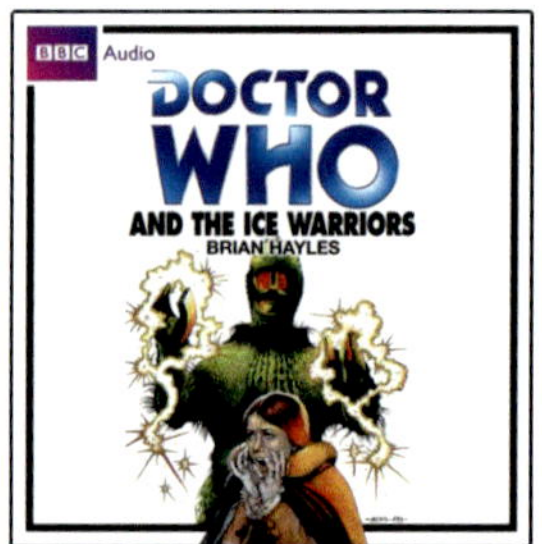

BBC Audiobook CD

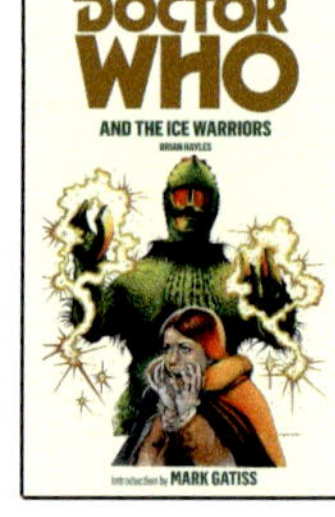

BBC Reissue

The Doctor Who and the Ice Warriors *BBC CD and book are available from retailers. See bibliography for details.*

"Victoria noticed with a shudder that instead of hands, or even webbed, reptilian claws, the arms ended in what looked like metallic clamps. And from the right forearm, compact and sleek, but as though part of the creature's physical anatomy, projected a strange tubular device — rather like the telescopic sights of a rifle."

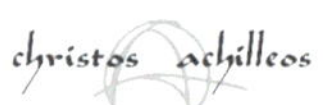

66 *The Ice Warriors* is one of my favourites. It's just perfect. I wouldn't change a single detail. I love the colours, the white background, and the silhouettes. I like the way the red clashes with the green. That's why I gave the green Ice Warrior red eyes. I also like the sparks coming out of its hands. As far as I know this does not happen in the episode. I think it really makes the cover! The reference photograph of Victoria they sent me was really good and quite dramatic. If I had more photos like this I would have included the companions more often in my covers. 99

The world is held in the grip of a second Ice Age, and faces total destruction from the rapidly advancing glaciers.

Doctor Who, with Victoria and Jamie, lands at a top scientific base in England, where they have just unearthed an ancient Ice Warrior. Aliens from Mars, preserved in the ice for centuries and now revitalised, the Ice Warriors feel ready to take over...

Can the Doctor overcome these warlike Martians and halt the relentless approach of the ice glaciers...?

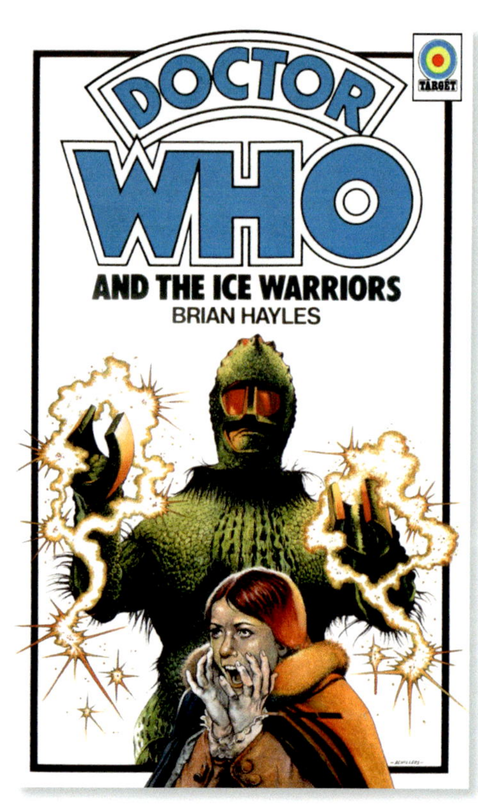

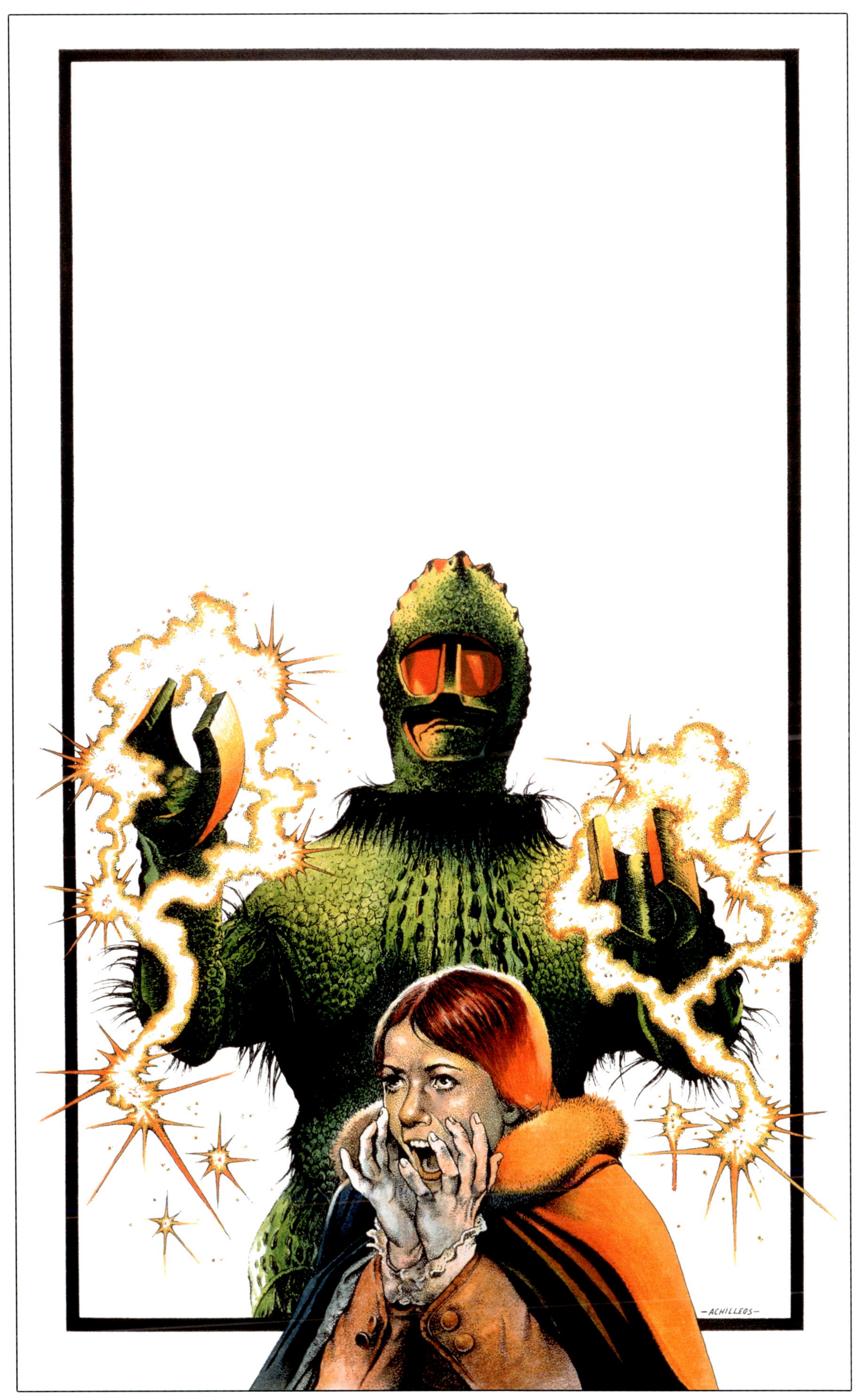

DOCTOR WHO AND THE REVENGE OF THE CYBERMEN

Writer: Terrance Dicks **Doctor:** Fourth **Release date:** 20 May 1976 **Release order:** 22

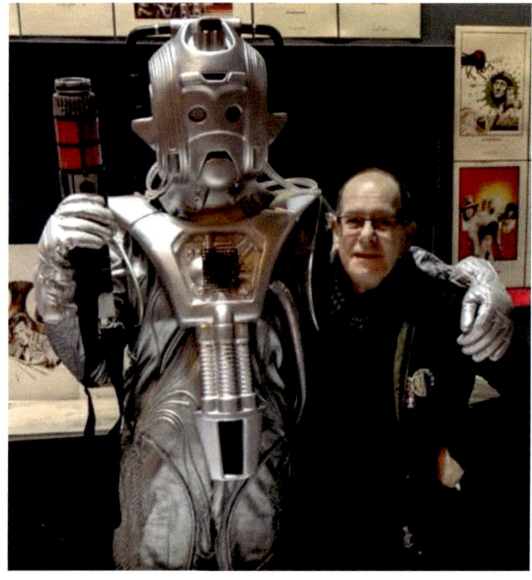

(below) Chris with the wrong Cyberman, again! John Williams, 15th Cyber Legion.

"'The trouble with you Cybermen is you've got hydraulic muscles and hydraulic brains to go with 'em.'
For some reason this childish insult broke through the Cyberleader's control. It took a final step forward, the silver arm sweeping upwards for a blow."

A mysterious plague strikes Space Beacon Nerva, killing its victims within minutes. When Doctor Who lands, only four humans remain alive. One of these seems to be in league with the nearby planet of gold, Voga… Or is he in fact working for the dreaded Cybermen, who are now determined to finally destroy their old enemies, the Vogans?

The Doctor, Sarah and Harry find themselves caught in the midst of a terrifying struggle to death – between the ruthless, power-hungry Cybermen and the desperate, determined Vogans.

❝ In some respects, I was back to what I had been doing previously in terms of layout. In retrospect, I think it could do with a background colour of some kind! Tom Baker's hair is a bit too curly, but the explosion behind him is very effective. The Cyberman and the Vogan facing each other completes the design. **❞**

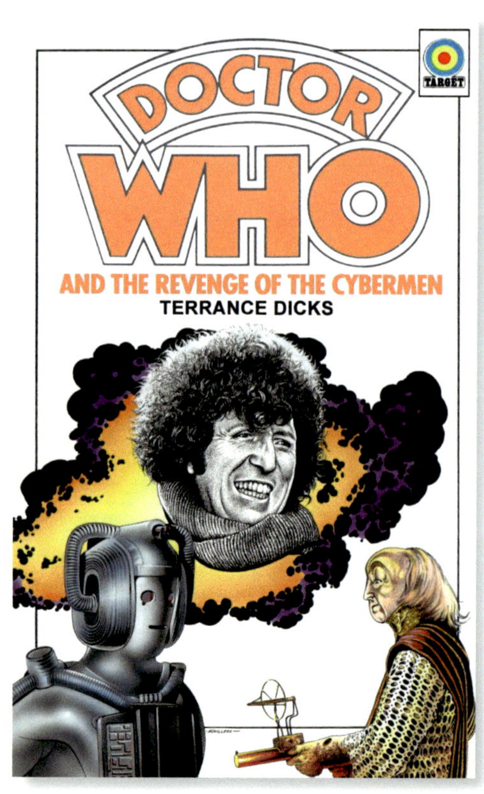

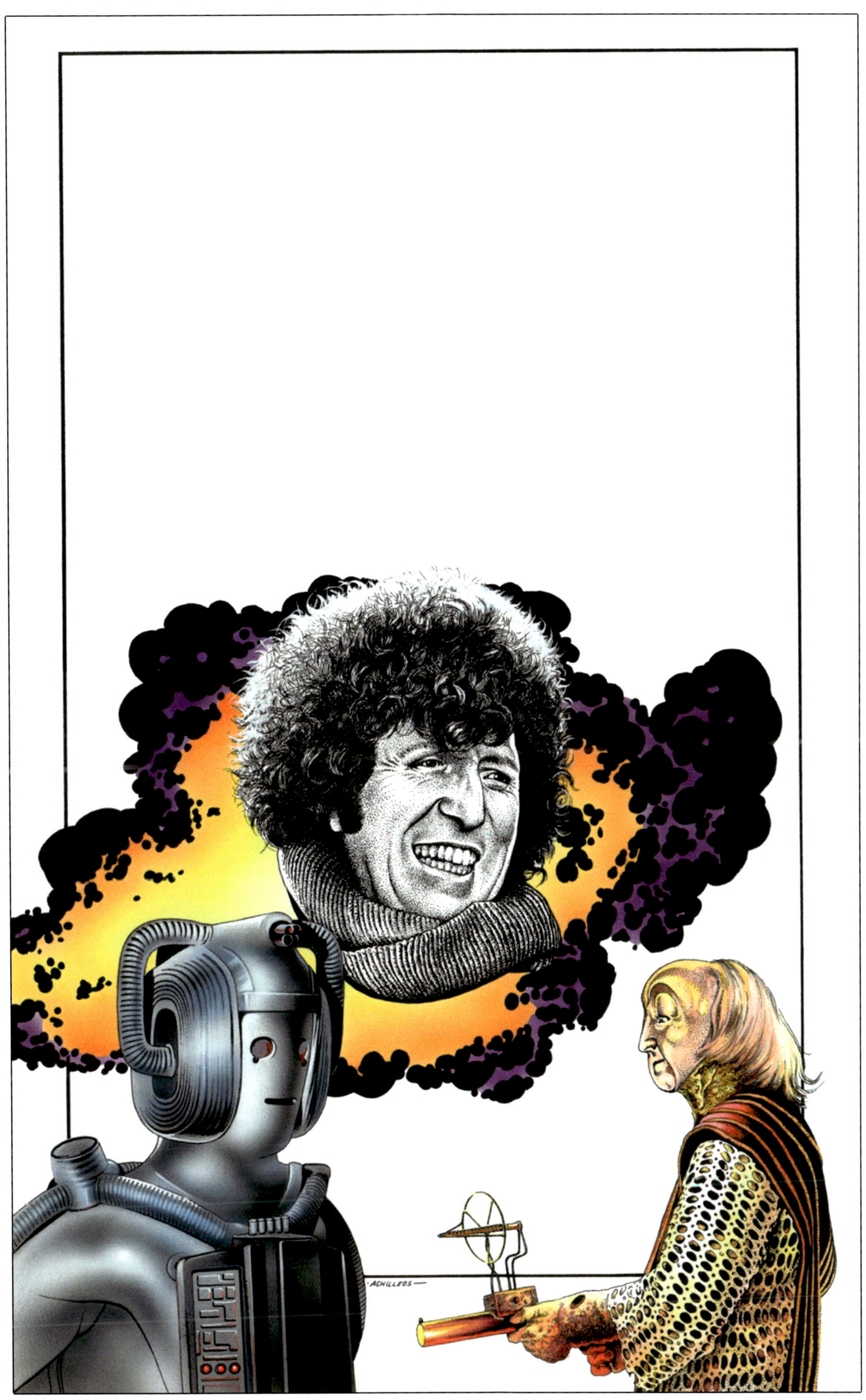

DOCTOR WHO AND THE GENESIS OF THE DALEKS

Writer: Terrance Dicks **Doctor:** Fourth **Release date:** 22 July 1976 **Release order:** 23

The Doctor Who and the Genesis of the Daleks *BBC CD and book are available from retailers, as well as* Doctor Who Magazine. *See bibliography for details.*

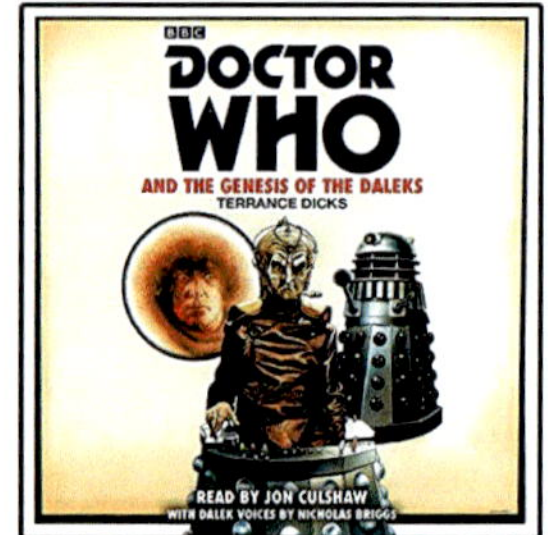

BBC Audiobook CD

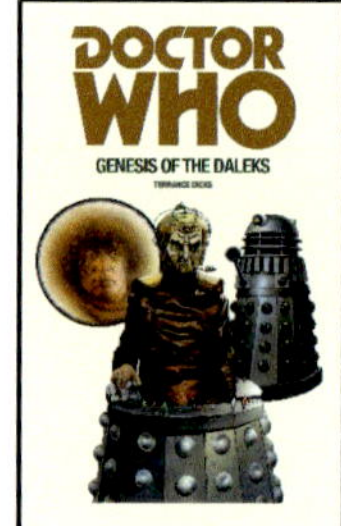

BBC Reissue

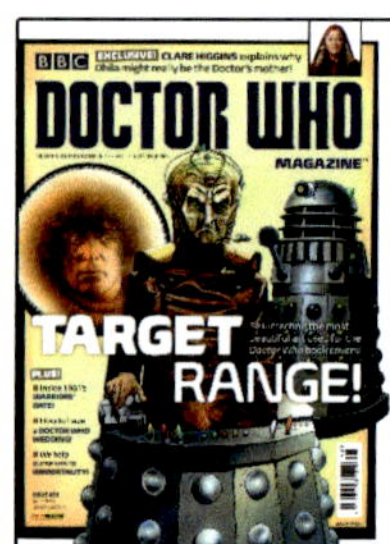

Doctor Who Magazine 449

"'Tell me, Davros, if you had created a virus in your laboratory, one that could destroy all life – would you use it?'

Davros seemed fascinated by the concept. 'To know that life and death on an enormous scale was within my choice ... That the pressure of my thumb breaking the glass of a capsule could end everything ... Such power would set me amongst the Gods ... Yes, I would do it! And through the Daleks I shall have such power!'"

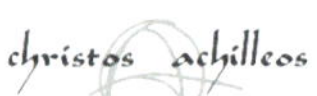

  I was constantly looking to do something different, so for this one I decided to paint the Doctor instead of using pointillism.

Arguably this cover is as simple as *Revenge of the Cybermen*, but I think it works at lot better. This earthy look is wonderful and quite a change to the previous bright colours. It's one of my favourites, because of Davros, mainly. Such a wonderful figure forming a pyramid design. It's a very clean and pleasing cover.

The Dalek's stalk is around the right way this time, and I like the way Tom Baker is looking worried at Davros. **"**

The place: Skaro
Time: The Birth of the Daleks
After a thousand years of futile war against the Thals, Davros has perfected the physical form that will carry his race into eternity – the dreaded Dalek. Without feeling, conscience or pity, the Dalek is programmed to exterminate.

At the command of the Time Lords, Doctor Who travels back through time in an effort to totally destroy this terrible menace of the future.

But even the Doctor cannot always win...

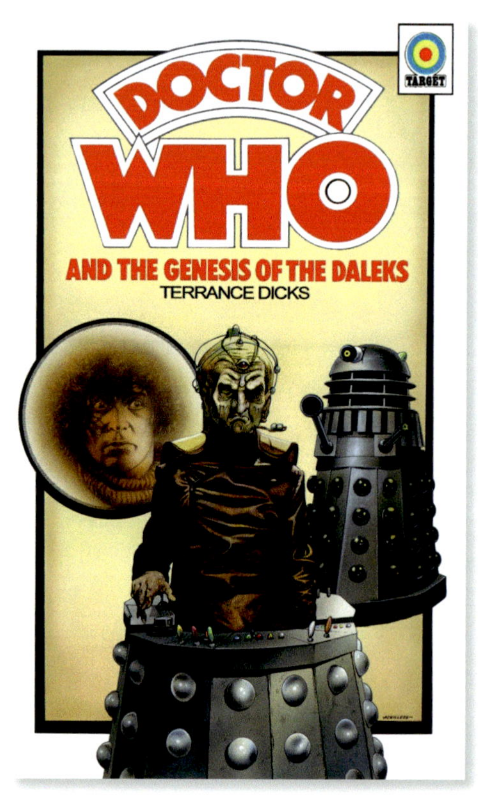

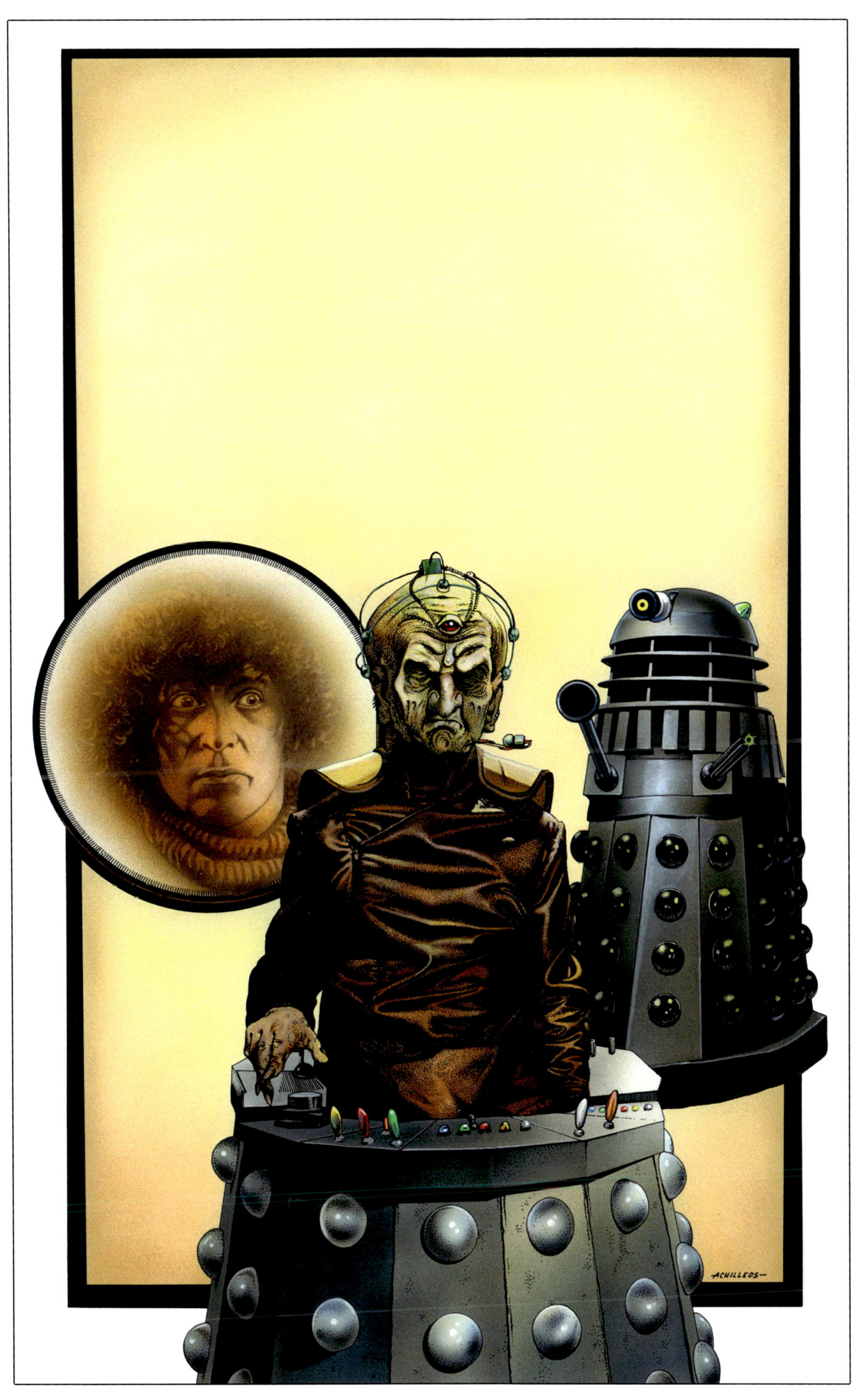

DOCTOR WHO AND THE WEB OF FEAR

Writer: Terrance Dicks **Doctor:** Second **Release date:** 19 August 1976 **Release order:** 24

The Doctor Who and the Web of Fear *BBC CD and book are available from retailers, as well as* Doctor Who Magazine. *See bibliography for details.*

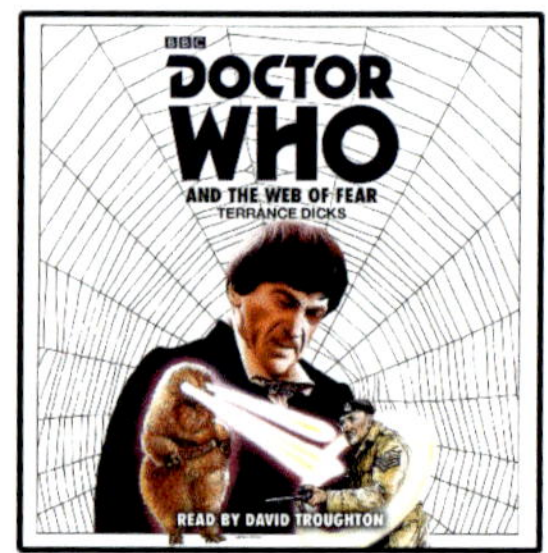
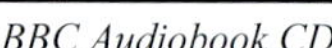

BBC Audiobook CD

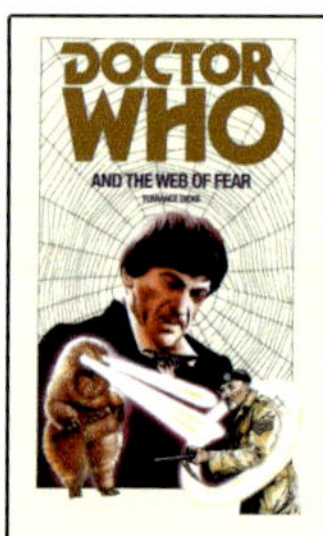

BBC Reissue

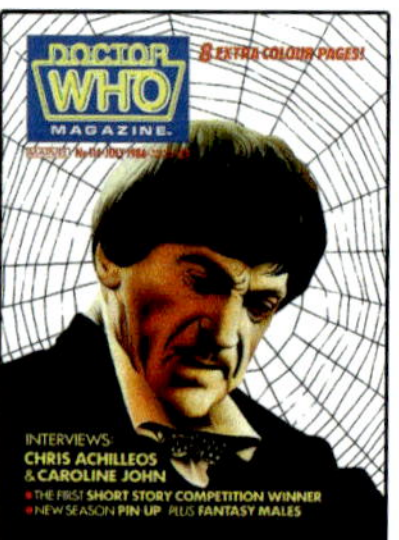

Doctor Who Magazine 114

"A tall figure appeared, torch in one hand, revolver in the other, covering the Doctor. It was a man in battledress, the insignia of a colonel on his shoulders. Even through the semi-darkness the Doctor caught an impression of an immaculate uniform and neatly trimmed moustache. The soldier peered down from his superior height at the small, scruffy figure of the captive. 'And who might you be?' he asked, sounding more amused than alarmed."

christos achilléos

❝ The spider's web going round the Doctor's head on this one is just great. I also like the energy beams coming out of the Yeti's eyes. As with *The Dinosaur Invasion* it would have been great to feature something similar to *'kklak'* in my design, but I didn't want to push it.

If truth be told, at the time, I do believe that I understood the mindset of the young readers better than the publisher. Being a comic fan since childhood and still in my twenties, I really knew how the kids' minds worked. But all the publishers really wanted to do was to sell books. **❞**

Forty years the Yeti had been quiet. A collector's item in a museum. Then without warning it awoke – and savagely murdered.

At about the same time patches of mist began to appear in Central London. People who lingered any time in the mist were found dead, their faces smothered in cobwebs. The cobweb seeped down, penetrating the Underground System. Slowly it spread...

Then the Yeti reappeared, not just one but hordes, roaming the misty streets and cobwebbed tunnels, killing everyone in their path. Central London was gripped tight in a Web of Fear...

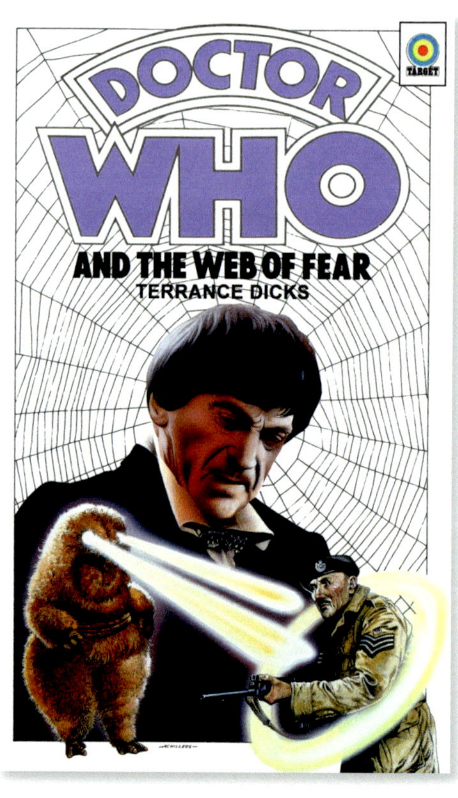

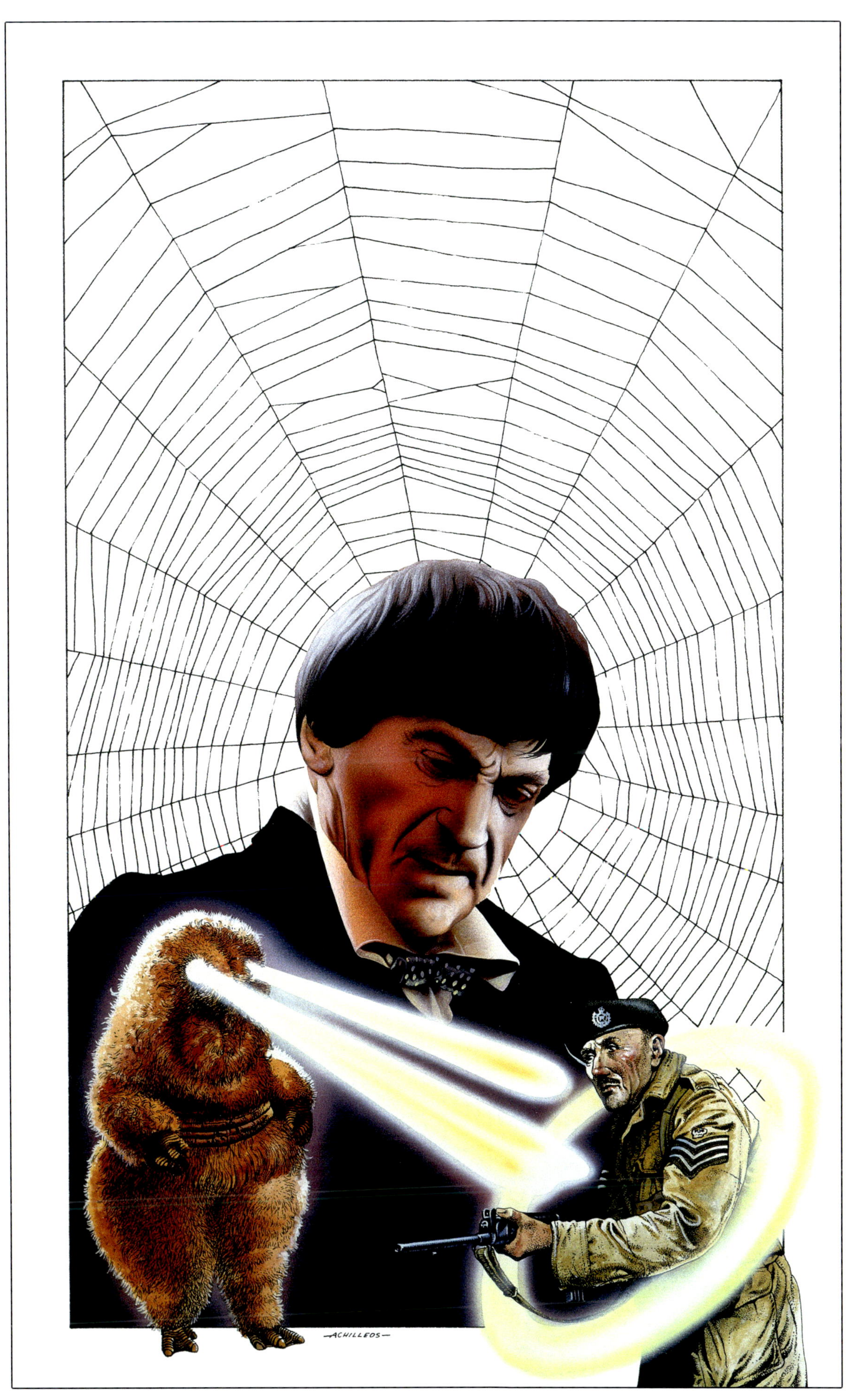

DOCTOR WHO AND THE SPACE WAR

Writer: Malcom Hulke **Doctor:** Third **Release date:** 23 September 1976 **Release order:** 25

The Doctor Who and the Space War *BBC CD is available from retailers. See bibliography for details.*

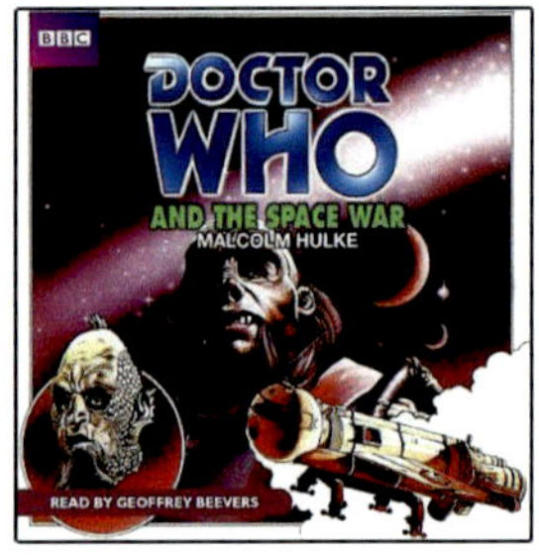
BBC Audiobook CD

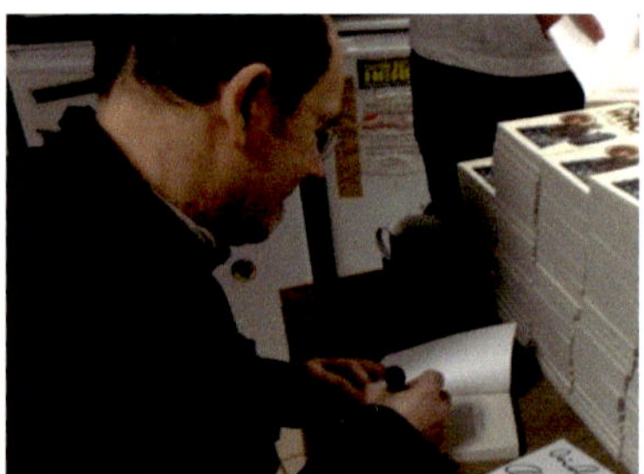
Chris signing books at Forbidden Planet

"'Are you a Draconian spy? When do they plan to attack us? Who first recruited you? Who are the other Draconian agents on Earth? Answer! Answer!'

Waves of intense pain poured through the Doctor's mind. On the television screen only whirling patterns appeared. Using all his energy, the Doctor tried to overcome the pain. Then, suddenly, the mind probe machine blew a fuse."

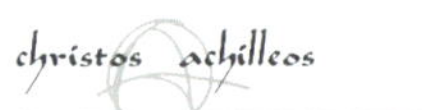

66 *The Space War* has a different look again.

Look at the circle with the Draconian in it. I originally had the head of the Doctor there. I changed it at the last minute. I thought the Draconian was such a good alien that the kids would like that better. They knew the Doctor's head anyway...

I also included a spaceship, which I hadn't done before on a cover. The Ogron has a great look as well. I like the three together. 99

"Doctor," screamed Jo. "Look at that thing. It's coming straight at us!" A small black spaceship, about a mile away, was approaching rapidly.

It had no lights, no markings. But some instinct told Jo that the tiny craft meant danger.

The year is 2540, and two powers loom large in the Galaxy – Earth and Draconia. After years of peace, their spaceships are now being mysteriously attacked and cargoes rifled. Each suspects the other and full scale war seems unavoidable. The Doctor, accused of being a Draconian spy, is thrown into prison. And only when the Master appears on the scene do things really begin to move...

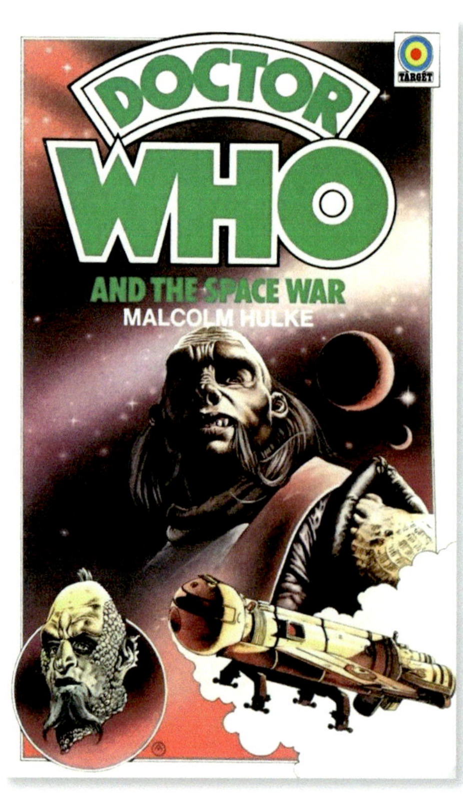

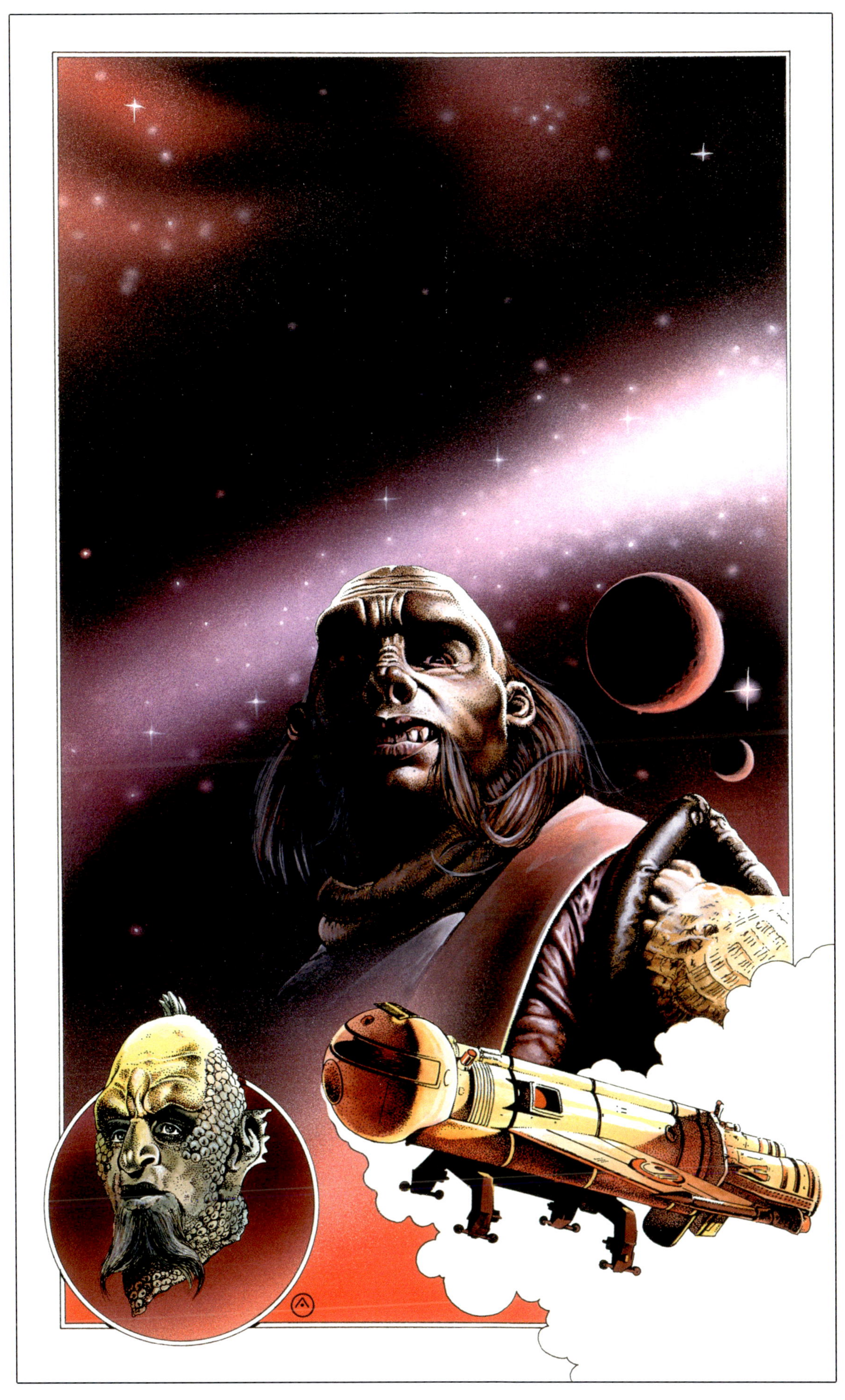

DOCTOR WHO AND THE PLANET OF THE DALEKS

Writer: Terrance Dicks **Doctor:** Third **Release date:** 21 October 1976 **Release order:** 26

The Doctor Who and the Planet of the Daleks *BBC CD is available from retailers. See bibliography for details.*

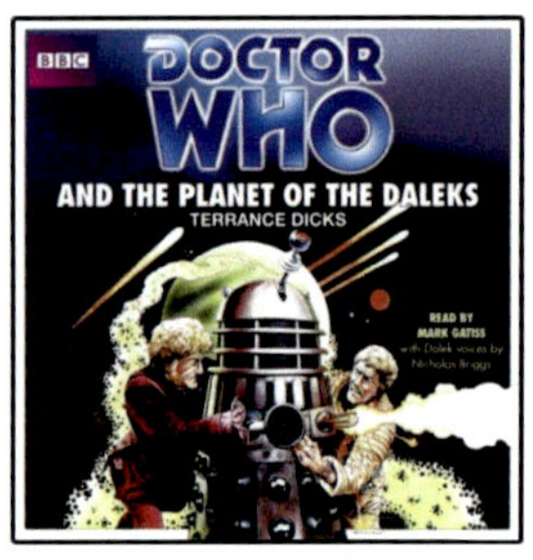

BBC Audiobook CD

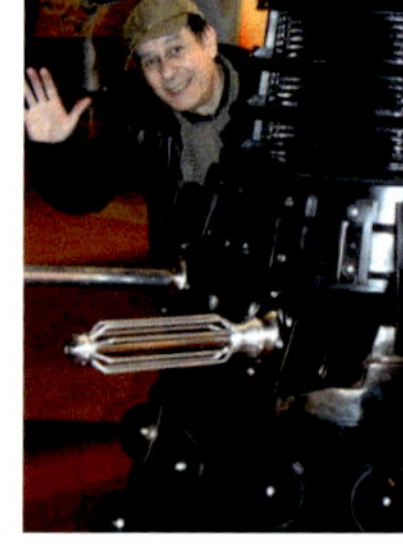

German Edition

Chris behind a Dalek

"The clock-hand on the third bomb had almost reached detonation point. And several Daleks were advancing towards [Jo] along the trail.

Jo grabbed the two switched-off bombs and scrambled up the rocky slope. The Daleks increased their pace. 'Halt. Halt and surrender or you will be exterminated!'"

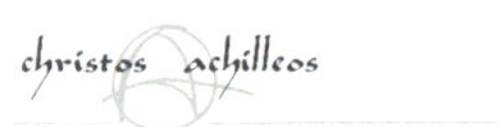

❝ I based this cover on a photograph of Jon Pertwee and the other guy attacking a Dalek. I did it my way, with the fire coming out of the Dalek's gun, and added spacey effects. It all fitted together perfectly.

The design works well, with the Dalek coming out of the bottom margin, and the fire projecting out into the right margin. That's something that I quite often use on my cover works. ❞

Jo peered through the panel and saw nothing. Yet someone had entered the cabin. She could hear hoarse breathing and stealthy padding footsteps. A beaker rose in the air of its own accord, then dropped to the floor ... THE INVISIBLE ENEMY.

After pursuing the Daleks through Space, Doctor Who lands on the Planet of Spiridon, in the midst of a tropical jungle ... and finds more than Daleks. Vicious plants spitting deadly poison, invisible Spiridons attacking from all sides and, in hiding, a vast army, waits ... for the moment to mobilise and conquer.

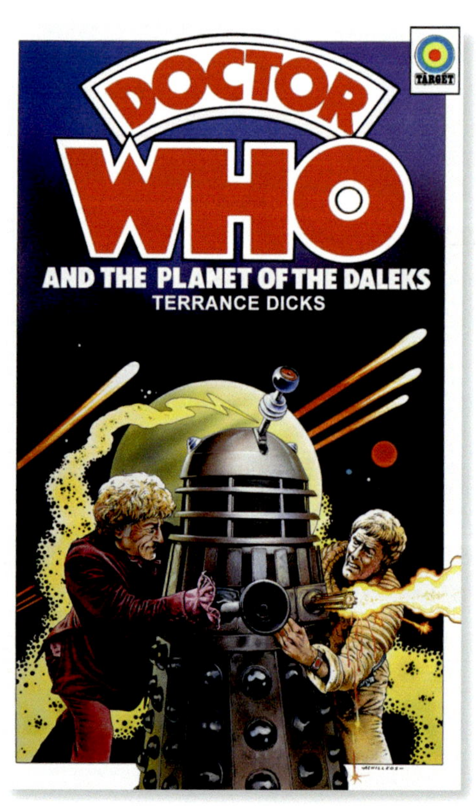

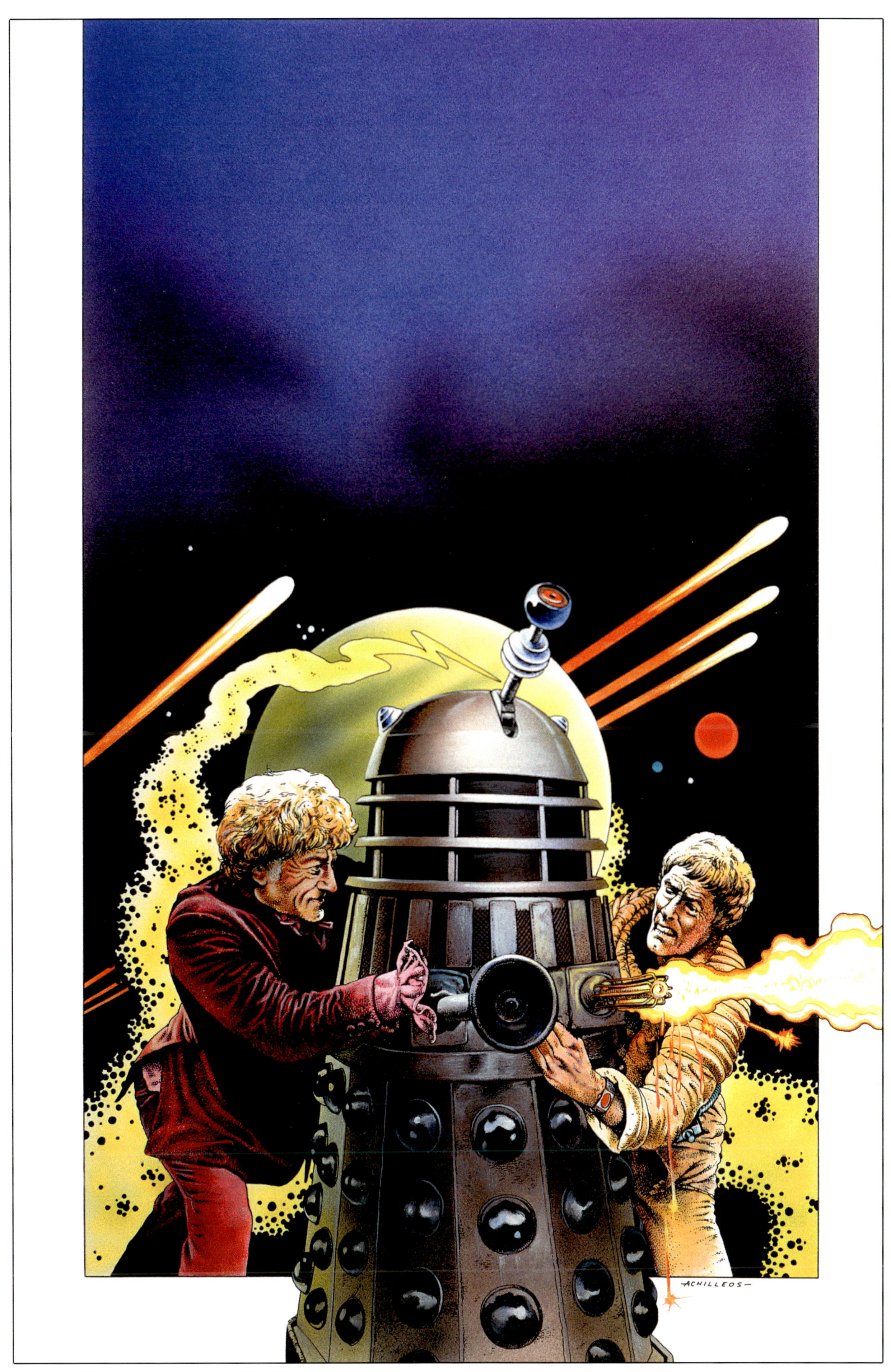

DOCTOR WHO AND THE PYRAMIDS OF MARS

Writer: Terrance Dicks **Doctor:** Fourth **Release date:** 16 December 1976 **Release order:** 27

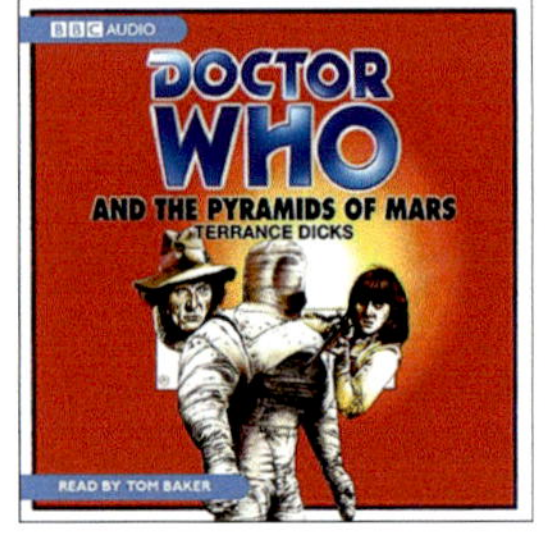

BBC Audiobook CD

The Doctor Who and the Pyramids of Mars *BBC CD is available from retailers. See bibliography for details.*

"As the figure advanced towards him he cringed back in sudden fear.

"Oh, master, spare me," he shrieked.

"Spare me. I am a true servant of the great Sutekh."

The figure's hands clamped down on Namin's shaking shoulders. Immediately Namin's whole body twisted. He let out a shuddering scream and struggled to break free. His clothing began to smoulder beneath the figure's hands."

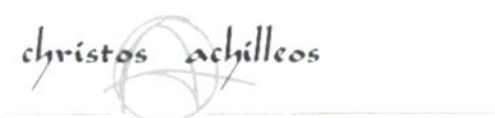

❝ This one I had to do very quickly. I like the central mummy figure very much, but Tom Baker looks a bit too grumpy, and Sarah Jane's not drawn very well at all.

All in all, it's a crass design. The white box is to hold Tom Baker and Sarah Jane together. Perhaps it should have been a different colour, but if you don't put the box there, they look as if they're floating like ghosts. You need something to ground them. Could do better! **❞**

For many thousands of years Sutekh had waited … trapped in the heart of an Egyptian Pyramid. Now at last the time had come – the moment of release, when all the force of his pent-up evil and malice would be unleashed upon the world...

The TARDIS lands on the site of UNIT headquarters in the year 1911, and the Fourth Doctor and Sarah emerge to fight a terrifying and deadly battle … against Egyptian Mummies, half-possessed humans – and the overwhelming evil power of Sutekh!

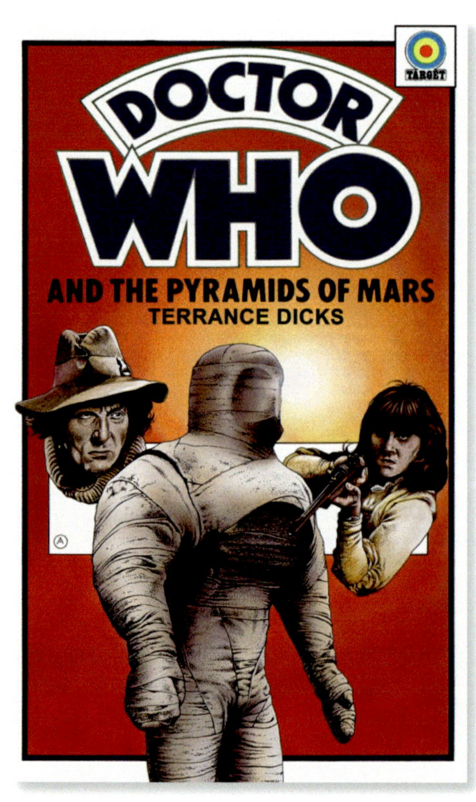

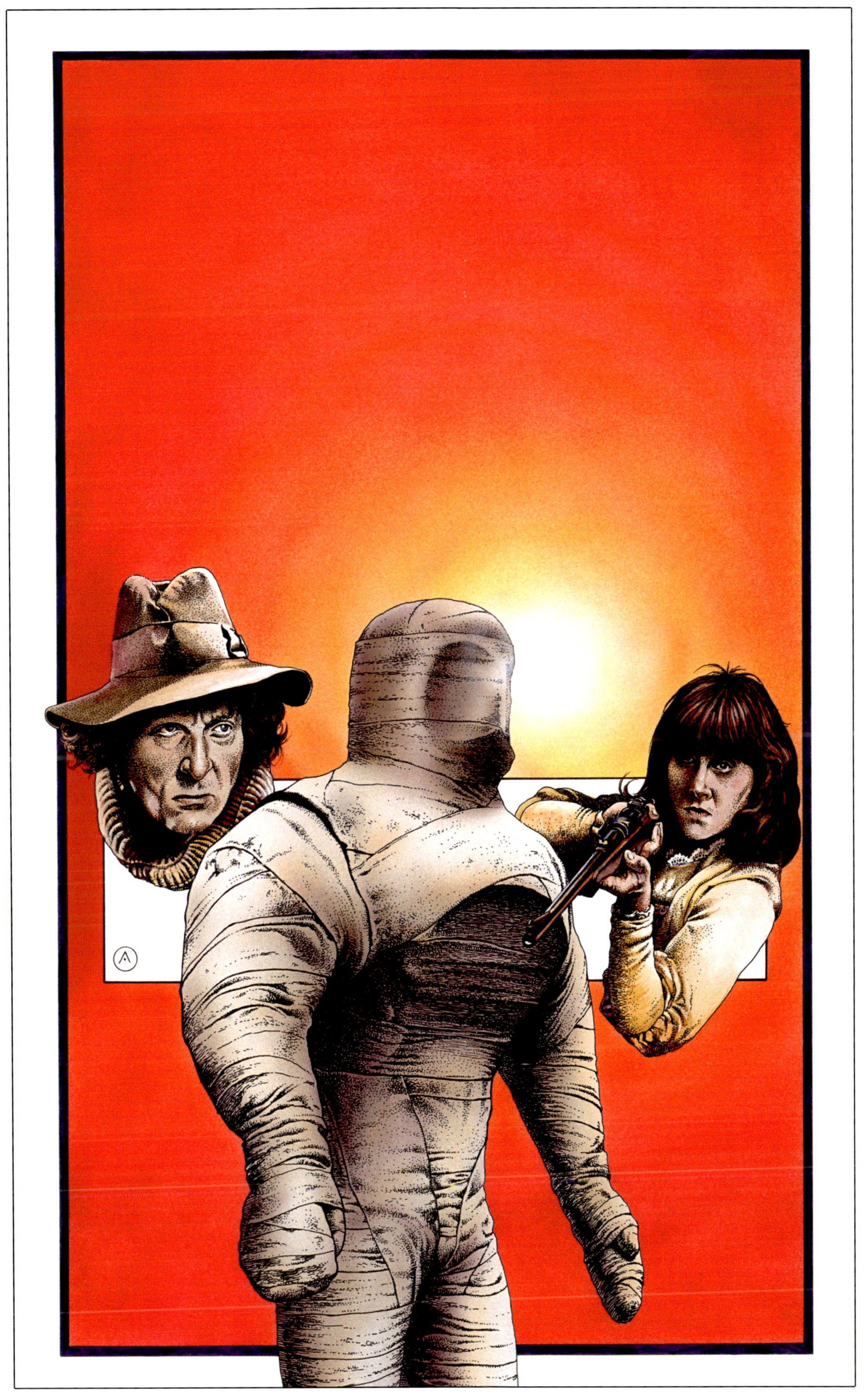

DOCTOR WHO AND THE CARNIVAL OF MONSTERS

Writer: Terrance Dicks **Doctor:** Third **Release date:** 20 January 1977 **Release order:** 28

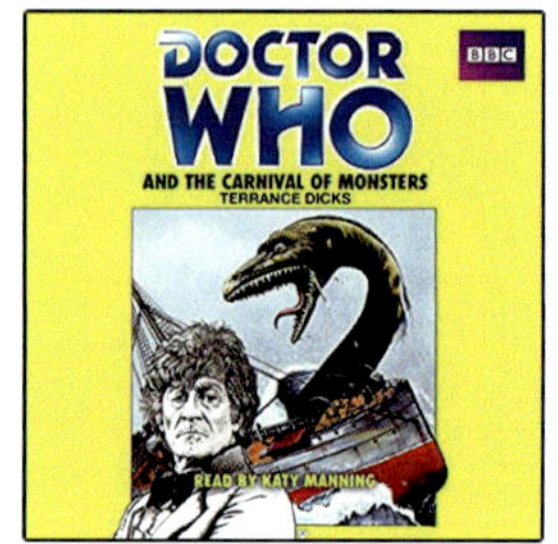

BBC Audiobook CD

The Doctor Who and the Carnival of Monsters *BBC CD is available from retailers. See bibliography for details.*

"There was another roar, and a jolting crash shook the ship as something huge slammed against it.

The Doctor led Jo to a porthole and they looked out. An enormous sea-creature was swimming around the boat, its savage head waving about on the end of a fantastically long neck.

The monster roared once again, then plunged back into the sea. They saw it swimming for a while, then it disappeared beneath the waves."

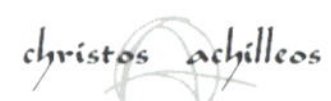

“ The *Carnival of Monsters* cover is very nice. I owned a beautifully illustrated book of ships, and I used it to find the correct reference for the ship of that era.

It's a good design: the waves, the ship's bow just breaking out of the border, and the looming sea monster – it's just right.

I can't remember if I designed the creature from a model or not. I do remember it didn't look particularly great on television. My approach with all these covers was to make the final product look good and exciting for the kids. That's what I did with whatever I was given to work with – or not given.

I like the drawing of Jon Pertwee. He looks very imposing here. ”

The Doctor and Jo land on a cargo ship crossing the Indian Ocean in the year 1926.

Or so they think.

Far away on a planet called Inter Minor, a travelling showman is setting up his live peepshow, watched by an eager audience of space officials

On board ship, a giant hand suddenly appears, grasps the Tardis and withdraws.

Without warning, a prehistoric monster rises from the sea to attack.

What is happening? Where are they? Only the Doctor realises, with horror, that they might be trapped ...

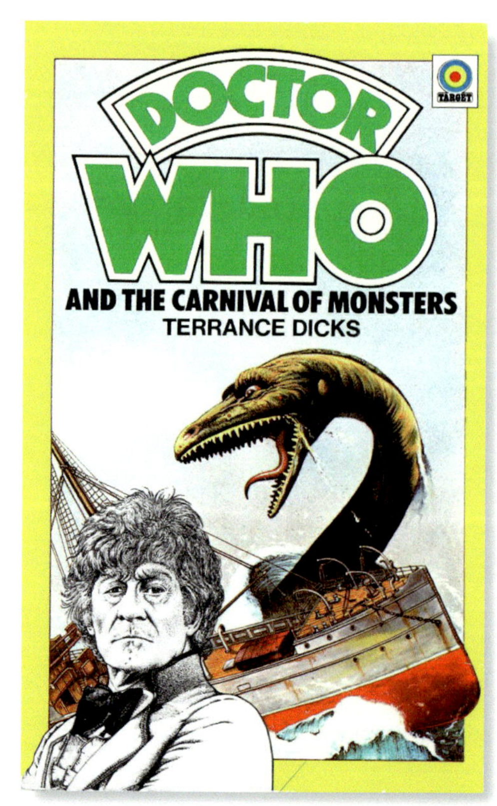

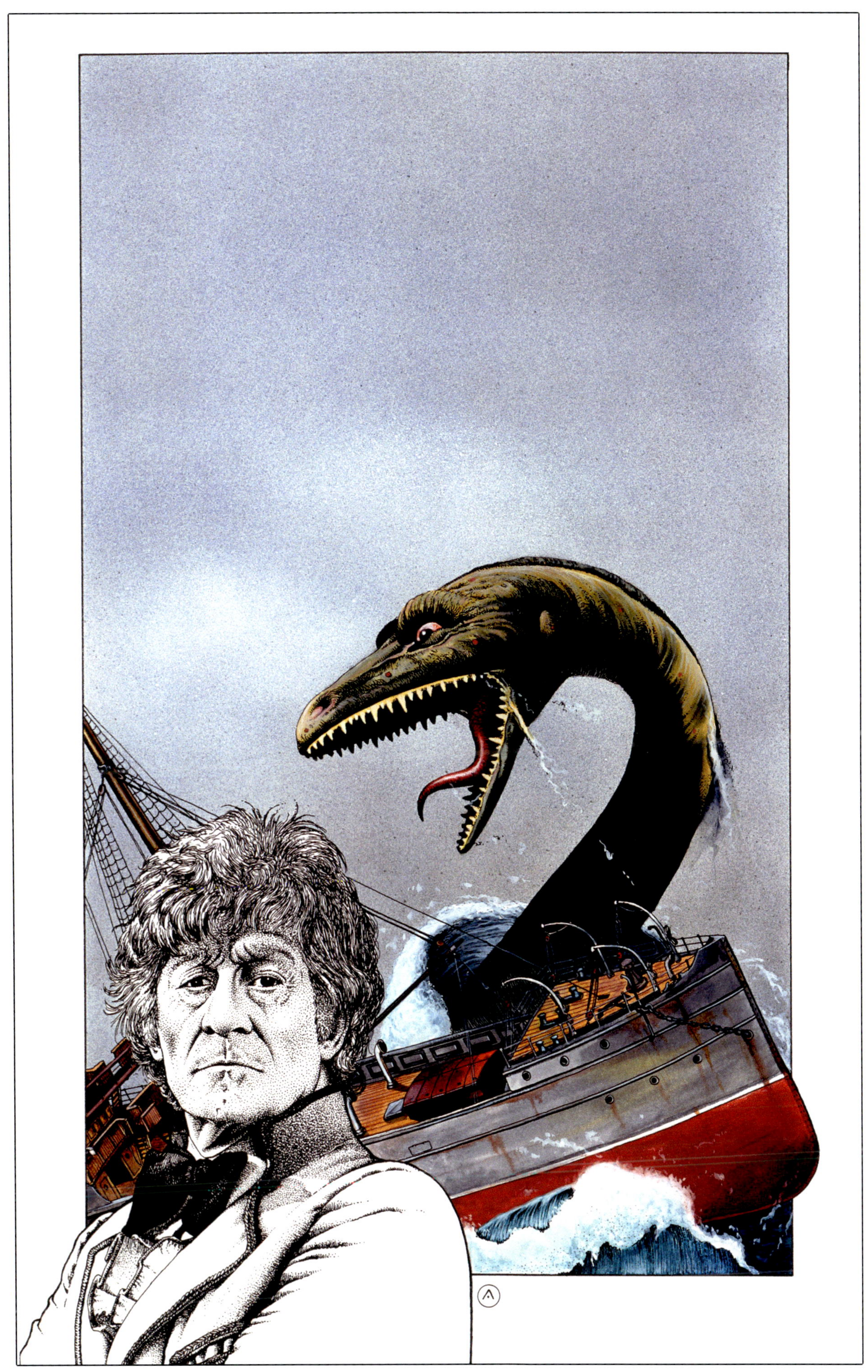

DOCTOR WHO AND THE SEEDS OF DOOM

Writer: Philip Hinchcliffe **Doctor:** Fourth **Release date:** 17 February 1977 **Release order:** 29

"All at once, Chase let out a piercing yell and his iron grip slackened. His feet were trapped in the rollers and he was being sucked into the gaping maw of the crusher. Frantically the Doctor tried to pull him free but the monstrous machine would not disgorge its victim and suddenly, with a hideous scream, Chase was gone."

christos achilleos

❝ This one's interesting. It's unusual because it has a full picture of the Doctor and Sarah Jane. Despite this, I don't really like the colour scheme or anything else. The only exception is the explosion. It's my least favourite *Doctor Who* cover.

But to this day I do sell prints of it. Some people really love it. I guess it's connected to a very popular story. **❞**

In the snowy wastes of blizzard-swept Antarctica, a strange pod-like object is unearthed, buried deep in the ice. Curiosity turns to alarm as the pod begins to grow – then horror when suddenly it cracks open and a snaking green tendril shoots out, mercilessly seeking the nearest live victim...

In London, the botanical experts are bewildered. Doctor Who is called in to fight this unknown horror. But will he be in time to save the Earth from the rapidly spreading tentacles of the Krynoid, giant man-eating monster from an alien world?

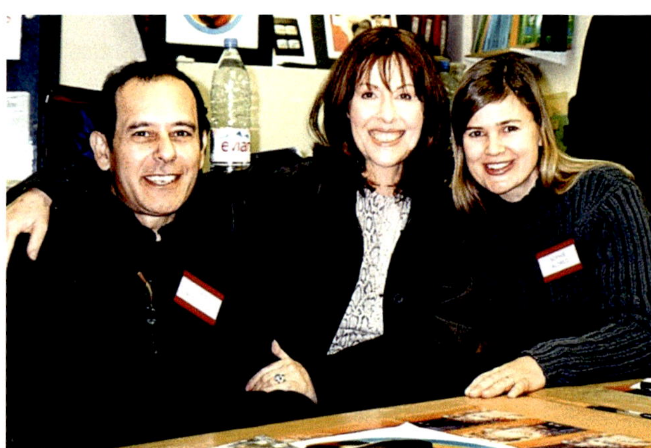

(above) Chris, Elisabeth Sladen and Sophie Aldred at the Stamp Centre, 2000.

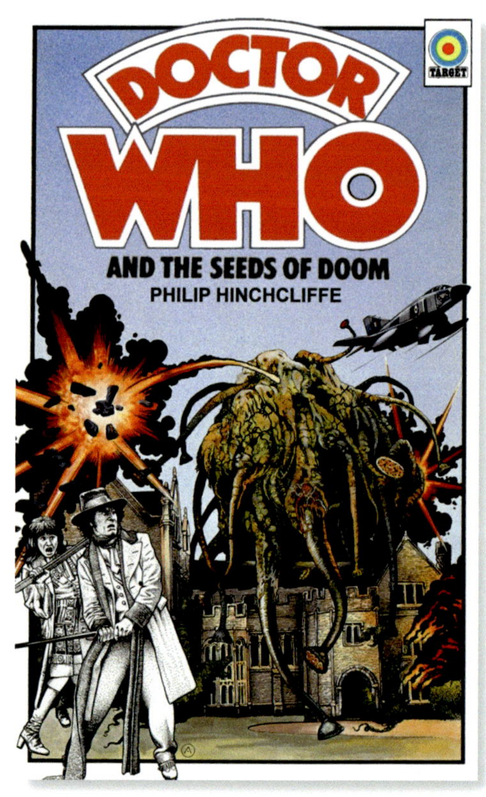

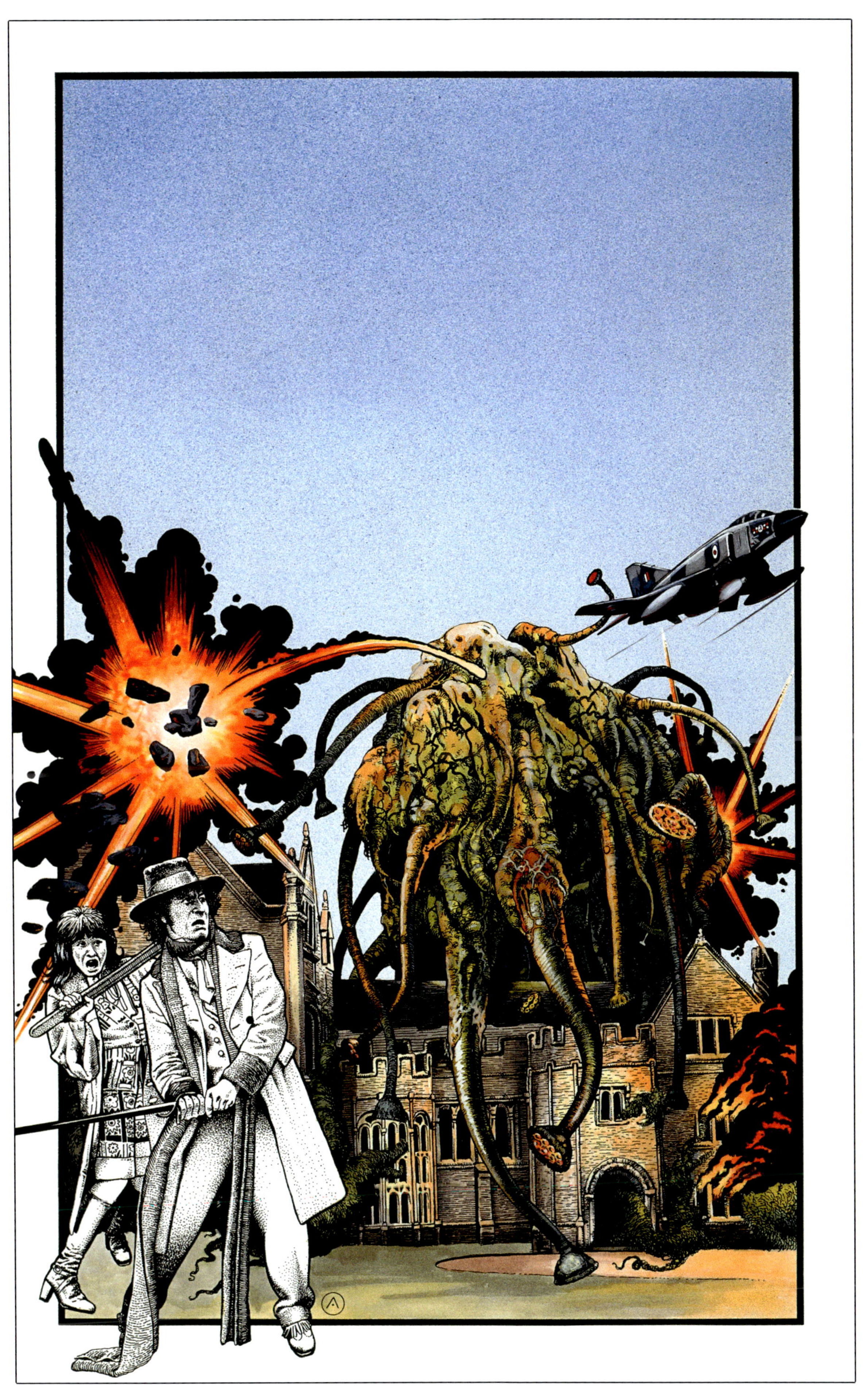

DOCTOR WHO AND THE DALEK INVASION OF EARTH

Writer: Terrance Dicks **Doctor:** First **Release date:** 24 March 1977 **Release order:** 30

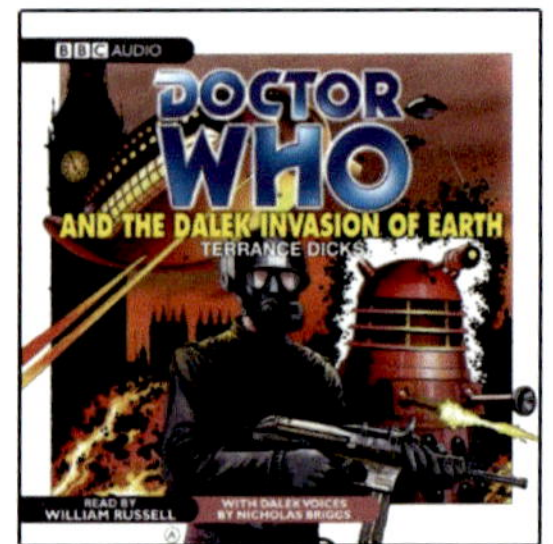

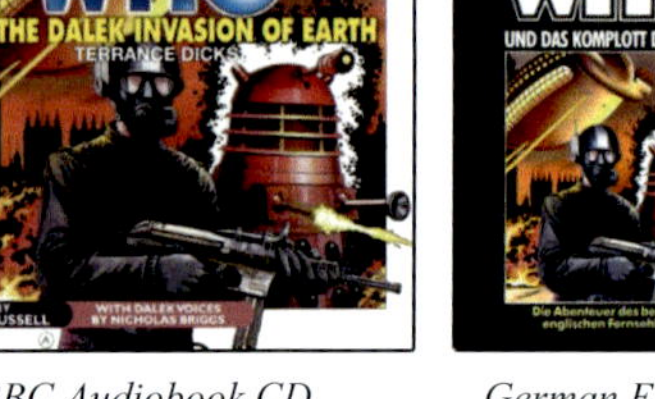

BBC Audiobook CD   *German Edition*

The Doctor Who and the Dalek Invasion of Earth *BBC CD and book are available from retailers. See bibliography for details.*

"The voice of the Dalek Supreme seemed to shake the little radio set. "Rebels of London. This is your final warning. Leave your hiding places. Show yourself in the open streets. You will be fed and watered. Work is needed, but in return the Daleks offer you life. Continue to resist and we will destroy London. You will all die, the males, the females, the young of the species. Rebels of London, come out from your hiding place."

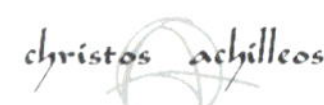

❝ They didn't give me any reference at all for this one, and I had to make up the Dalek spaceships. I found a film magazine, I forget what it was called, which had an article on Peter Cushing as Dr Who in a movie. I ended up using references from that, but almost everything in it is wrong and inaccurate.

I didn't think the kids would mind, and the publishers never noticed. I just tried to make an exciting cover and meet my tight deadline. **❞**

The TARDIS lands in a London of future times — a city of fear, devastation and holocaust... a city now ruled by Daleks.

The Doctor and his companions meet a team of underground resistance workers, among the few survivors, but after an unsuccessful attack on the Dalek spaceship, they are all forced to flee the capital.

A perilous journey through England finally brings them to the secret centre of Dalek operations... and the mysterious reason for the Dalek invasion of Earth!

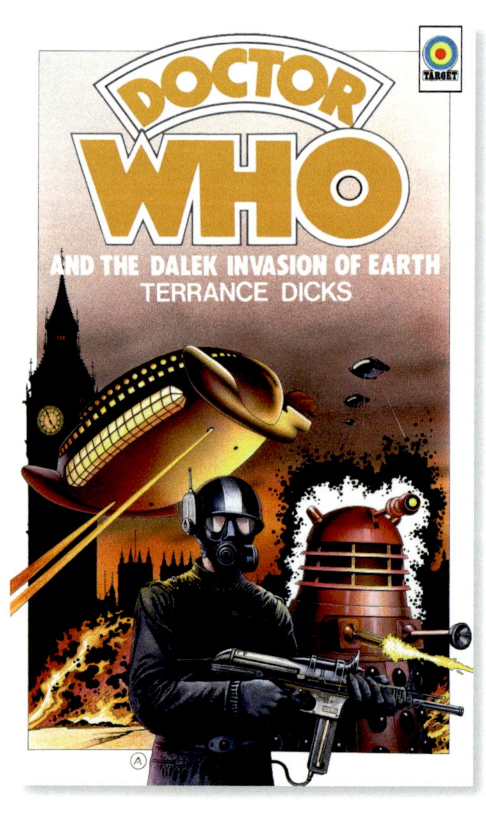

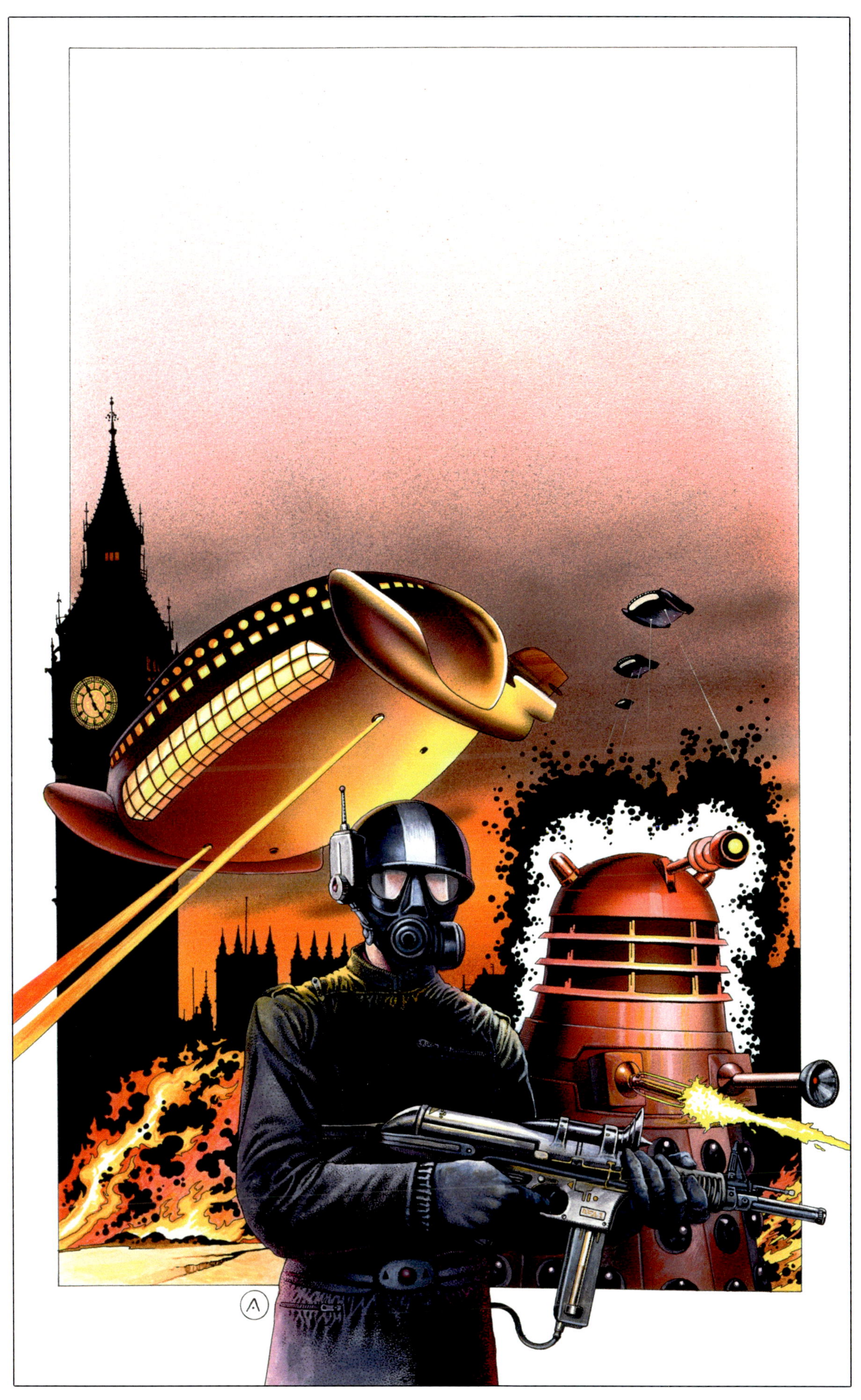

DOCTOR WHO AND THE CLAWS OF AXOS

Writer: Terrance Dicks **Doctor:** Third **Release date:** 21 April 1977 **Release order:** 31

"It moved through the silent blackness of deep space like a giant jellyfish through the depths of the sea. Its shape was constantly changing, pulsating with energy and life, and a myriad of colours flickered over its glistening surface. Unerringly it sped towards its chosen target, the planet known as Earth. Soon the instruments of the humans would detect its approach. It knew this, and was undisturbed. Detection was the first stage of its plan..."

christos achilléos

❝ This is class, to me. This has become one of my top three covers. I don't know how I drew that creature. If you zoom in on the ink work, it's really drawn well.

It's a really punchy and powerful concept design. I put it all together, but there was something missing, something to add to it; I came up with the idea of these rays coming out from the sides of the Axon's head.

You can easily mess the whole thing up, making changes like that. That's the difference between digital and real painting work. You can easily ruin the whole thing with just the airbrush deciding to start spitting. With digital computer work, all you have to do is press the undo button and go back a step or two.

I never do any thumbnail roughs to work out the colours when I'm developing a cover. I sense the colours that are needed by instinct.

In this case, when it was all put together, I thought it was just right. It's a perfect design and I love it to this day. **❞**

'Axos calling Earth, Axos calling Earth...'

The creatures stood before them, beautiful golden humanoids, offering friendship and their priceless Axonite, in return for – what?

Only Doctor Who remains suspicious. What is the real reason for the Axon's sudden arrival on Earth? And why is the evil Master a passenger on their spaceship? He very soon finds out...

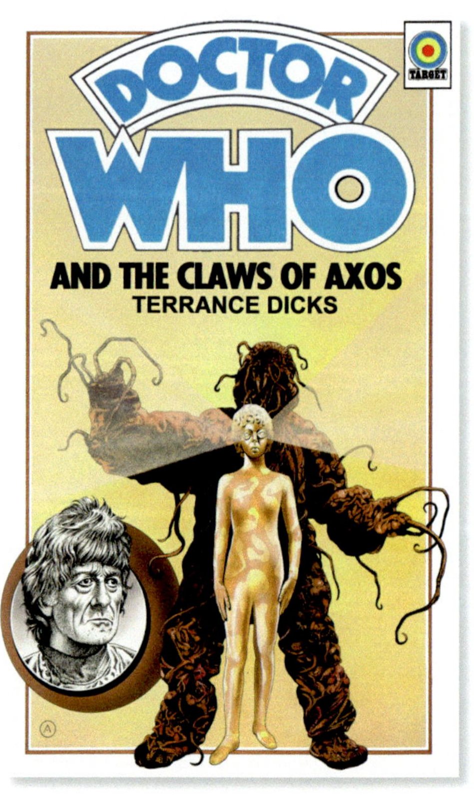

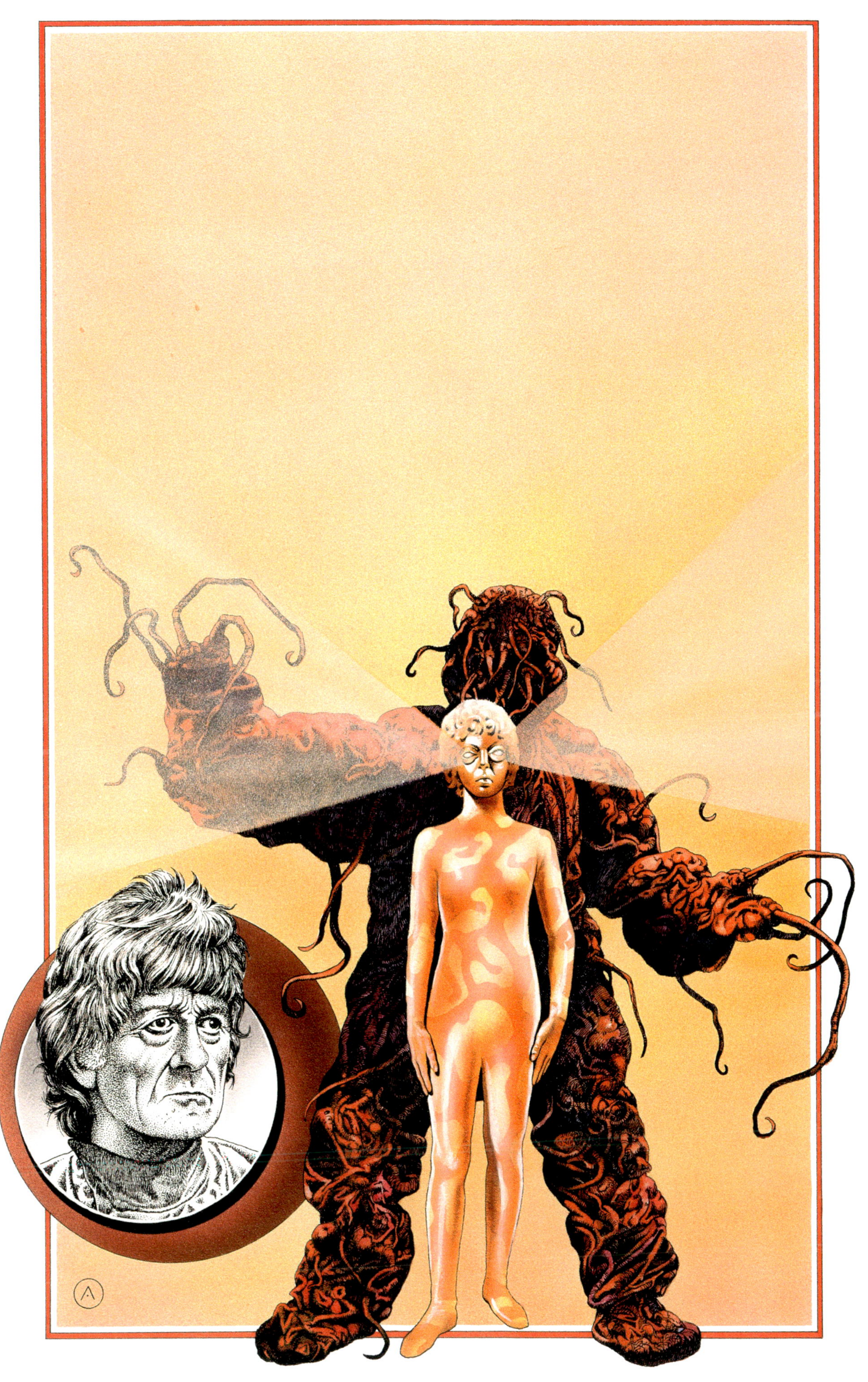

DOCTOR WHO AND THE ARK IN SPACE

Writer: Ian Marter **Doctor:** Fourth **Release date:** 21 April 1977 **Release order:** 32

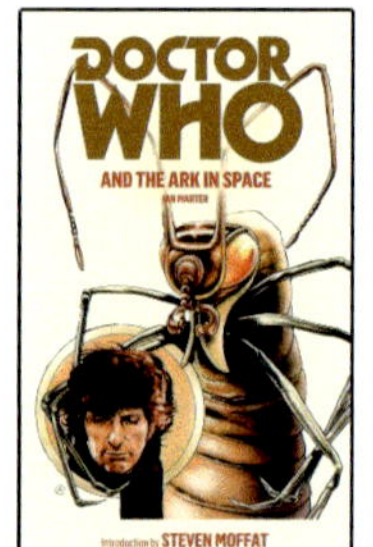

BBC Reissue

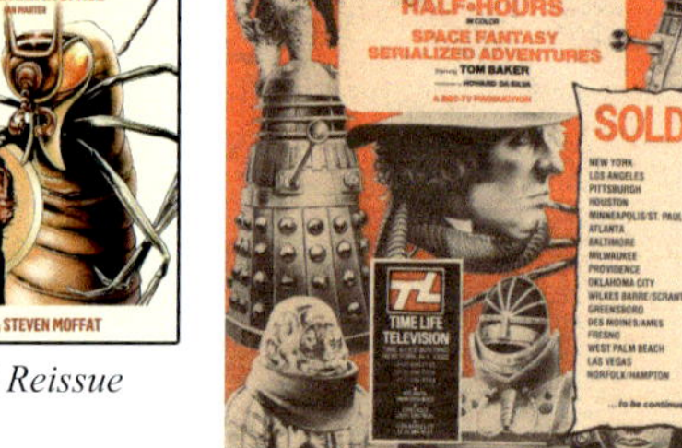

(left) Time Life Television
US TV syndication
advertisement.

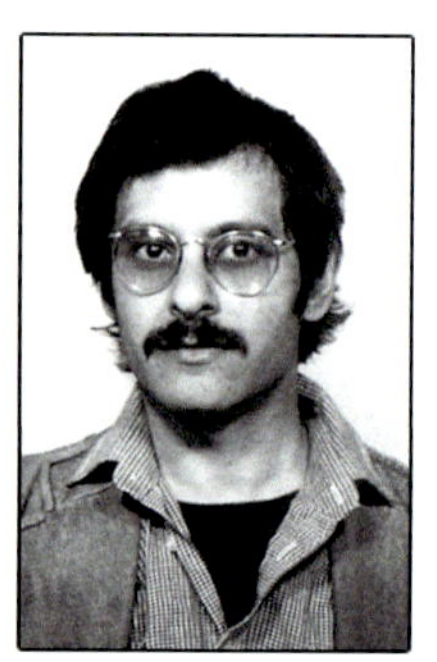

(left) Chris'
passport photo
around 1977.

"The Doctor wandered into the shadows of the next bay, peering through the shields as if examining exhibits in a museum. 'These people are not dead, Harry, they're asleep.' He continued to speak, his voice rising and echoing majestically around the vast vaults. '...Homo Sapiens... what an indomitable species... it is only a few million years since it crawled up from the sea and learned to walk... a puny defenceless biped... it has survived flood, plague, famine, war... and now here it is out among the stars...'"

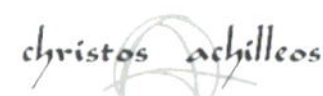

66 *The Ark in Space* was the last one I did for the main range. Basically, the publishers and I'd had a massive falling out.

I told the publishers that I had enough of the way they treated me and that I was not prepared to do any more *Doctor Who* covers for them. The newish art director said, 'Fine, Chris, no problem,' not realising how difficult it would be to replace me. I knew how popular I was with the fans. It wasn't too long before I received a call practically begging me to take on three more covers in order for him to have time to find another illustrator.

The three were *The Ark in Space, The Dalek Invasion of Earth,* and *The Seeds of Doom. The Ark in Space* was the last one I did. 99

At a time in the far-off future, Earth has become uninhabitable. A selection of humanity is placed, deep-frozen, in a fully automated space station, to await the day of their return to Earth...

Thousands of years later, Doctor Who arrives. He finds things going suspiciously wrong, and the station under attack from the giant Wirrn, deadly creatures who, in their lust for power, now threaten the future of the whole Human Race...

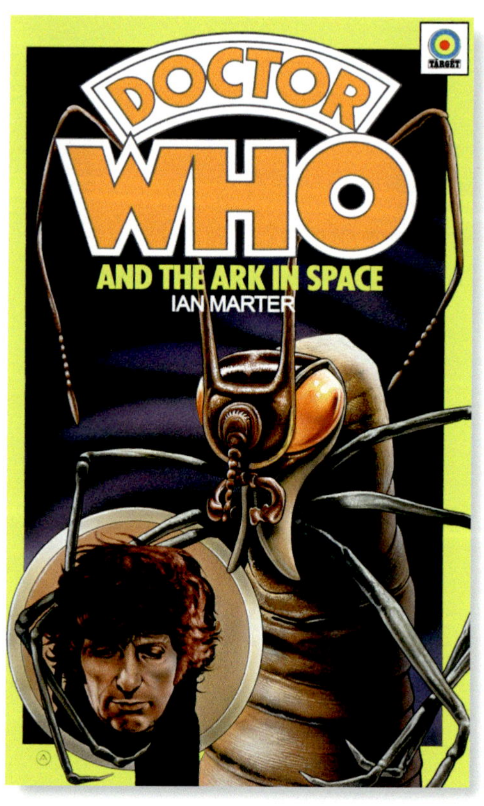

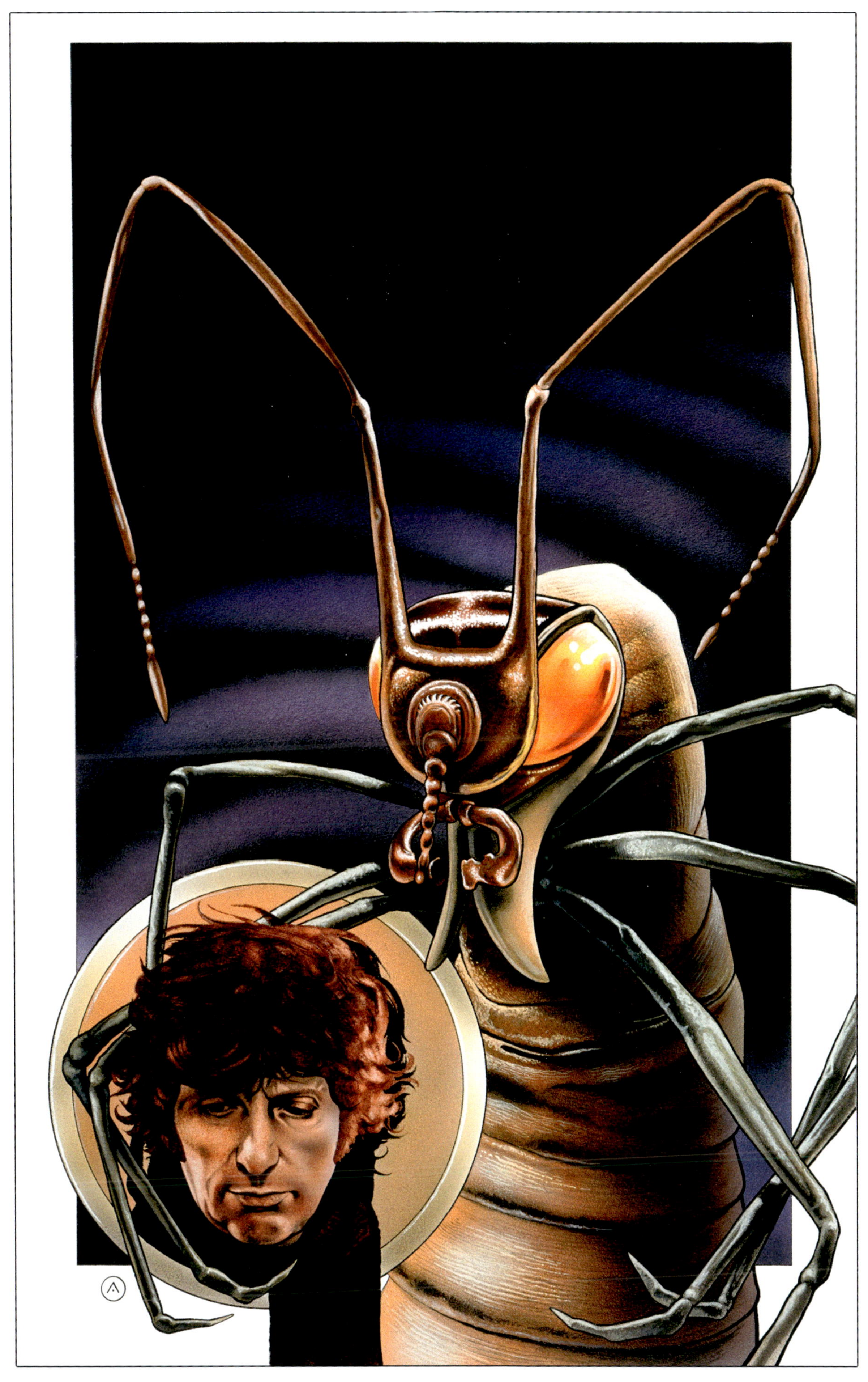

THE DOCTOR WHO MONSTER BOOK

Writer: Terrance Dicks **Doctor:** 1, 2, 3, 4 **Release date:** 20 November 1975

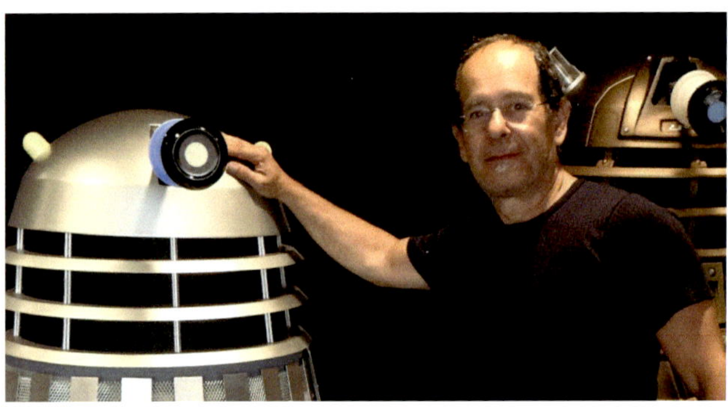

(below) Chris and the Daleks visiting the Doctor Who *Experience Target Exhibition* in 2016.

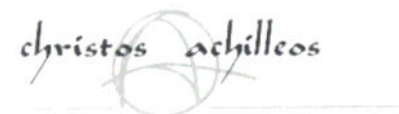

66 This has a somewhat different approach again. It's a combination of techniques. There's a lot of airbrush in it: the Daleks and the Cyberman are airbrushed, as is Tom Baker. It's a combination of drawing and airbrushing. Davros, the Silurian and the Sontaran are hand-coloured, and detailed with a more pointillist approach.

The standard of the effects and creature design on the show had really improved by this point, and as such, so had the reference images I was given to work from. In particular, I like the Cyberman here, staring straight out at you. 99

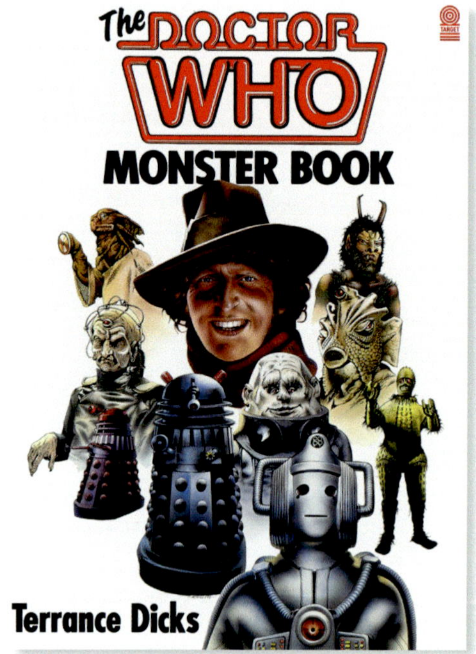

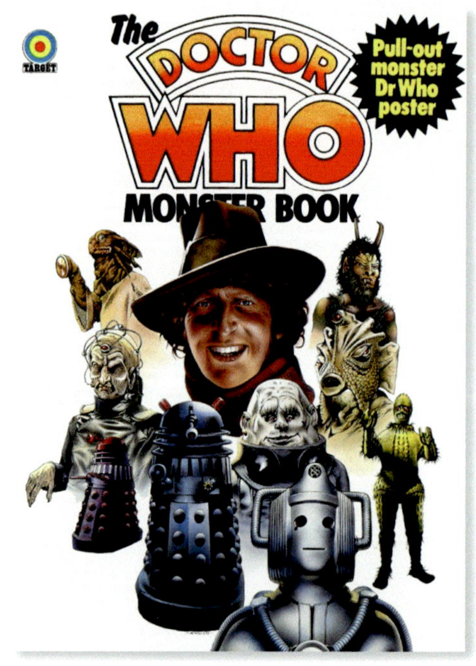

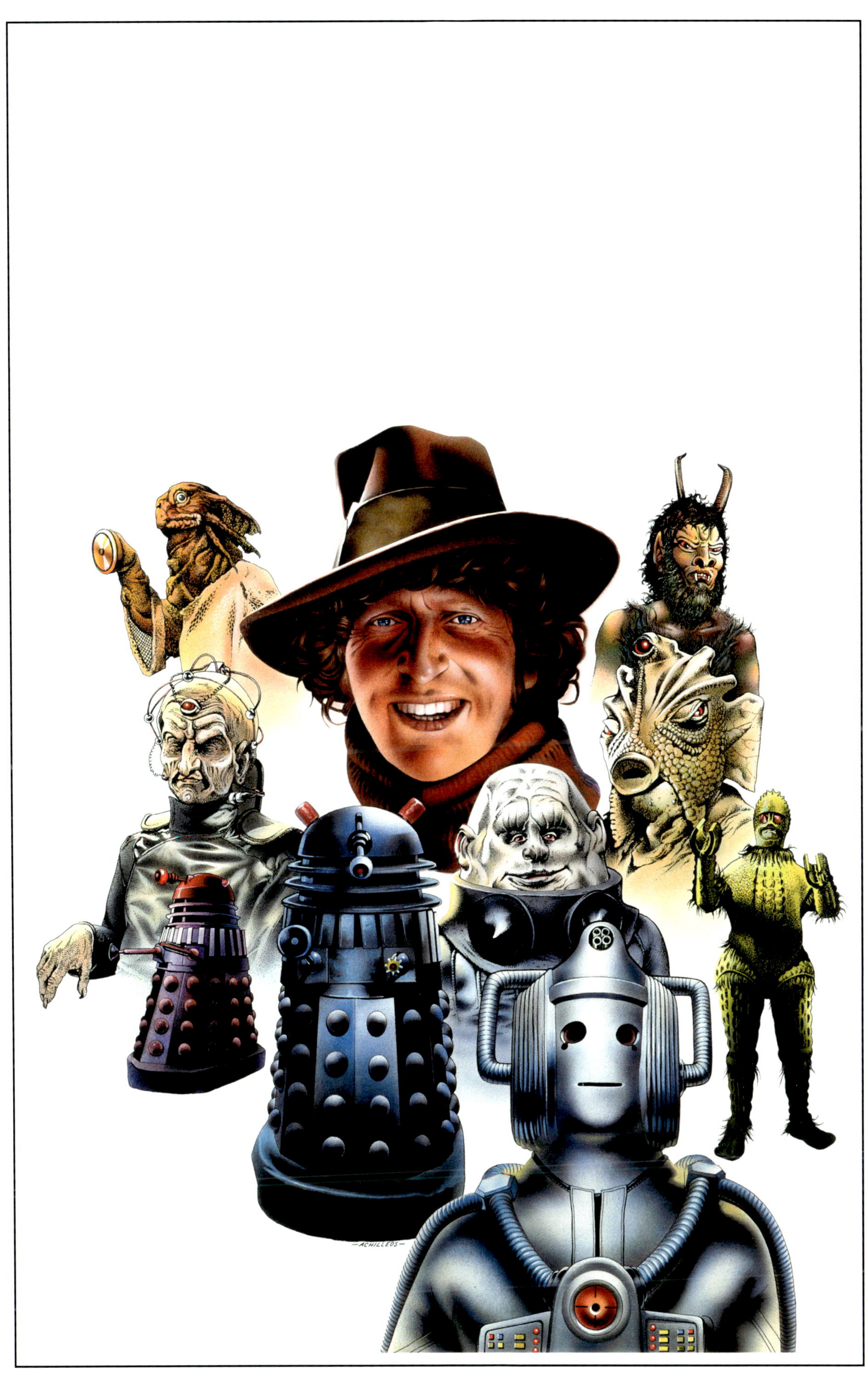

THE AMAZING WORLD OF DOCTOR WHO

Doctor: Fourth **Release date:** 1976

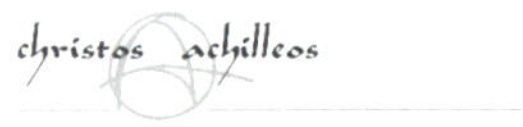

❝ I secured this job through an advertising agency I had previously worked for. The agency was, of course, familiar with my *Doctor Who* stuff, and things fell into place. I was asked to illustrate the *Doctor Who* Ty-Phoo Tea card sets, as well as an accompanying poster.

The lettering on the top on the logo was all painted by hand. The bottom part of the image, where you see all the special effects, was left largely empty because there was supposed to a lot of promotional writing there.

It was quite a big piece of artwork, and I wish I still had it; the rights are mine, but when I asked for it, the art director said he gave it to his nephew or son or something – maybe his boss's son, who knows? I didn't want to kick up a fuss and lose the client, so I just let it go. Bear in mind that *Doctor Who* stuff was not as sought after as it is today; nowadays I'd press my case!

The image was also used for the cover of a book that came with the cards; I have the transparency of the cover, but that's it. I remember that there were a lot of graphics within the book itself, but I wasn't responsible for any of those.

Tom Baker as Doctor Who *(right)*

I did this for the back cover of *The Amazing World of Doctor Who*. I worked from a picture of Tom just after he accepted the role. As you can see, he was already channelling the Marx Brothers! ☺ **❞**

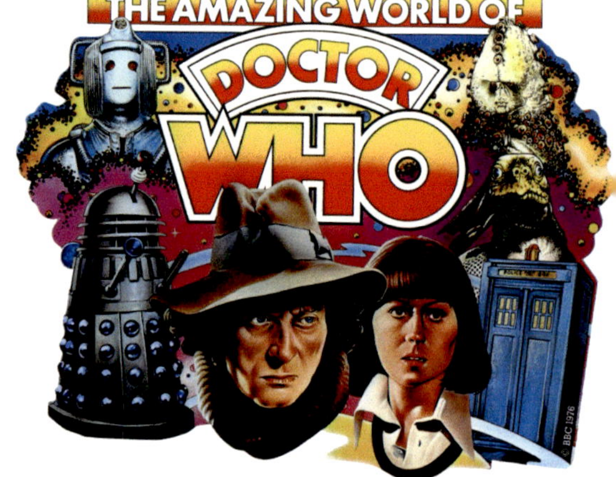

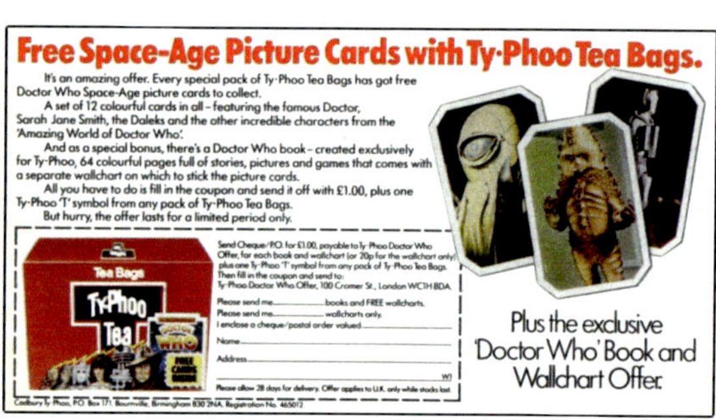

Ty-Phoo Tea Coupon to get book

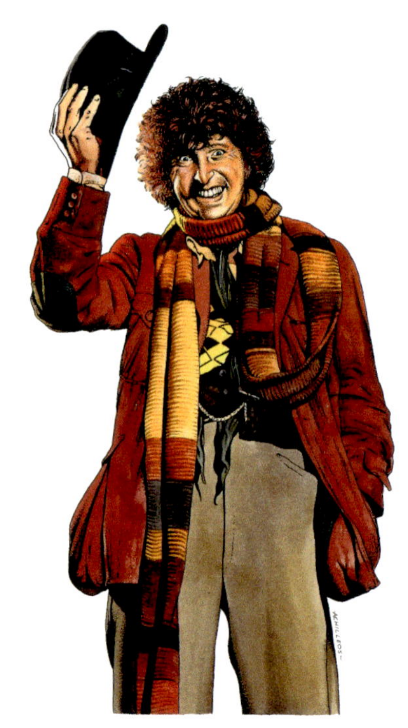

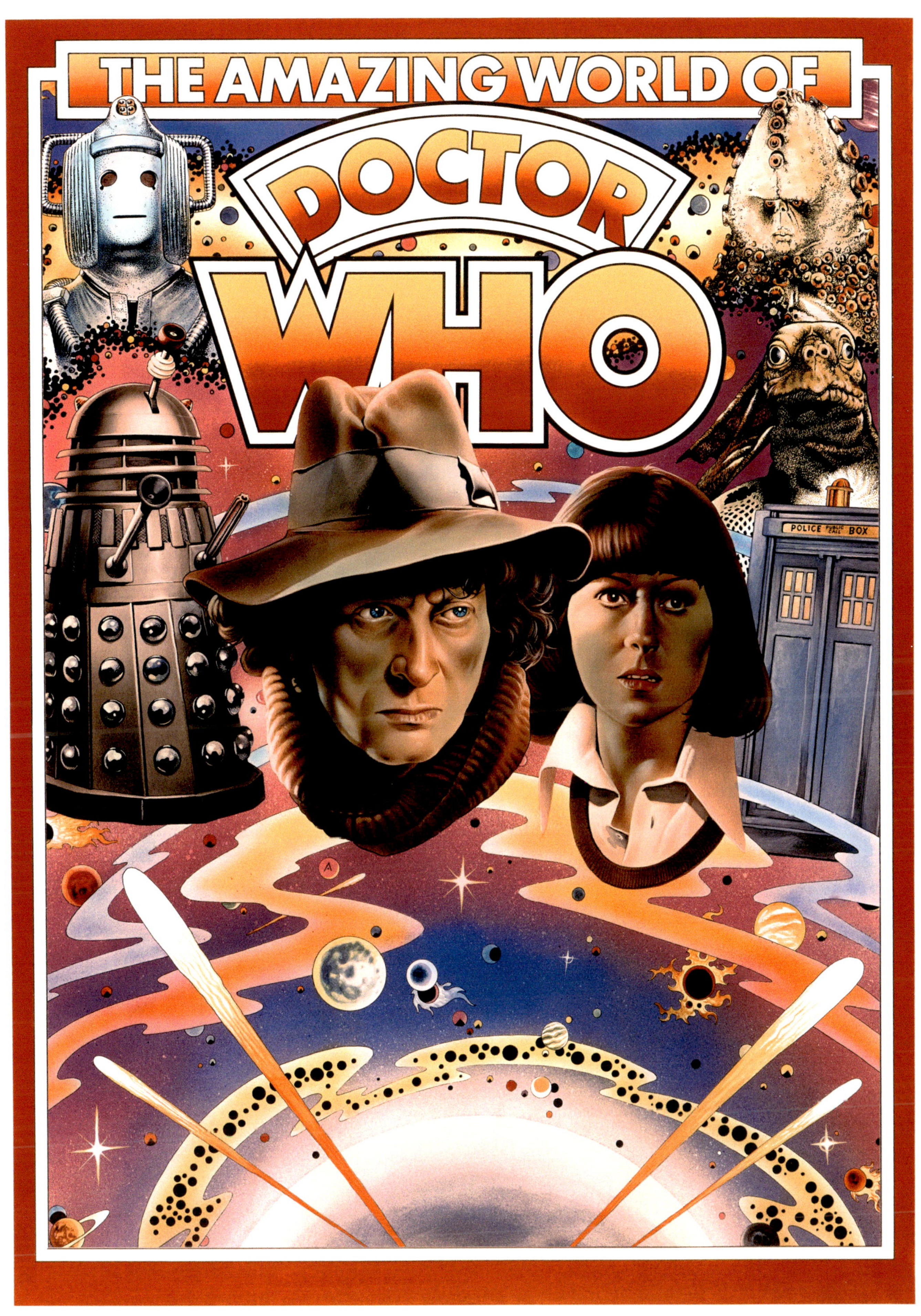
THE AMAZING WORLD OF
DOCTOR
WHO
POLICE BOX

THE MAKING OF DOCTOR WHO

Writer: Terrance Dicks & Malcolm Hulke **Doctor:** 1, 2, 3, 4 **Release date:** 16 December 1976

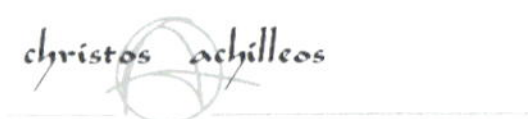

> **"** At the time I was working on other projects and I received a call to do this cover. This was a reprint of a previous book from another publisher and Target wanted to aim this edition at a younger audience. I decided to do something very simple – a nice portrait of the Doctor and put the Target logo behind him. I suggested that this would be a nice, clean, punchy cover. The publisher agreed, and it was quickly done. Looking at it now, I think it's great. It's become an iconic image from 1970s *Doctor Who*. The fans seem to like it very much too. **"**

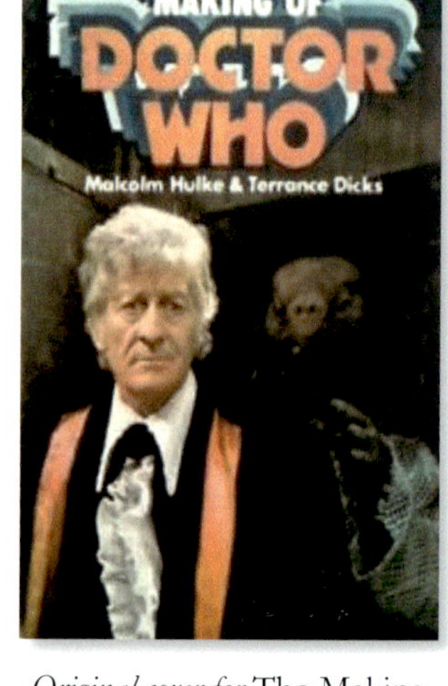

Original cover for The Making of Doctor Who *published by Piccolo. The book was extensively rewritten by Terrance Dicks for the Target release.*

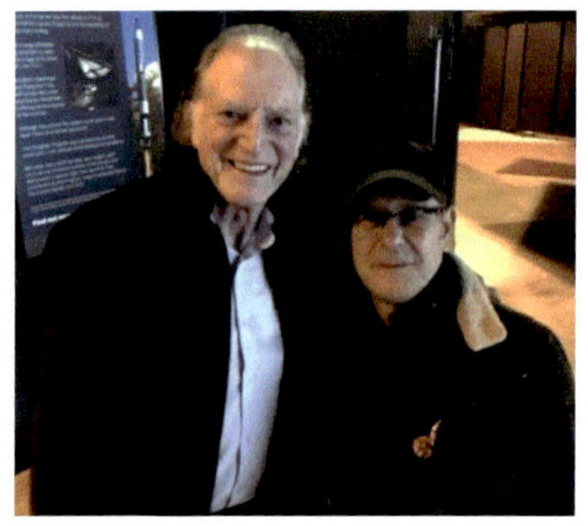

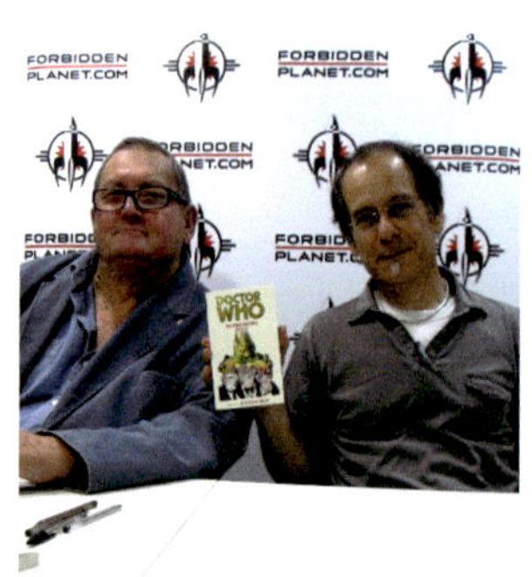

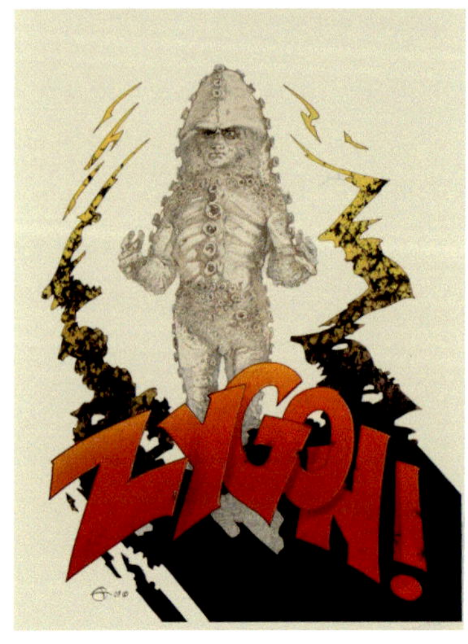

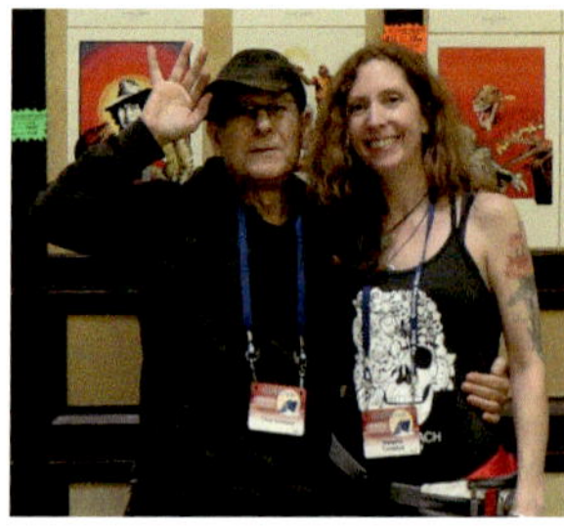

(top left) Chris meets first Doctor actor David Bradley.
(top right) Terrance Dicks and Chris.
(bottom left) Zygon, *a private commission.*
(bottom right) Chris and Natasha.

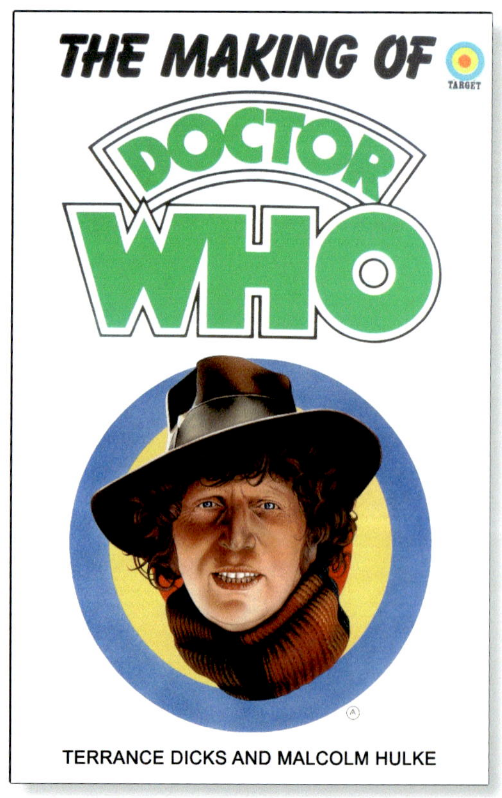

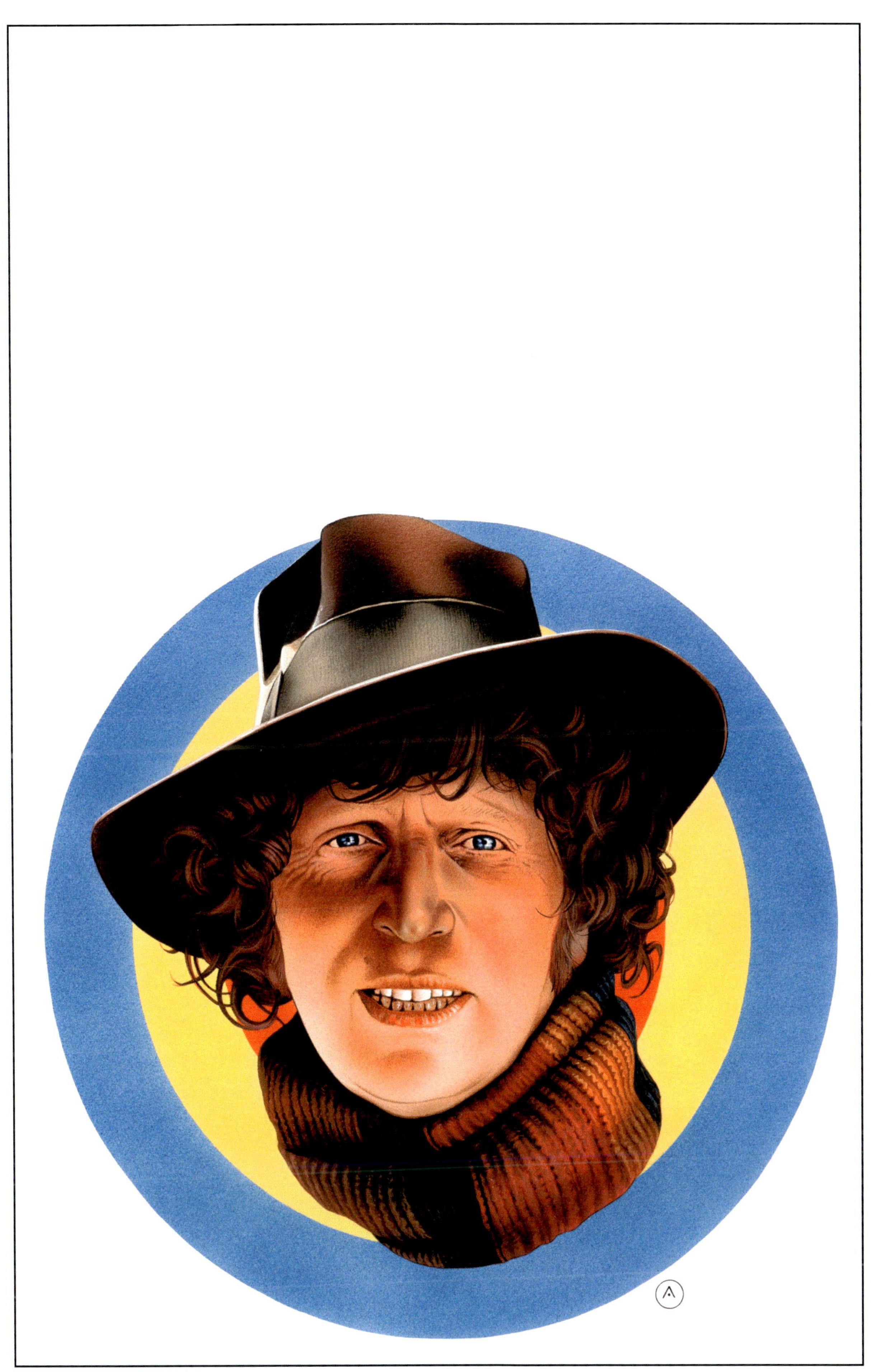

THE SECOND DOCTOR WHO MONSTER BOOK

Writer: Terrance Dicks **Doctor:** 1, 2, 3, 4 **Release date:** 20 October 1977

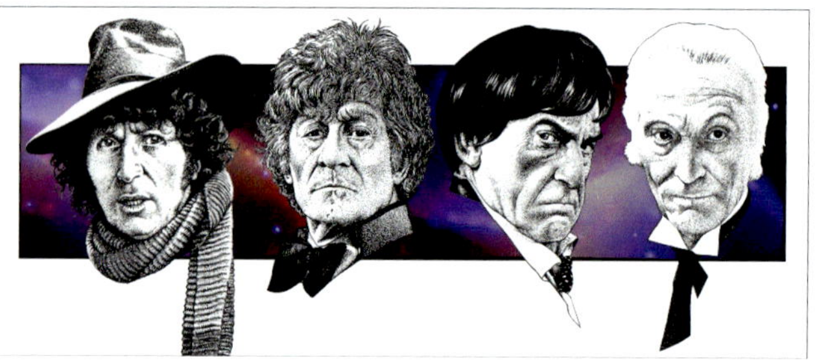

The four Doctors as they appear on the mugs and t-shirts.

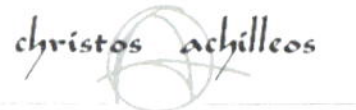

❝ This was two years later, but I used similar techniques. I remember I was very busy when they came to me with other fantasy work, but I managed to fit it in.

I like Tom Baker with his long scarf coming down, and I tried to make the most possible use of the area around him, dotting it with figures as much as I could. **❞**

FROM THE PUBLISHER:
Here in *The Second Doctor Who Monster Book* is the story of the new Doctor in his fourth, most exciting incarnation. How and why he changed his form... the story of his companions, adventures and, above all, the fresh array of monstrous enemies he encountered on the way.

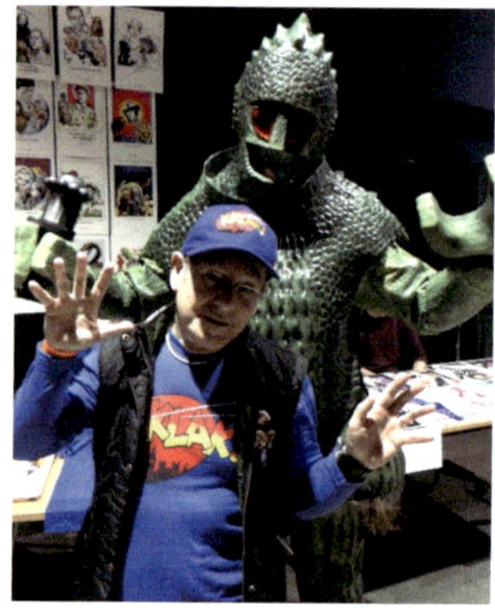

Chris with an Ice Warrior.

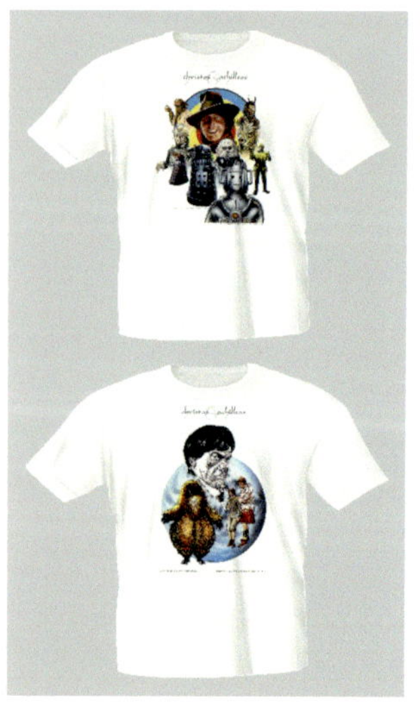

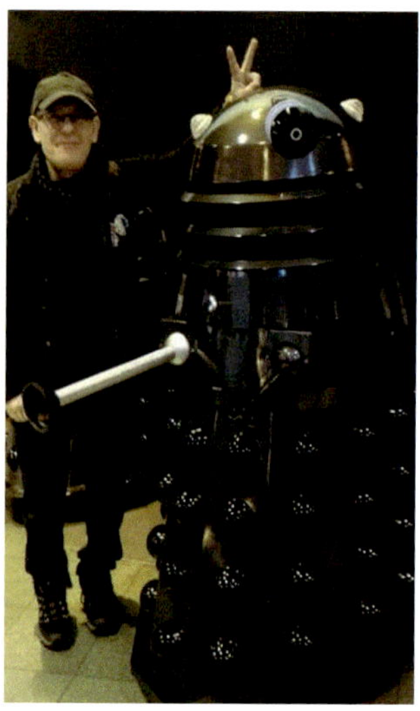

(above) Achilléos' long-awaited t-shirts.
(right) Chris having fun with a Dalek.

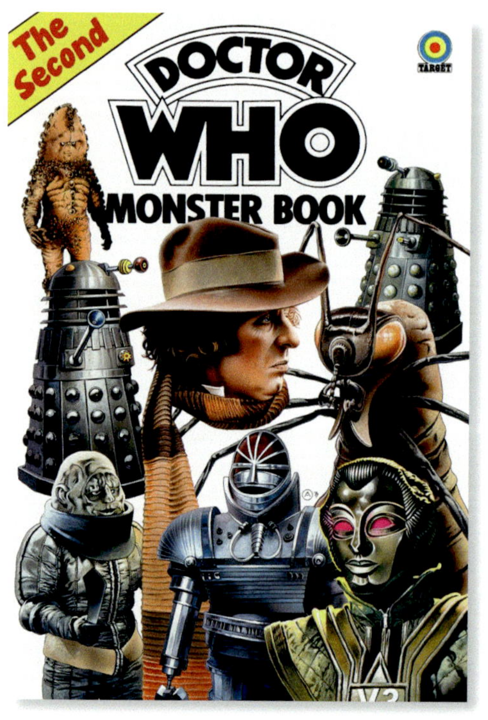

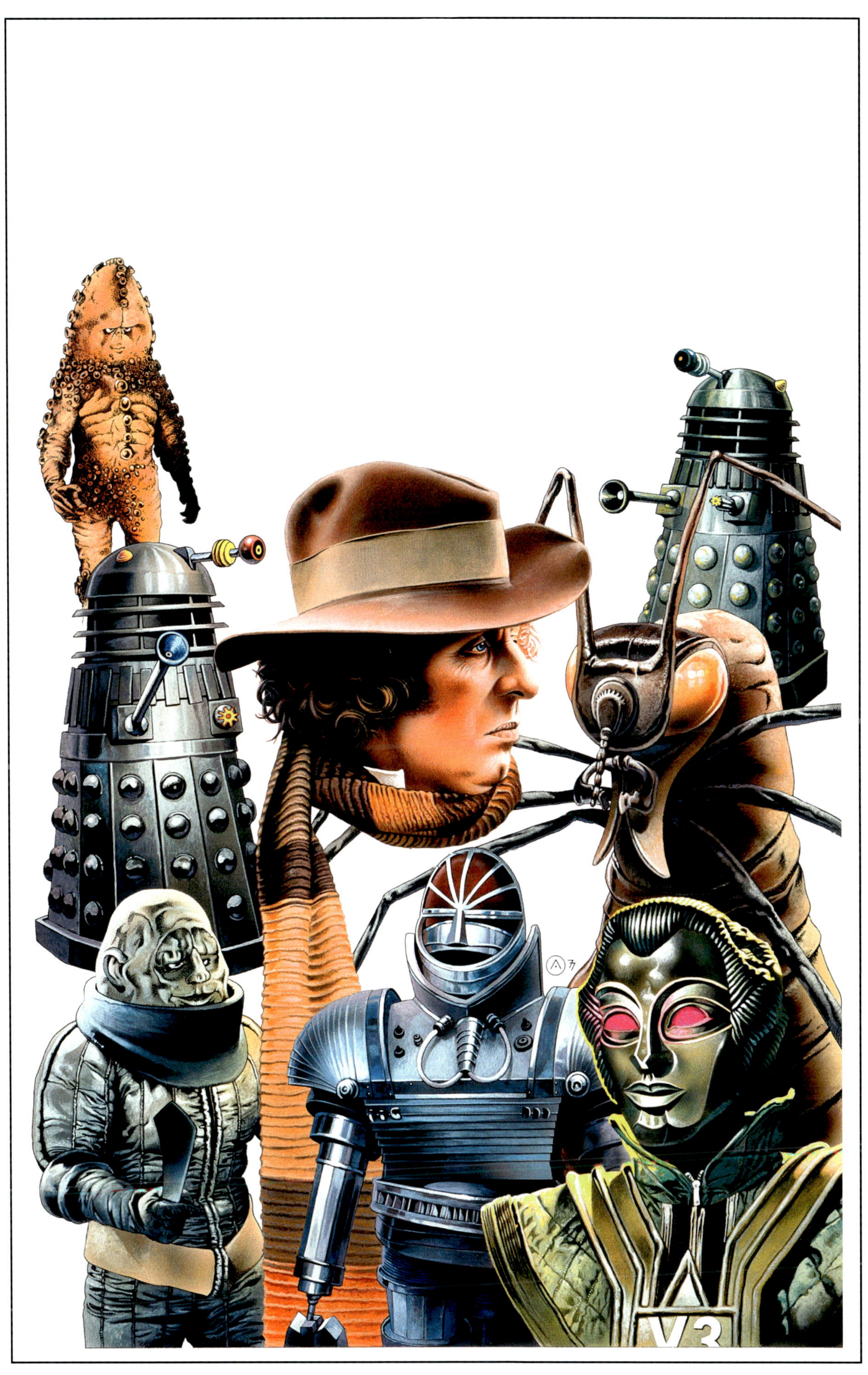

THE DOCTOR WHO APPRECIATION SOCIETY

Doctor: 1, 2, 3, 4, 5 **Release date:** 1983

BACK TO THE FOLD BY DAVID HOWE

The twentieth anniversary of *Doctor Who* fell in November 1983, and at that time I was running the reference department of the *Doctor Who* Appreciation Society and wanted to publish a 'Making Of' magazine to cover the adventure.

For the cover, I knew I wanted something special, so I contacted Chris about whether he might be interested in doing a new painting for the cover.

I had two options: an A4 piece which would just be on the cover; or an A3 piece which would wrap-around to the back. Chris produced a sketch of the proposed artwork, which included all five Doctors in a sweep across the page, surrounded by a variety of monsters. Chris suggested the Giant Robot, Sontaran, Cybermen (of two different designs), Daleks (again, several different designs), a small spaceship (taken from *The Invasion of Time*) and, of course, the TARDIS. We discussed it and added more monsters down the left hand side of the 'sweep', with a space above the TARDIS top right so I could add the *Doctor Who* logo and magazine title in foil.

The original sketches and idea included the Richard Hurndall version of the first Doctor, and I was torn as to whether the art should include that, or the original William Hartnell version. In the end we went with Hartnell, and it worked better as a piece to celebrate twenty years of the show, rather than just the one story in which Hurndall appeared. Chris also produced a sketch of a Cyberman pointing, which was ultimately not used on the art.

This was the first piece of *Doctor Who* art that Chris had completed since his work on the Target novelisations, and I was so pleased and proud to 'bring him back to the fold, so to speak' with this new creation, celebrating twenty years of *Doctor Who*!

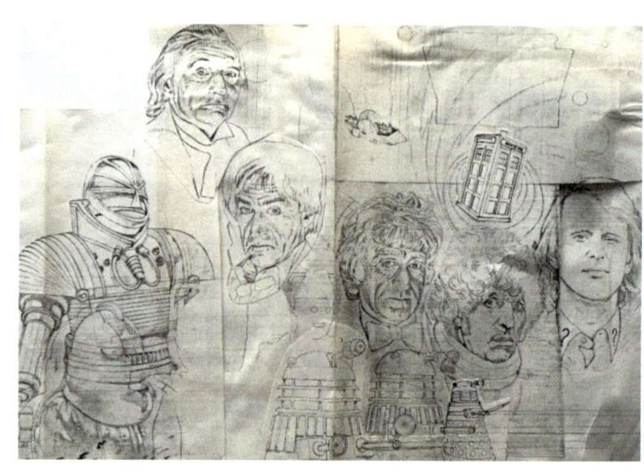

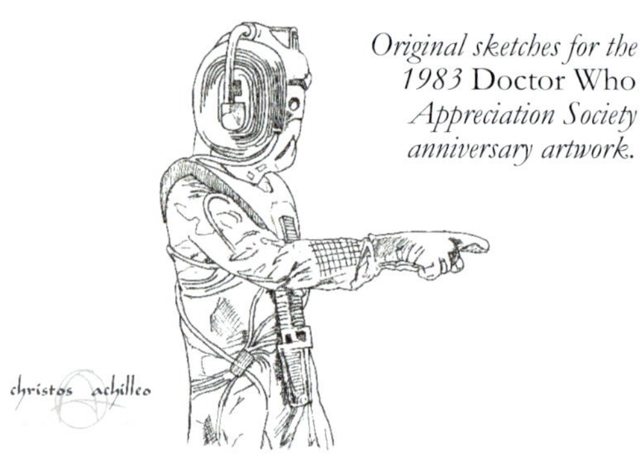

Original sketches for the 1983 Doctor Who *Appreciation Society anniversary artwork.*

66 This is interesting, because it has all five Doctors up to that point. Apart from an updated version of this image, this is the one of two times I did Peter Davison. He was new to the role, and as in other cases, I had virtually nothing to work from.

To be honest, when he was cast, personally, I thought that was the end of *Doctor Who* as we know it. No reflection on the actor, I just thought that he was much too young for the role. He wasn't a slightly nutty professor like the others have been. It was the beginning of a long, slow, agonising decline of the show, in my opinion. 99

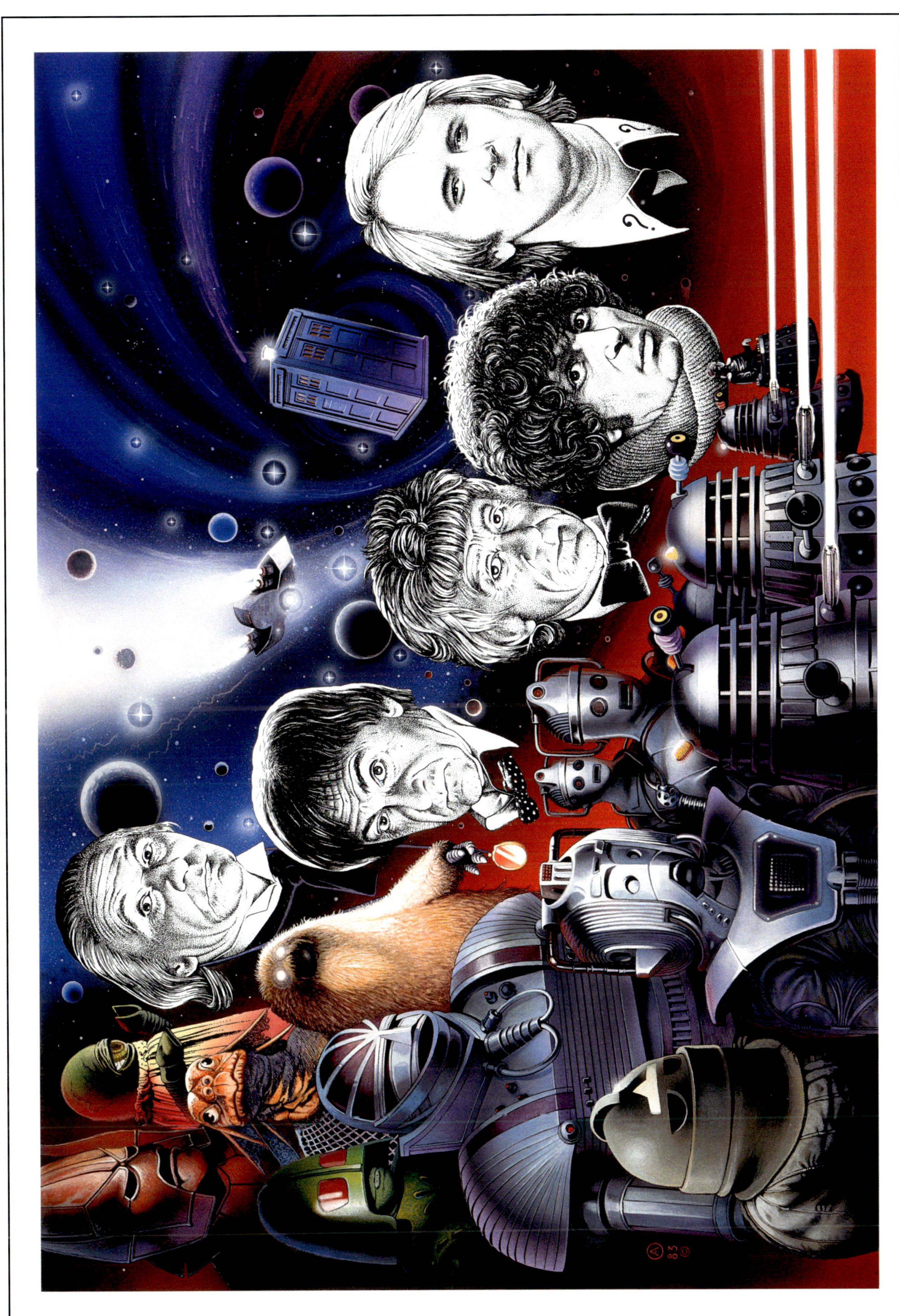

DOCTOR WHO SKETCH CARDS

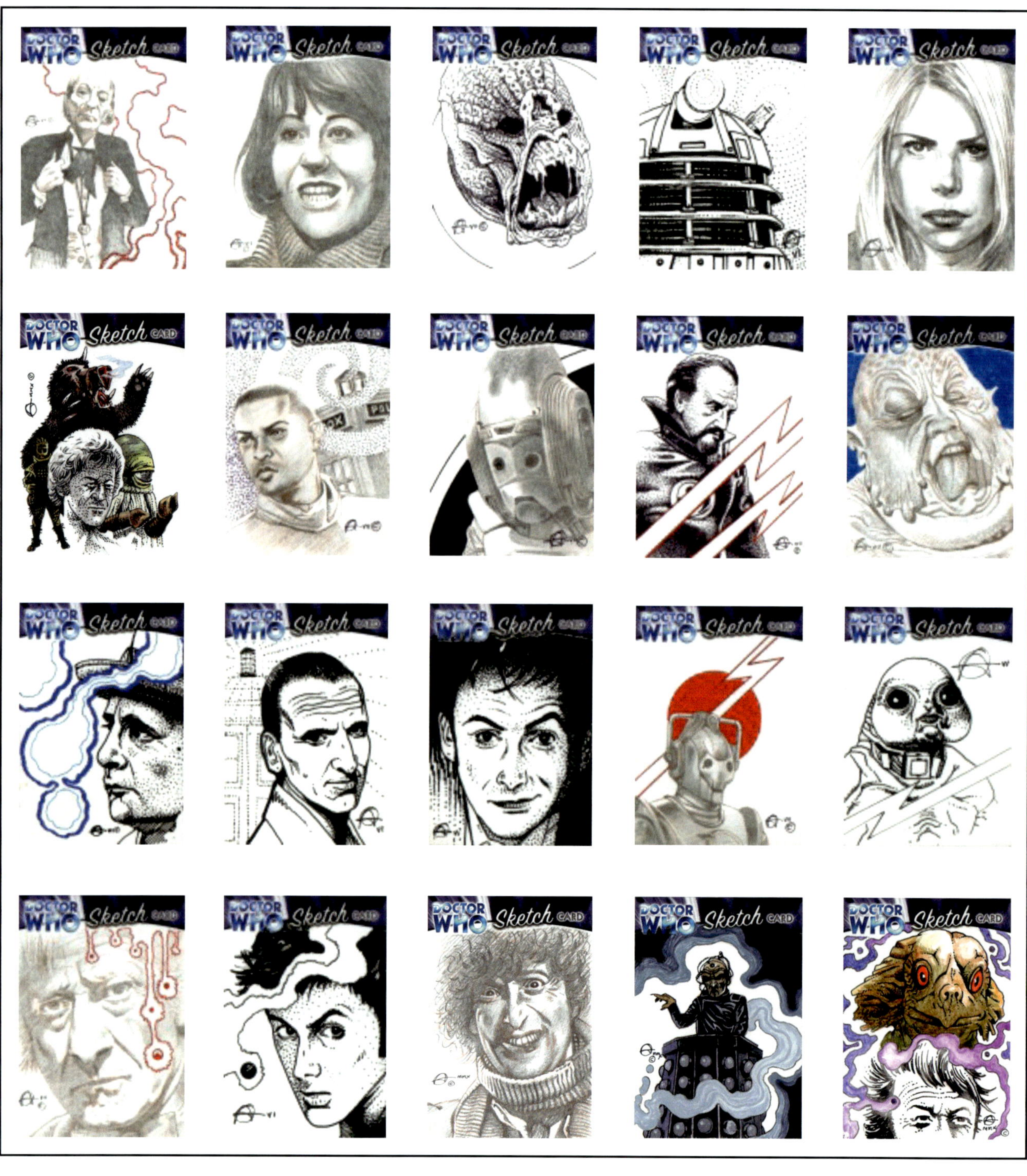

This set of sketch cards were commissioned back in 2006, but I'm not sure if they were ever sold or distributed.

(above) Doctor Who *trading cards. Published 2006. (Right page) Covers for the reprints of* The Daleks, Web of Fear, Day of the Daleks & Ark in Space. *These are still available from retailers. ISBN details can be found in the bibliography.*

DRAWING THE DOCTORS

William Hartnell

For William Hartnell, I used a reprograph pen. I had previously used this for scientific illustration work, using the dot effect. I did all right with the first two books, but for some reason I decided to use a smaller size pen for his head in *The Crusaders*, and it was a big mistake. It just drove me mad dotting away for hours. I never made the same mistake again.

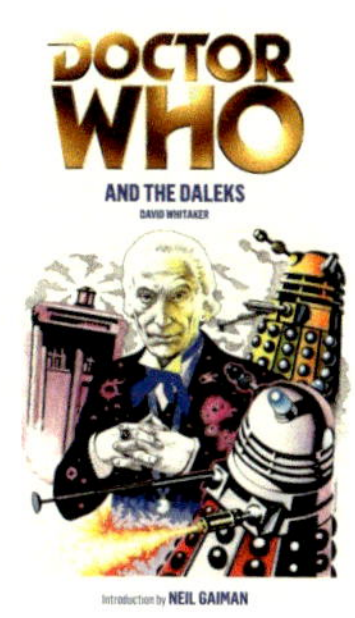

Patrick Troughton

Patrick Troughton was my favourite Doctor to draw. His face is so interesting and full of character. He was a very playful Doctor, but I always tried to give him a serious edge on the covers. In *The Abominable Snowmen* he almost looks villainous; all he needs is a Hitler moustache! I think that's a particularly good drawing; it's a story where Earth is in danger, and I tried to encapsulate that through his expression.

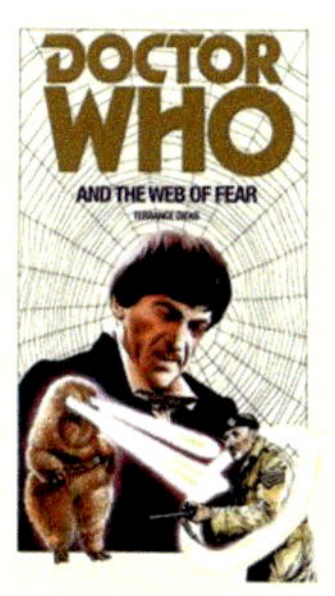

Jon Pertwee

For me drawing an older Doctor is easier than drawing a young one. They have more character in their faces. I enjoyed drawing Jon Pertwee as he also had very defined lines that made it quite easy to get his likeness. Unfortunately, he didn't think so. ☺ I found Pertwee difficult to engage with. When we would meet at signings, he always seemed distant and unapproachable. This was a shame because he was a great actor and I would have loved to spend a little time with him. I thought he was a genius playing Worzel Gummidge.

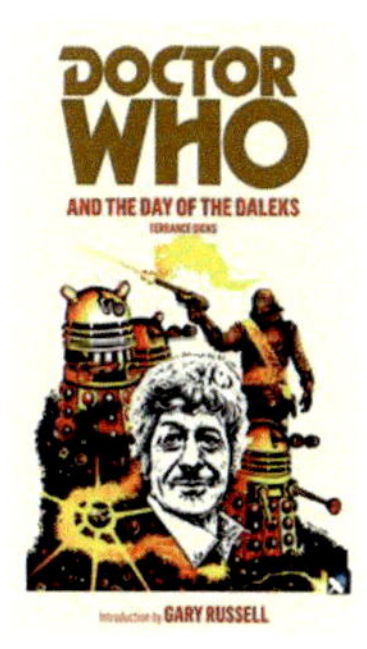

Tom Baker

Tom Baker was great to draw and good fun to be with. He has such an iconic look. The only problem was his curly hair, which was very hard to draw and quite time consuming.

Looking at the *Doctor Who Appreciation Society* artwork from '83, his hair is just too much. I'm pretty sure the reference I used for that was from *the Horror of Fang Rock*.

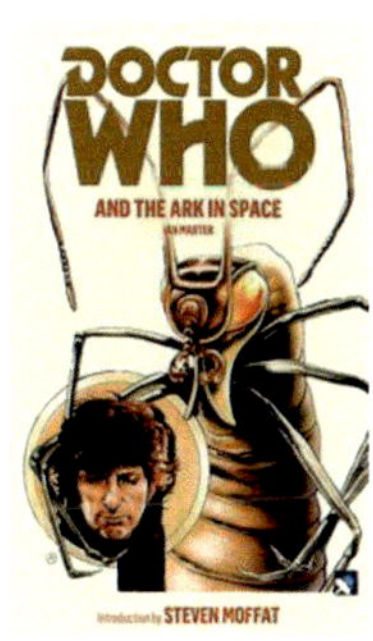

DOCTOR WHO: THE VISITATION

Writer: Eric Saward **Doctor:** Fifth **Reprint release date:** 28 April 2016 **Release order:** 69

"'Is that supposed to be Heathrow?' [Tegan] shouted, a rigid finger pointing at the screen.

'It is,' said Adric firmly.

'Well, they've let the grass grow since I was last here.'

'Actually they haven't built the airport yet,' Adric continued. 'We're about three years early.'

'That's great! Perhaps I should slip outside and file a claim on the land. When they get around to inventing the aeroplane, I'll make a fortune!'"

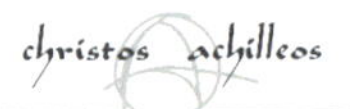

> **"** For many years I had been out of touch with *Doctor Who.* I didn't watch the programme, and I had no idea they were still publishing books. If they had phoned me with work, I would have taken it on, but art directors came and went, and the phone never rang.
>
> Despite this, I ended up getting back to *Doctor Who* for the fiftieth anniversary, when I was commissioned by the BBC to illustrate three new covers featuring the three 1980s Doctors. When I look back on them now, I don't think they're bad, except for the first one, *The Visitation*, where I didn't draw Peter Davison very well. Sorry, Peter! ☹ **"**

Trying to get Tegan back to Heathrow in 1981, the Doctor brings the TARDIS to the right place, but over 300 years early – to 1666. They are not the only visitors as Death stalks the local woods, complete with cloak, scythe and a skull like face.

In fact, 'Death' is an android bought by a group of alien Terileptils whose spaceship has crashed. Criminals and fugitives from their own race, they now plan to take over Earth. With Adric and Tegan captured, the Doctor and Nyssa try to deal with the deadly android, and a group of local villagers under the control of the Terileptils.

But even if they succeed, can they prevent the Terileptils from unleashing an even more deadly form of the Black Death?

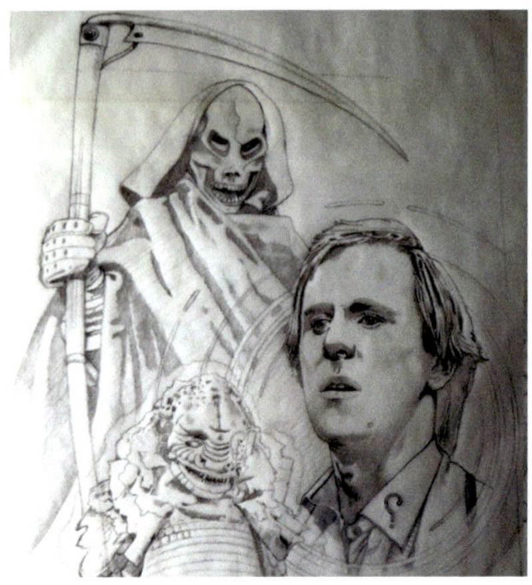

(left) original drawing for The Visitation.

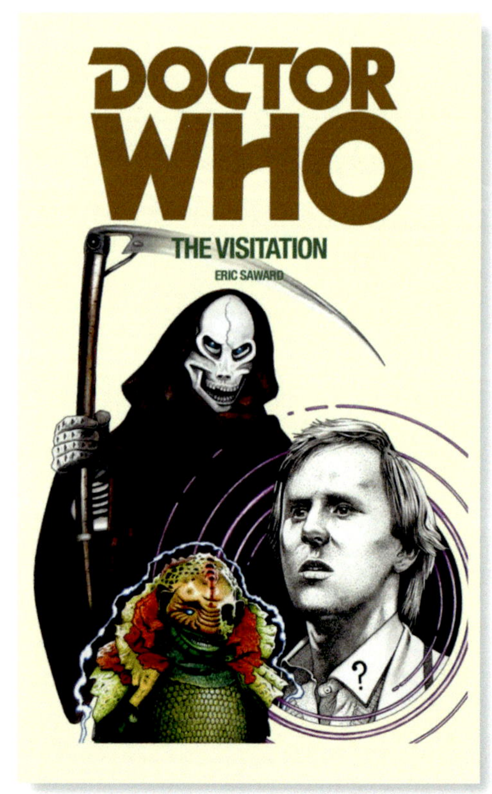

*The Visitation is still available from retailers.
ISBN details can be found in the bibliography.*

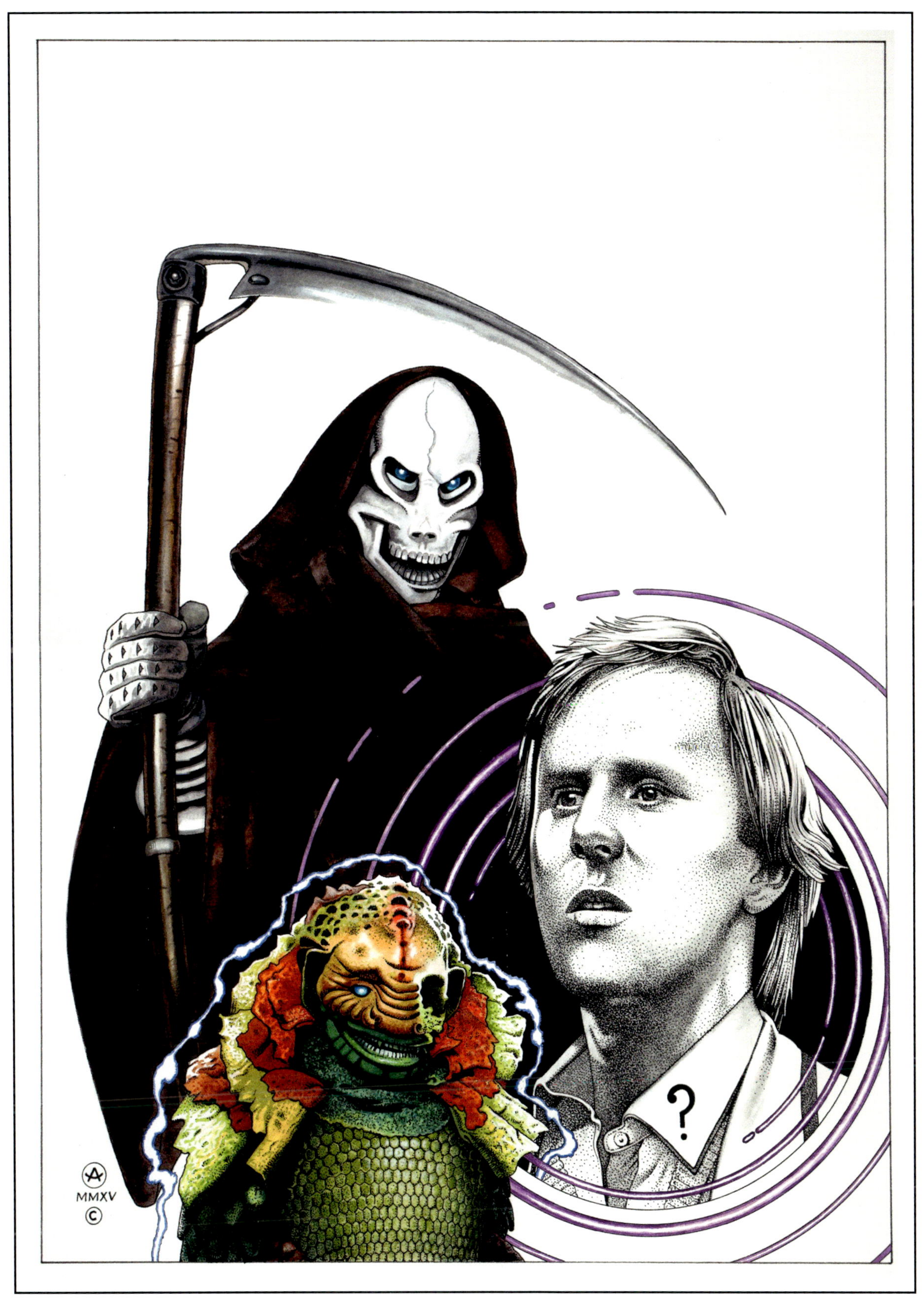

DOCTOR WHO: VENGEANCE ON VAROS

Writer: Philip Martin **Doctor:** Sixth **Reprint release date:** 28 April 2016 **Release order:** 127

"'What now, sir?' Bax turned to the Governor.

'Go in close, establish there is no flicker of life.'

'Yes, sir.' Bax shifted his cameras into a big close-up that brought the Doctor's waxen face so close that it filled the screen. Not a muscle twitched nor was a tremor of breath evident.

'He's dead, sir.'

'I agree.' The Governor watched the Doctor for a moment more, then snapped his fingers.

'Cut it now, Bax...'

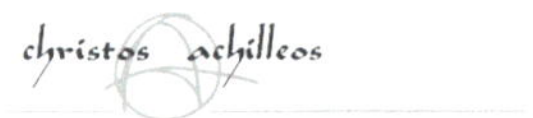

“ *Vengeance on Varos* is better, but to my amazement the BBC asked me to remove the noose from my original design. I said, sorry I'm not doing that, I'm a traditional artist, and if I do, then I have to start the whole thing again. I asked them to remove it digitally, reasoning that there must be people in the BBC who could do it in five minutes. But it did spoil the whole design. It just diluted it. ”

Bax shifted his camera into a big close-up that brought the Doctor's waxen face so close that it filled the screen. Not a muscle twitched nor was a tremor of life evident. 'He's dead, sir.'

In need of Zeiton-7 to repair the TARDIS, the Doctor and Peri travel to the planet Varos. A former prison for the criminally insane, Varos is now ruled by the descendants of the guards. The population is kept in check and entertained by broadcasts of torture and execution from the Punishment Dome – where the TARDIS lands.

Soon the Doctor and Peri, together with rebel fugitives Jondar and Areta, find themselves trying to escape the Dome's traps and challenges – all on live television.

Can the Doctor and Peri escape the Punishment Dome, and help the Governor ensure the people of Varos get a fair deal for their Zeiton-7?

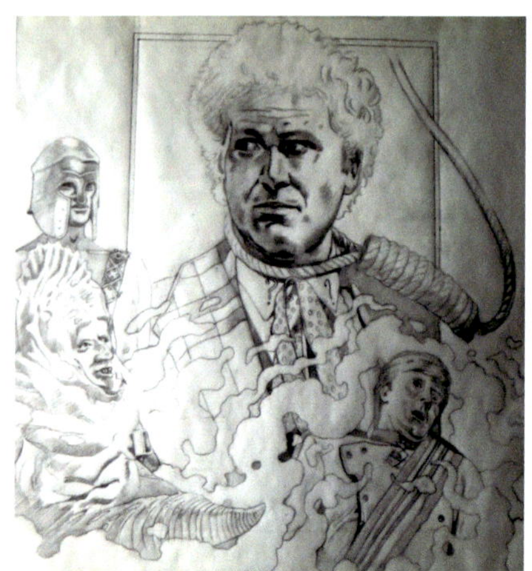

(left) original drawing for Vengeance on Varos.

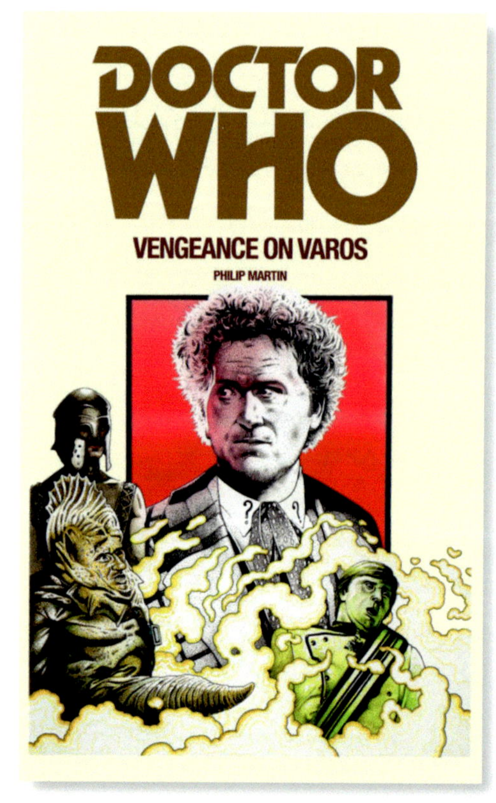

Vengeance on Varos is still available from retailers. ISBN details can be found in the bibliography.

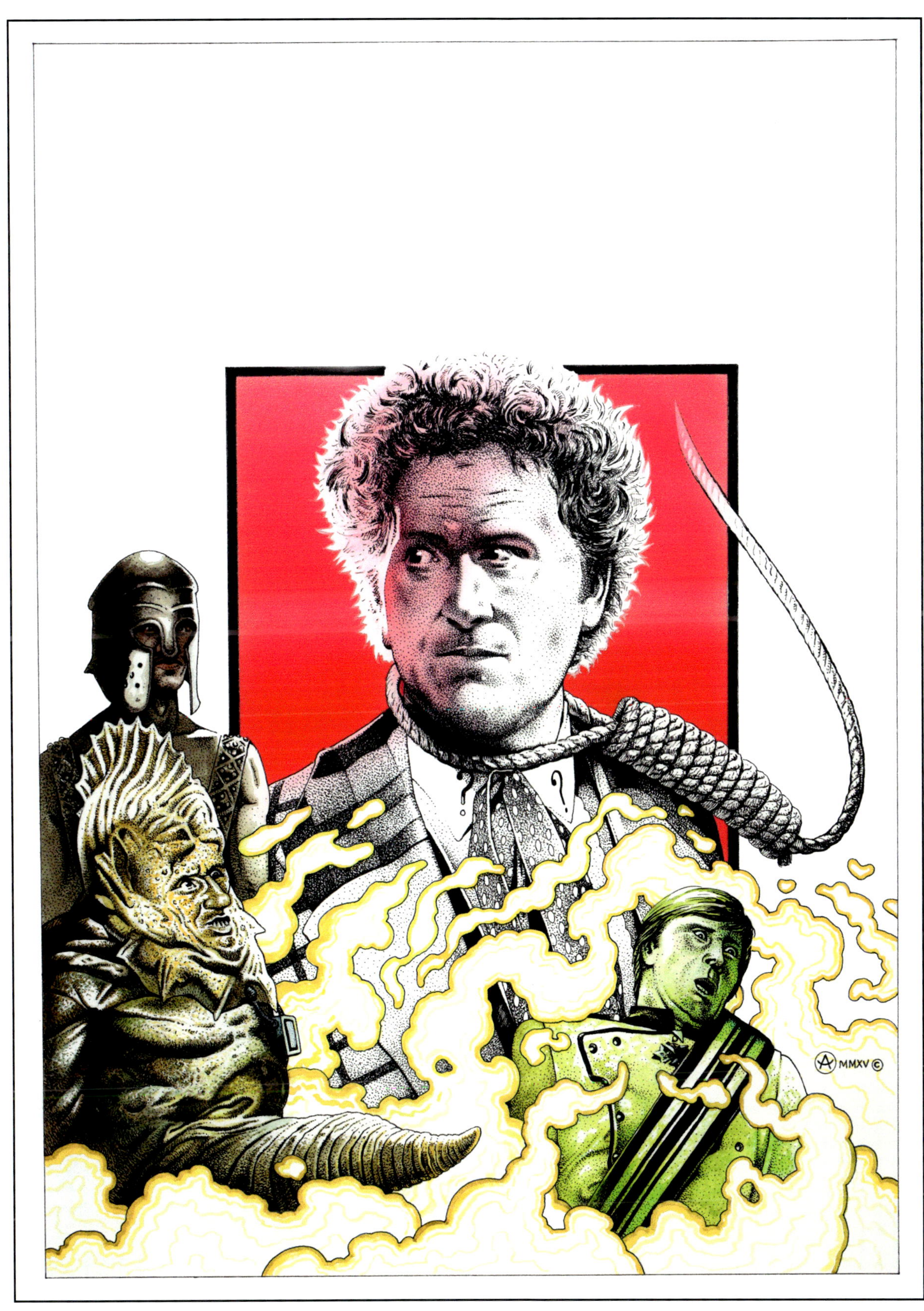

DOCTOR WHO: BATTLEFIELD

Writer: Marc Platt **Doctor:** Seventh **Reprint release date:** 28 April 2016 **Release order:** 154

"The Doctor sat up oblivious of the concerned faces that surrounded him. 'I cannot allow your interference,' he said.

And he could see her now. A proud regal warrior armoured in gold, lit by torchlight. She raised her hand aggressively and made a fist. 'Then let this be our last battlefield!'"

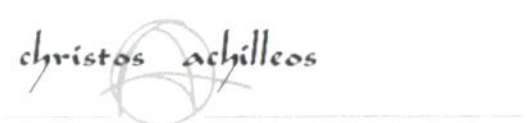

❝ For *Battlefield* I watched the video as I wasn't a regular viewer of the programme in the 1980s. I thought the Destroyer was the best thing in it, but I thought they didn't use him enough in the story. Luckily, I had a decent photo of him to use on the cover. I kept McCoy quite simple. I wanted to show him with more expression, but unfortunately, I could not find the reference. With hindsight, I should have used a different colour for the energy bolts.

I do believe that all three books are OK, but I didn't have my heart in them. This was not my era. I think the BBC asked me to do them because of my success in the '70s. **❞**

'How do you do?' the Doctor said. 'This is Ace, and I am...'

'Merlin!' cried the Black Knight. His smile broadened in wonder and recognition. 'Merlin, against all hope!'

A UNIT nuclear convoy, stranded on the shores of Lake Vortigern, becomes the focus of an incursion by knights from a parallel reality. In this other world, technology and magic exist side by side, and the legends of King Arthur are fact. Close to the lake, the sinister Mordred battles against his enemy Ancelyn and summons his mother, the powerful witch Morgaine.

Is the Doctor really Merlin? And will he discover what actually happened to King Arthur? But time is running out for everyone as Morgaine takes control of the nuclear weapons and summons the Destroyer – Lord of Darkness and Eater of Worlds...

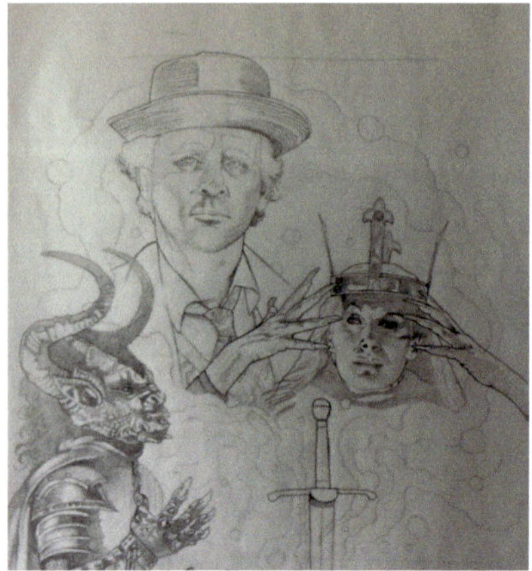

(left) original drawing for Battlefield.

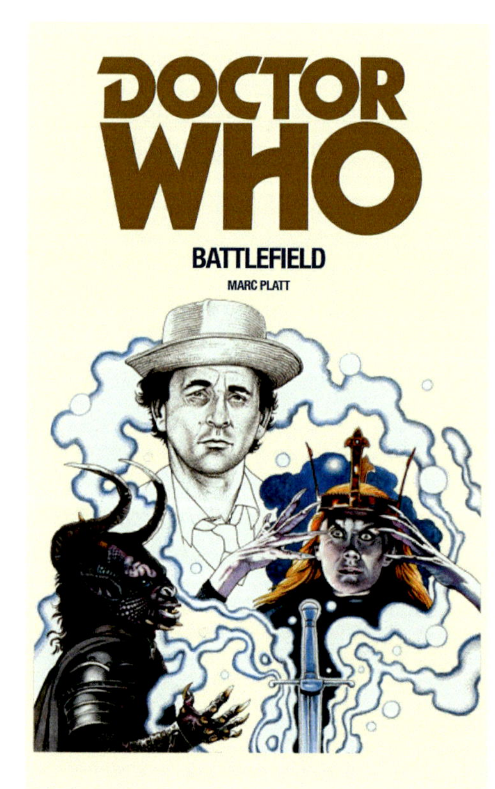

Battlefield *is still available from retailers.*
ISBN details can be found in the bibliography.

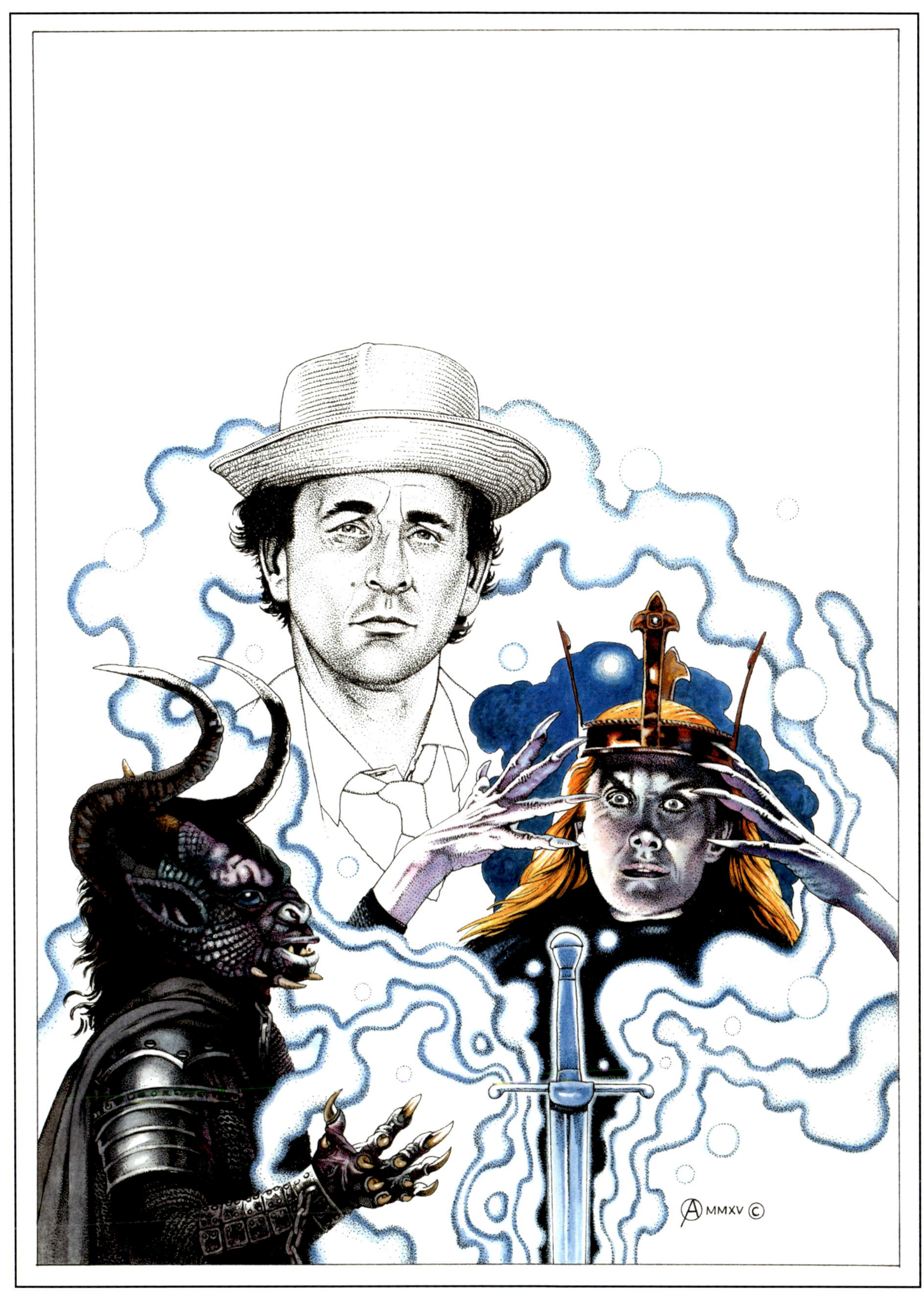

DOCTOR WHO AND THE KEYS OF MARINUS

Writer: Philip Hinchcliffe **Doctor:** First **Release date:** 21 August 1980 **Release order:** 59

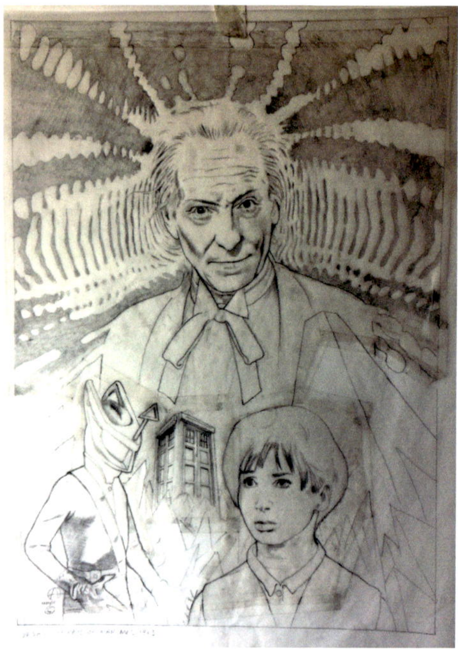

Original drawing for The Keys of Marinus.

MARINUS
a remote force-shielded island set in a
sea of acid, governed by
THE CONSCIENCE
the ultimate computer which rules
and balances the gentle life of
Marinus, guarded by
ARBITAN THE KEEPER
ruthless protector of a peace-loving
race threatened by
YARTEK
Warlord of the brutal sub-
human Voords, sworn enemy of
Arbitan and of Marinus, who has
within his grasp
THE KEYS OF MARINUS
the Conscience's vital micro-circuits,
the doors of good and evil.
Can the Doctor find the hidden
circuits in time? Arbitan's command
was 'Find them,
OR DIE!'

"Barbara recoiled in horror at the sight of the four brains glowing eerily inside their transparent domes ... Barbara looked around. There was no one else in the room apart from a girl attendant who stood motionless and glassy-eyed. Those monstrous brains had everyone in their thrall.

'We are the masters of this city,' rasped the Voice, echoing Barbara's thoughts."

christos achilleos

66 For this private commission of *The Keys of Marinus*, I used the special effects that were shown in the opening of the 1960s TV show. The fans tell me that this idea hasn't been done before. Of course, I did know that these effects were used in the Patrick Troughton era, and not the William Hartnell. 99

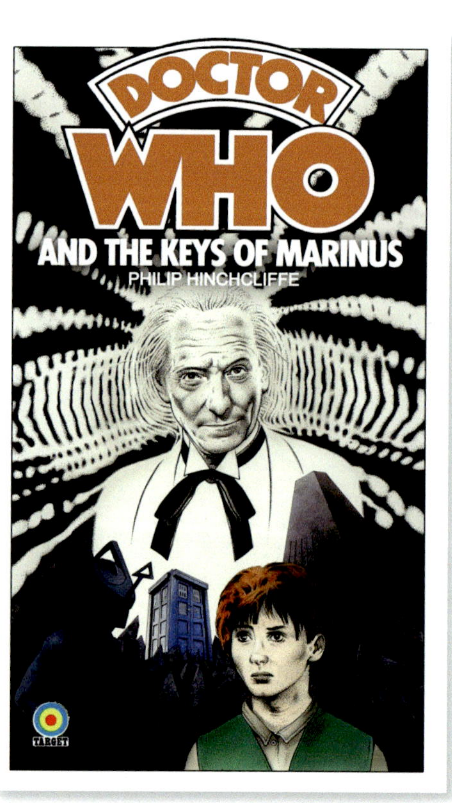

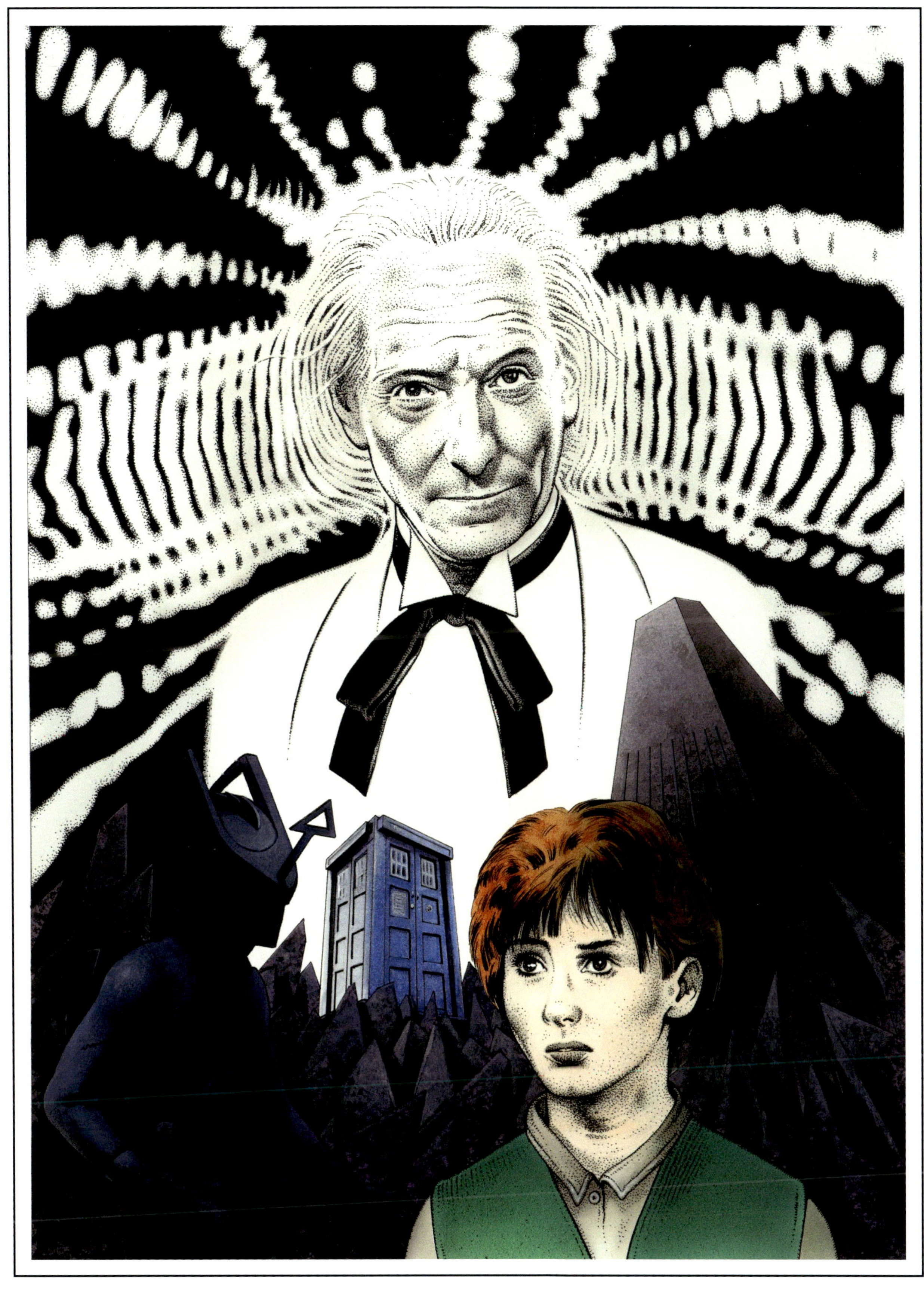

DOCTOR WHO: THE AZTECS

Writer: John Lucarotti **Doctor:** First **Release date:** 21 June 1984 **Release order:** 89

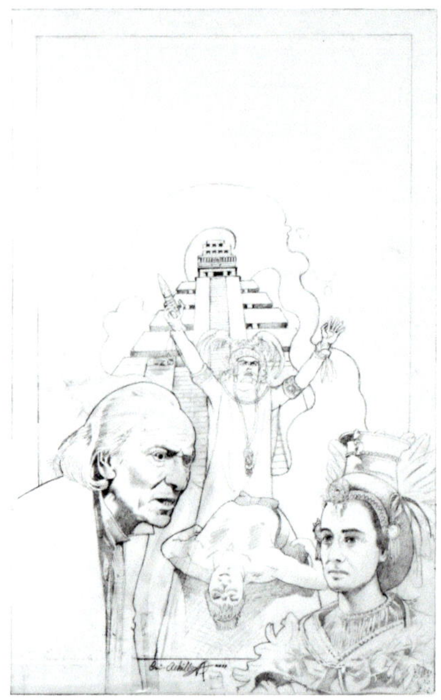

Original drawing for The Aztecs.

"The Doctor, Susan and Ian were in an antechamber below the temple. The walls were covered with colourful tapestries; the stone floor was carpeted; there were three couches to recline on, and a legless table laden with food and wine. Susan and Ian sat down while the Doctor paced up and down."

66 This is the first of the my new images painted exclusively for this book. I love historical stories. I originally wanted to do *The Myth Makers,* which is about Troy, but there are no useful images available, so I chose to do *The Aztecs* instead. The reference material for *The Aztecs* was good, and this makes all the difference. I like the pyramid design, this time literally, with energy flowing out, threatening to engulf the foreground figures. I like to think that the kids back in the '70s would have loved this one ☺ 99

The TARDIS materialises in Mexico during the Aztec civilisation. The Doctor and his companions step outside to discover they are inside a tomb – the tomb, it turns out, of Yetaxa, once High Priest of the Aztecs.

Barbara is hailed as Yetaxa's reincarnation by Autloc, High Priest of Knowledge, and Tlotoxl, High Priest of Sacrifice, when they find her in the precincts of the tomb wearing the bracelet of the deceased Priest, now revered as a god.

And she takes advantage of her position of unaccustomed power to try and dissuade the Aztecs from practising human sacrifice...

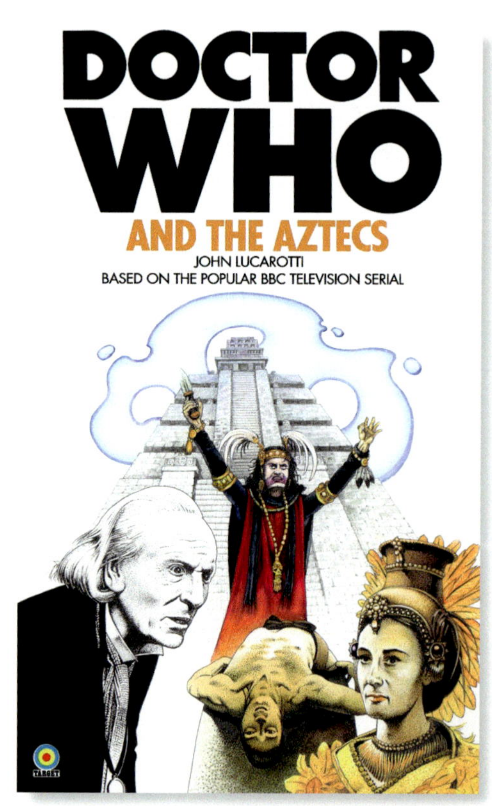

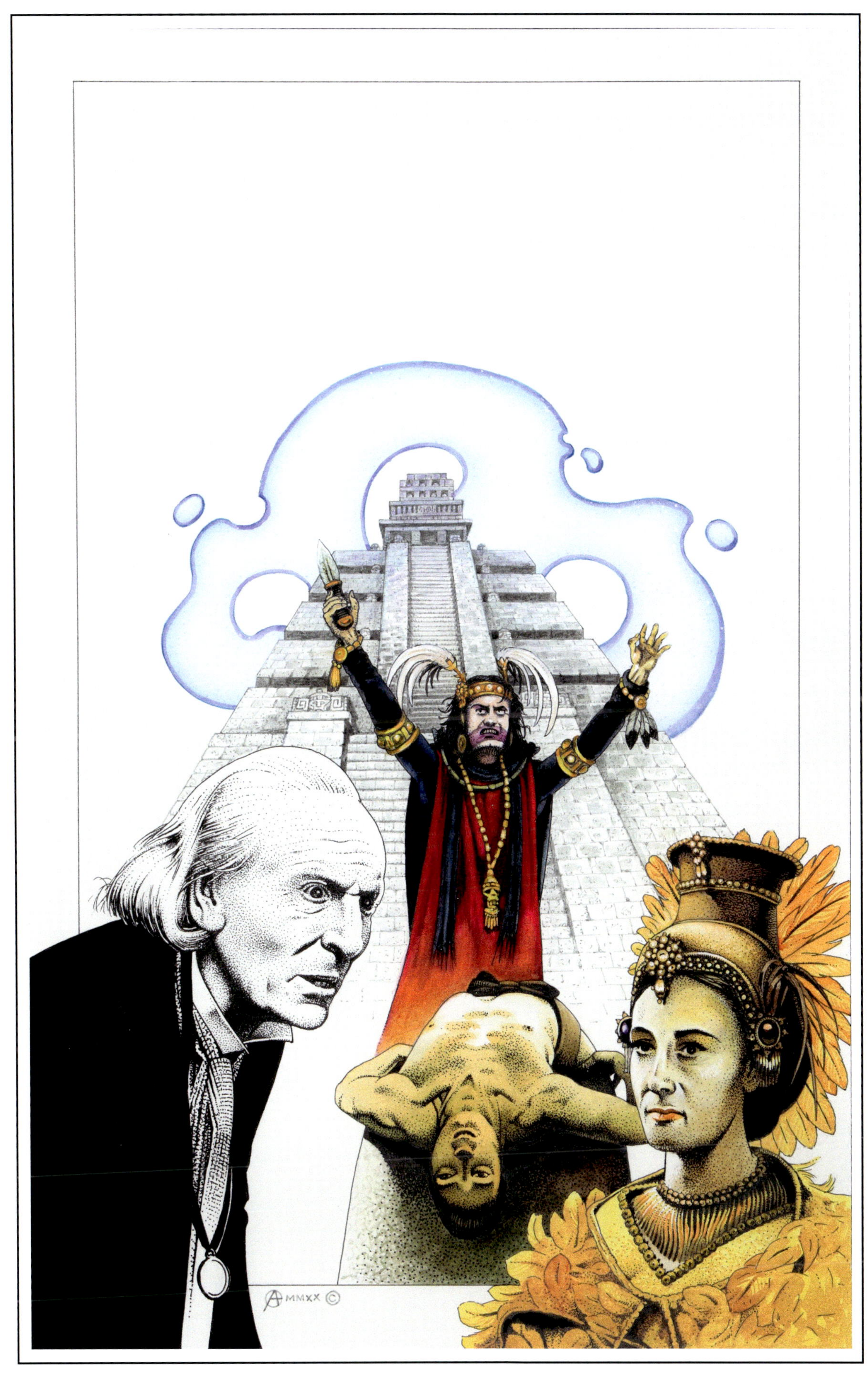

DOCTOR WHO AND THE DALEK INVASION OF EARTH

Writer: Terrance Dicks **Doctor:** First **Release date:** 24 March 1977 **Release order:** 30

" The Doctor stood at the TARDIS console, still holding Susan's shoe. Behind him Ian and Barbara stood hand in hand. They knew the dilemma the Doctor was facing, but there was nothing they could do to help.

Suddenly the Doctor stood very erect. He put Susan's shoe down carefully and reached for a particular control-switch and slammed it over, hard.

Susan had almost reached the TARDIS when its door closed in her face. She took the key from round her neck and tried to open it. Nothing happened.

'Grandfather,' she screamed. 'Grandfather!'"

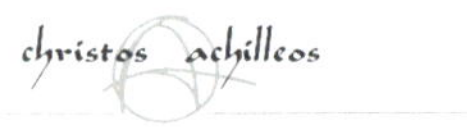

❝ I felt lucky to be given a second chance to do this cover. This is a private commission of *The Dalek Invasion of Earth* for Dale Santos, an avid collector of my *Doctor Who* work from the USA.

When I first did the cover back in the '70s, I used all the wrong elements. Now it has accurate Daleks and the correct flying saucers. I based the old artwork on the 1960s movie. In this new version I particularly like that it's mostly black and white. It's more atmospheric and faithful to the TV series. The Hartnell drawing is quite nice – even though I really hate drawing architecture – and all those straight lines on the Houses of Parliament nearly drove me mad. I left the Doctor's head in black and white pencil, and it really feels that he's connected to the building. I think this is a good one and it's proven to be very popular with the fans. **❞**

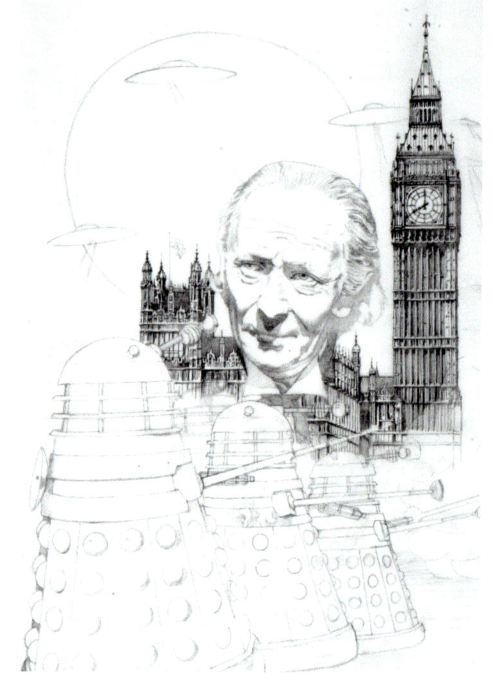

Original drawing for The Dalek Invasion of Earth.

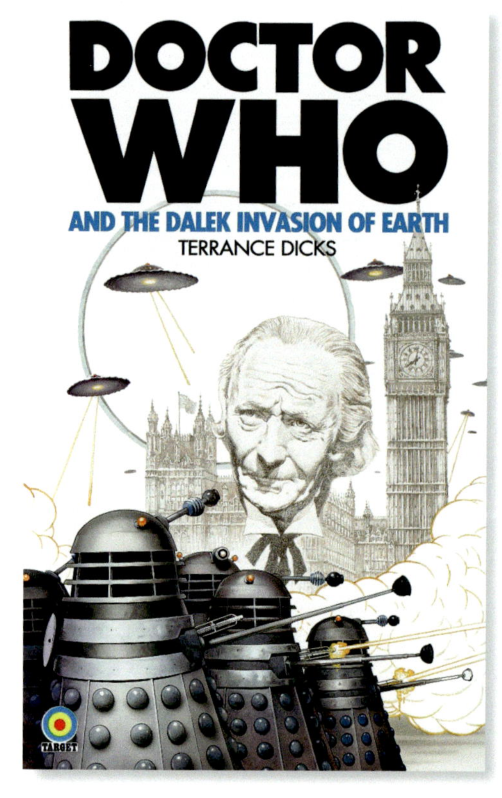

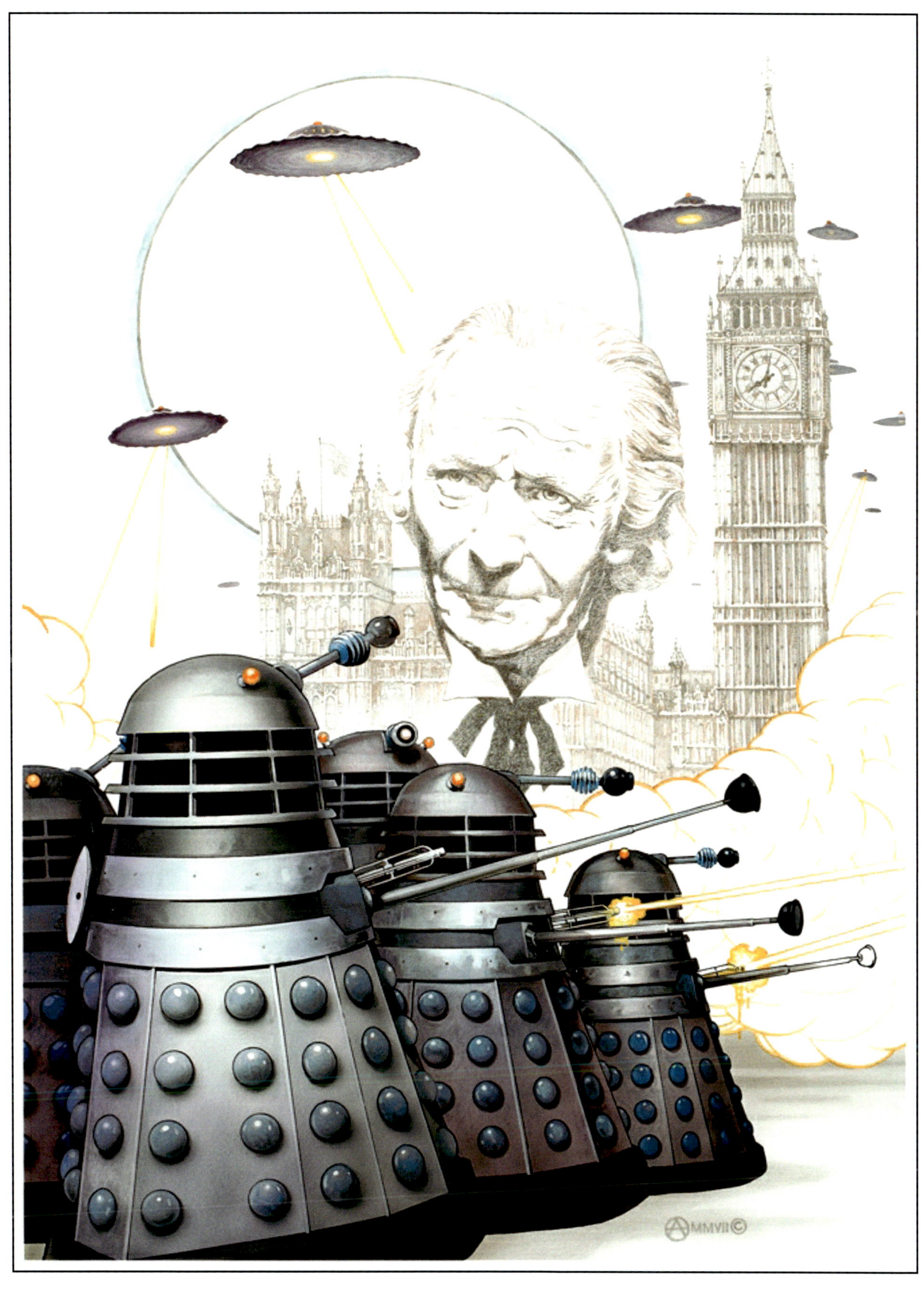

DOCTOR WHO: THE EVIL OF THE DALEKS

Writer: John Peel **Doctor:** Second **Release date:** 10 October 1985 **Release order:** 99

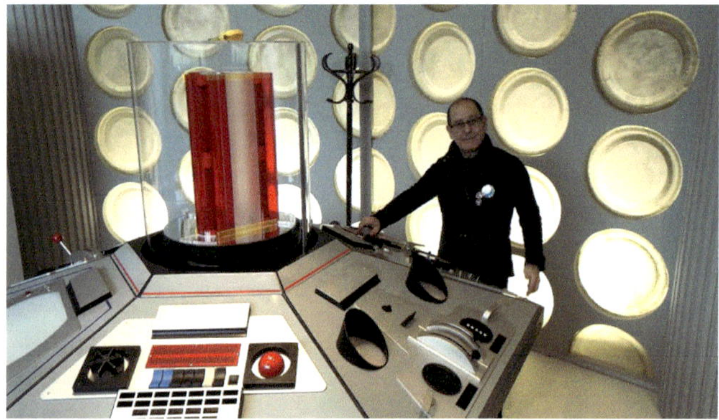

Chris flying the TARDIS.

"Over the entire time that the Daleks had existed, the mysterious Doctor had time and again arrived to defeat their plans. His appearance had changed many times, but never his unflagging devotion to the destruction of the Daleks' schemes. From the instant of their creation, the Doctor had been their greatest foe."

christos achilléos

❝ In this *Evil of the Daleks* cover I decided to leave the Doctor's head a pencil drawing as I felt it would stand out against the dark background. I really like the way the explosion brings the images together. Things are a lot more dramatic than the actual story, which is something I can do with private commissions. Once again the Daleks' sink plungers are the wrong way round. Sorry about that. **❞**

"The Daleks tell me I'm going to do something for them – something I would rather die than do."

Stranded in Victorian London, separated from his TARDIS and forced to cooperate with the Daleks, it seems that the Doctor's luck has finally run out.

The Daleks are searching for the elusive Human Factor, and want the Doctor to help them find it. With Victoria and Jamie held captive, the Doctor has no choice.

An army of Daleks stands poised to conquer the universe. Will the Human Factor be their ultimate weapon?

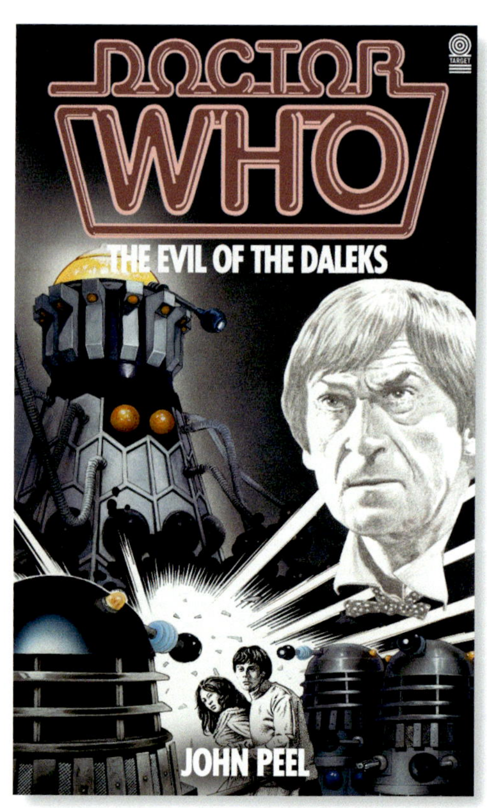

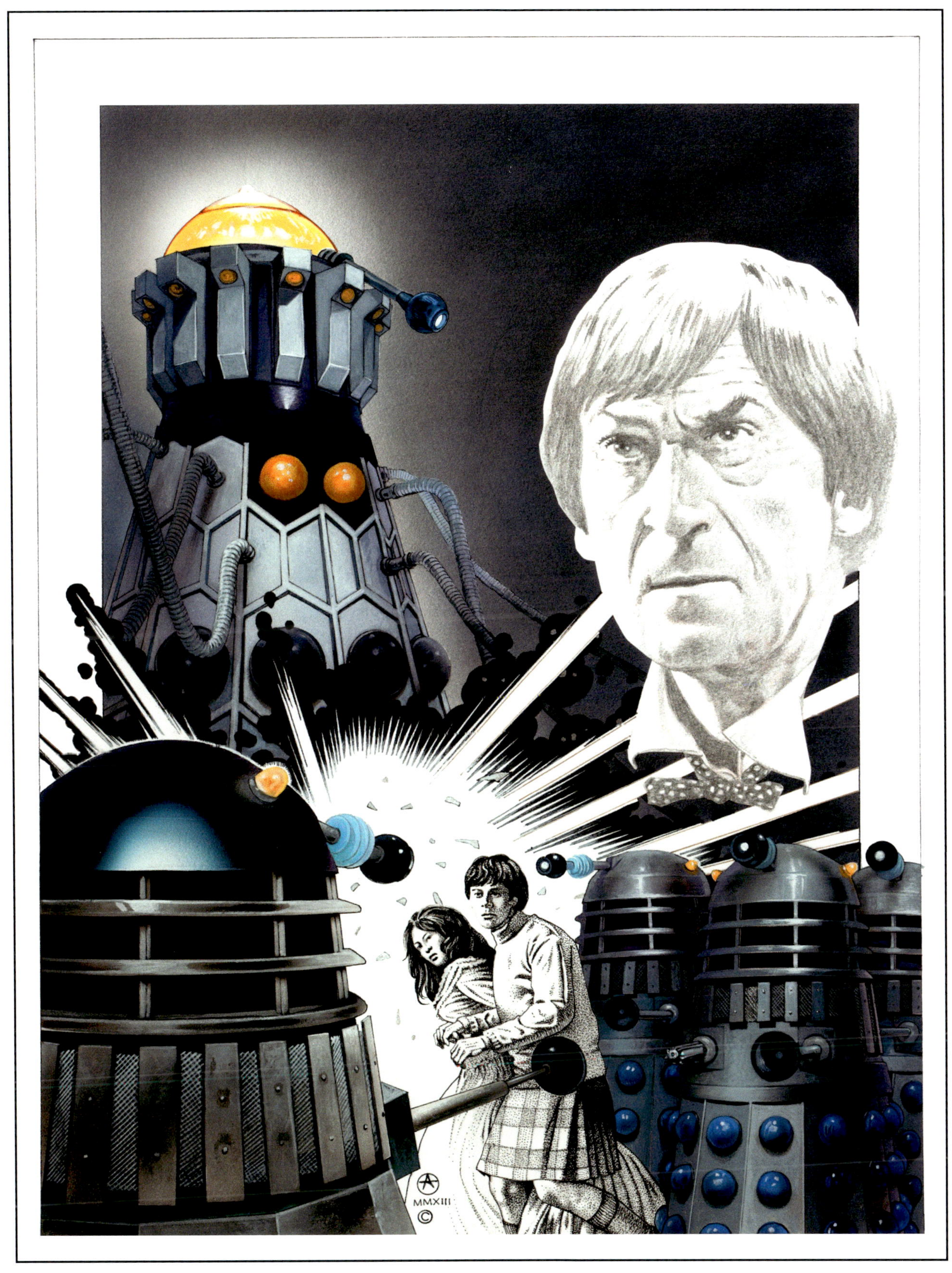

DOCTOR WHO AND THE TOMB OF THE CYBERMEN

Writer: Gerry Davis **Doctor:** Second **Release date:** 18 May 1978 **Release order:** 41

"'You'll find there is so much else to think about – to remember. Our lives are different from everybody else's, that's the exciting thing,' he said. 'Nobody in the universe, in the whole universe, can do what we're doing, be what we are. Nobody.'"

christos achilleos

❝ *The Tomb of the Cybermen* was another private commission. Jeff Cummins did the original artwork and made the same mistake; he also drew the wrong Cybermen! To be fair, it's confusing drawing Cybermen and Daleks as there have been so many versions of them over the years. I really like this version, despite it being difficult to find reference material that nobody has used before. **❞**

The Cybermen – silver, indestructible monsters whose only goal is power – seem to have disappeared from their planet, Telos. When a party of archaeologists, joined by the Doctor, Jamie, and Victoria, land on the Cybermen's barren, deserted planet, they uncover what appears to be their tomb.

But once inside it becomes clear that the Cybermen are not dead, and some in the group of archaeologists desperately want to re-activate these monsters! How can the Doctor defeat these ruthless, power-seeking humans and the Cybermen?

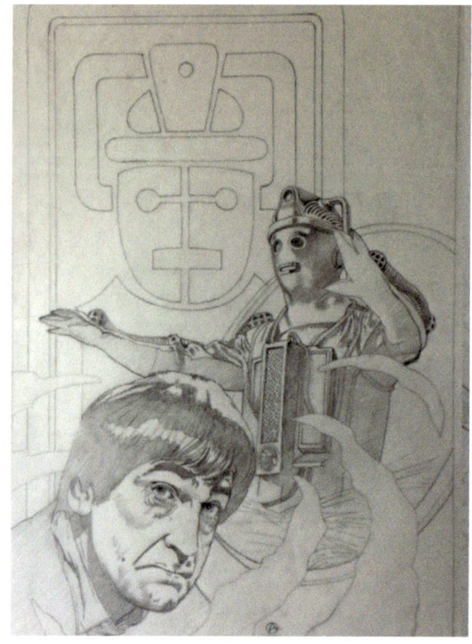

(left) original drawing for Doctor Who and The Tomb of the Cybermen.

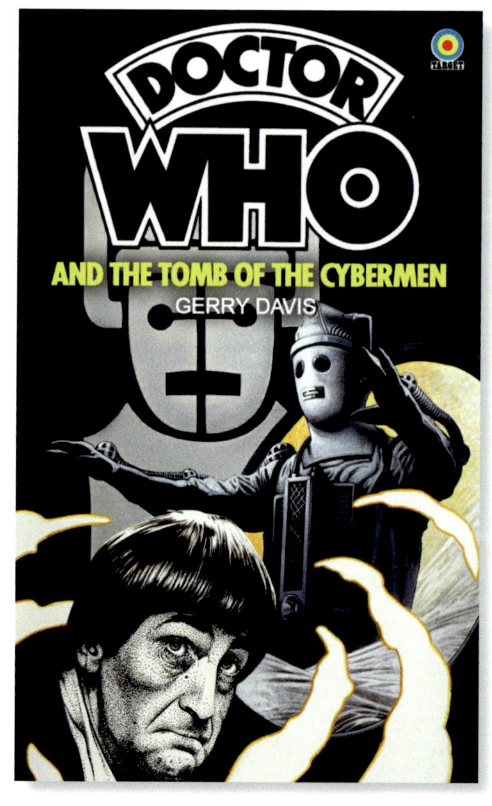

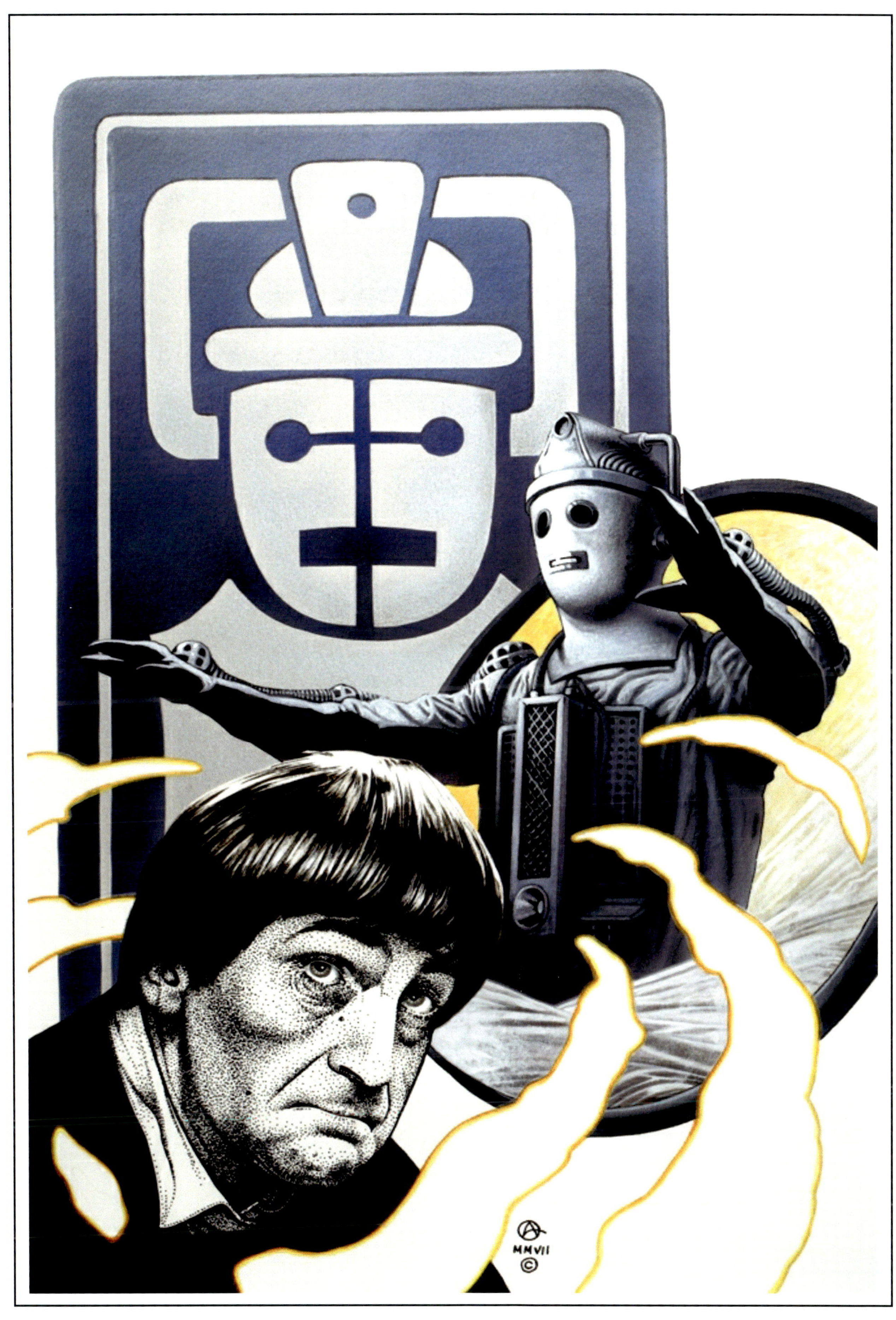

DOCTOR WHO: THE INVASION

Writer: Ian Marter **Doctor:** Second **Release date:** 10 October 1985 **Release order:** 97

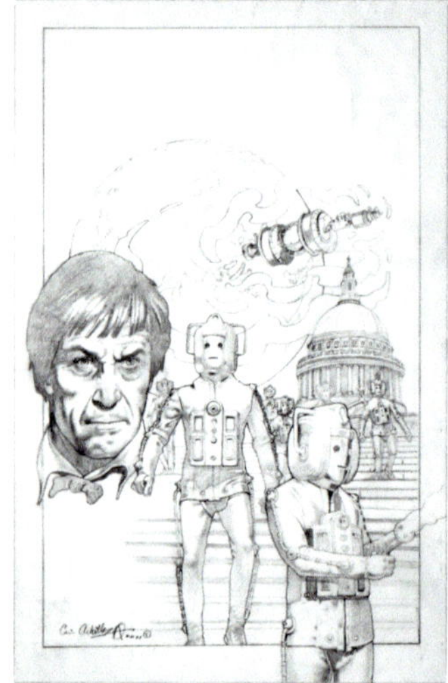

Original drawing for The Invasion.

"Silhouetted against the sunlit open doorway stood four Cybermen, their huge shadows stretching across the floor. The UNIT platoon concentrated its machine-gun fire on the advancing enemy, but it had no effect whatsoever. Then the Cybermen's laser units flashed with intense blue light and two troopers were flung against the corrugated steel wall of the factory amid splinters of wooden crate."

christos achilleos

" This is the second of the my new images painted exclusively for this book. I enjoyed combining the classic image of Troughton and the 1960s Cybermen. This is another cover where I attempted to encapsulate the story in one overall design. I decided to use the classic, but perhaps a bit overused, image of the Cybermen on the steps of St Paul's Cathedral. I wanted the two front Cybermen to look threatening, with one staring right at you and the other one firing his weapon. **"**

Materialising in outer space, the TARDIS is attacked by a missile fired from the dark side of the moon.

Back on Earth, the newly-formed United Nations Intelligence Taskforce, led by Brigadier Lethbridge-Stewart, is disturbed by a series of UFO sightings over Southern England.

Meanwhile, a large consignment of mysterious crates is delivered to the headquarters of International Electromatix, the largest computer and electronics firm in the world.

Three seemingly unconnected events – but in reality the preparations for a massive Cyberman invasion of Earth with one aim – the total annihilation of the human race.

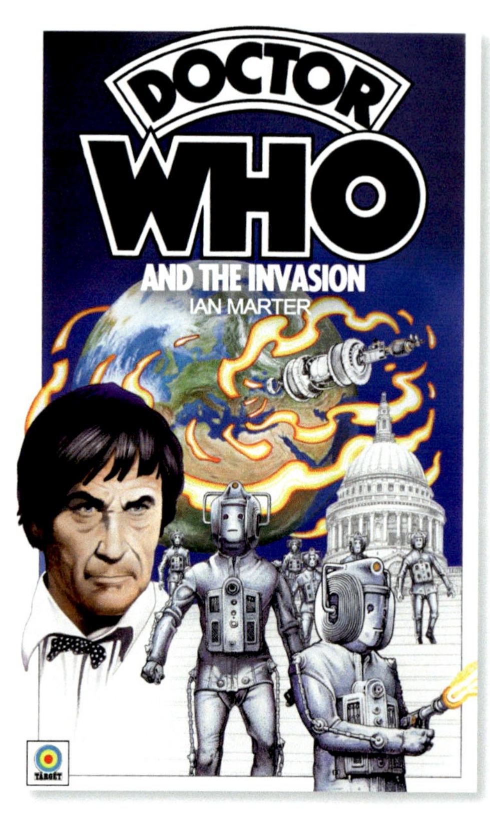

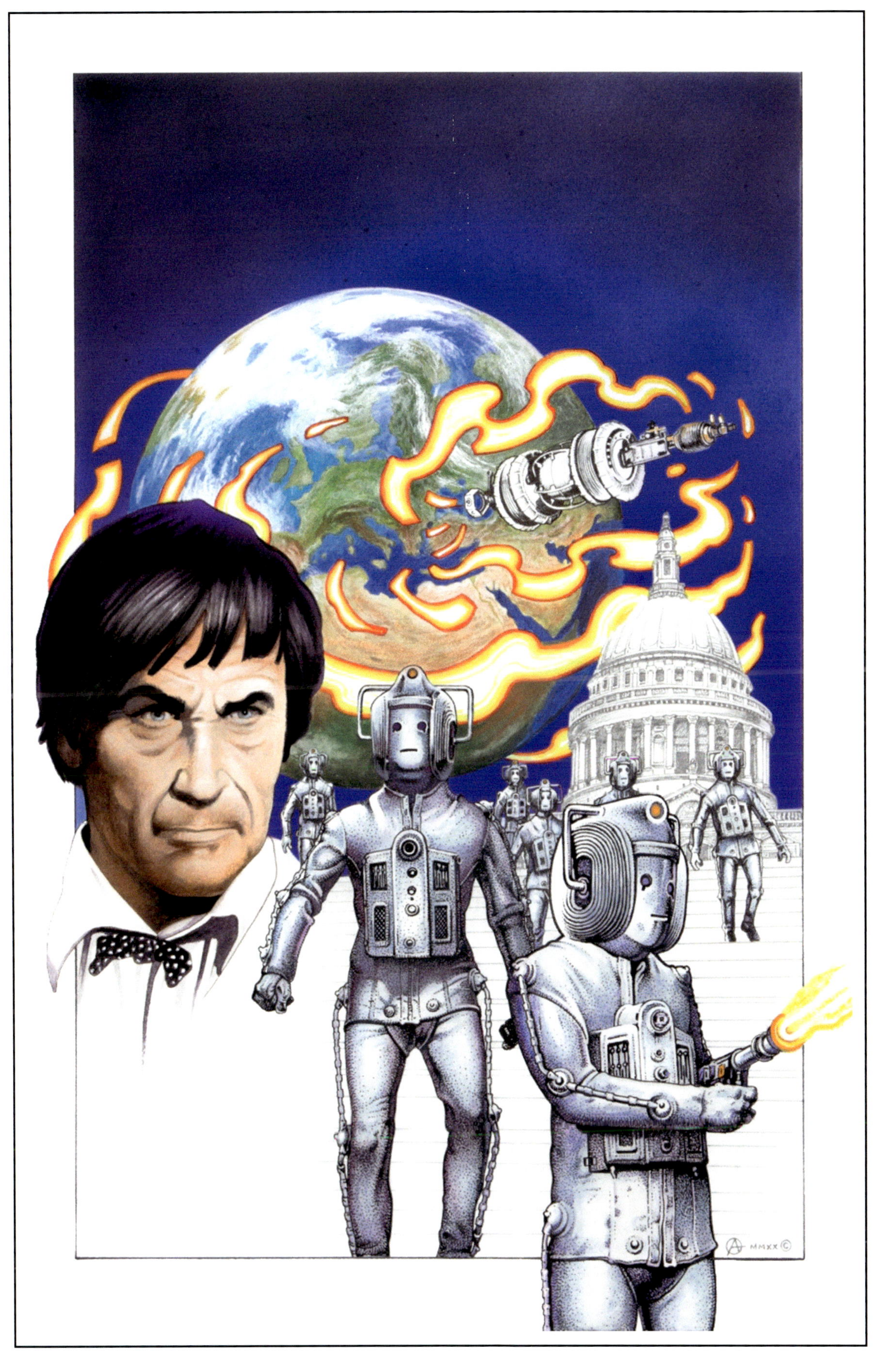

DOCTOR WHO: INFERNO

Writer: Terrance Dicks **Doctor:** Third **Release date:** 18 October 1984 **Release order:** 90

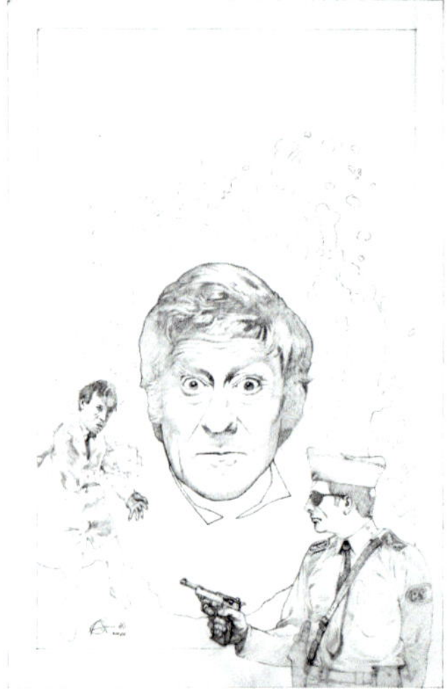

Original drawing for Inferno.

"For what seemed a very long time the Doctor had been whirling helplessly in some kind of limbo, a place where not only time and space but the fabric of reality itself seemed to be distorted. He felt as if he was being split off, so that there were not one but ten, a hundred, a thousand, a million Doctors – with a million TARDIS consoles and a million Bessies to go with them."

christos achilléos

❝ This is the third of the my new images painted exclusively for this book. For *Inferno* I watched the DVD to immerse myself in this classic story. I love the alternate universe stuff, especially the Brigadier with his eye patch. This is such an iconic image, and I just had to get it in. The reference image of Jon Pertwee was not something I'd seen of him before. I feel that the pencil works well against the fiery background. It's my favourite of the most recent images I have done. To me it fits in nicely with the covers of 1972-77. It tells a story. **❞**

Inferno is the name of a top-secret drilling project to penetrate the Earth's crust and release a major new energy source.

A crisis develops when a noxious liquid leaks out as drilling progresses – the green poison has a grotesquely debilitating effect on human beings.

As the Earth's plight worsens, the Doctor is trapped in a parallel world, unable to rescue the planet and its inhabitants from the destructive force of Inferno...

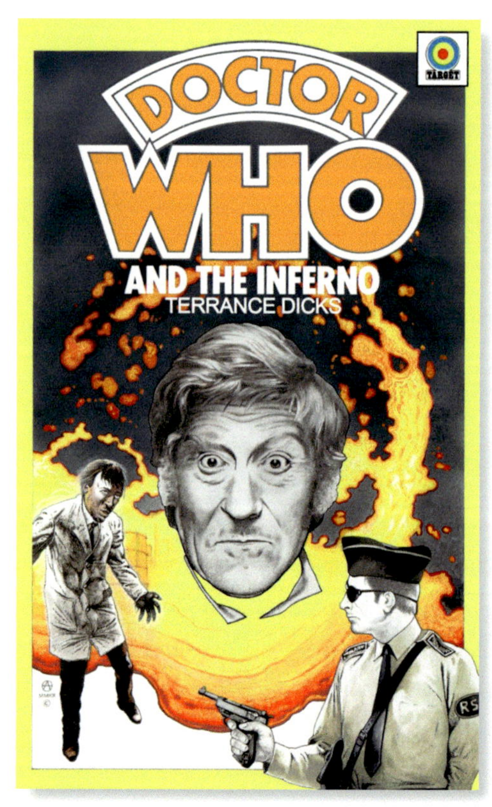

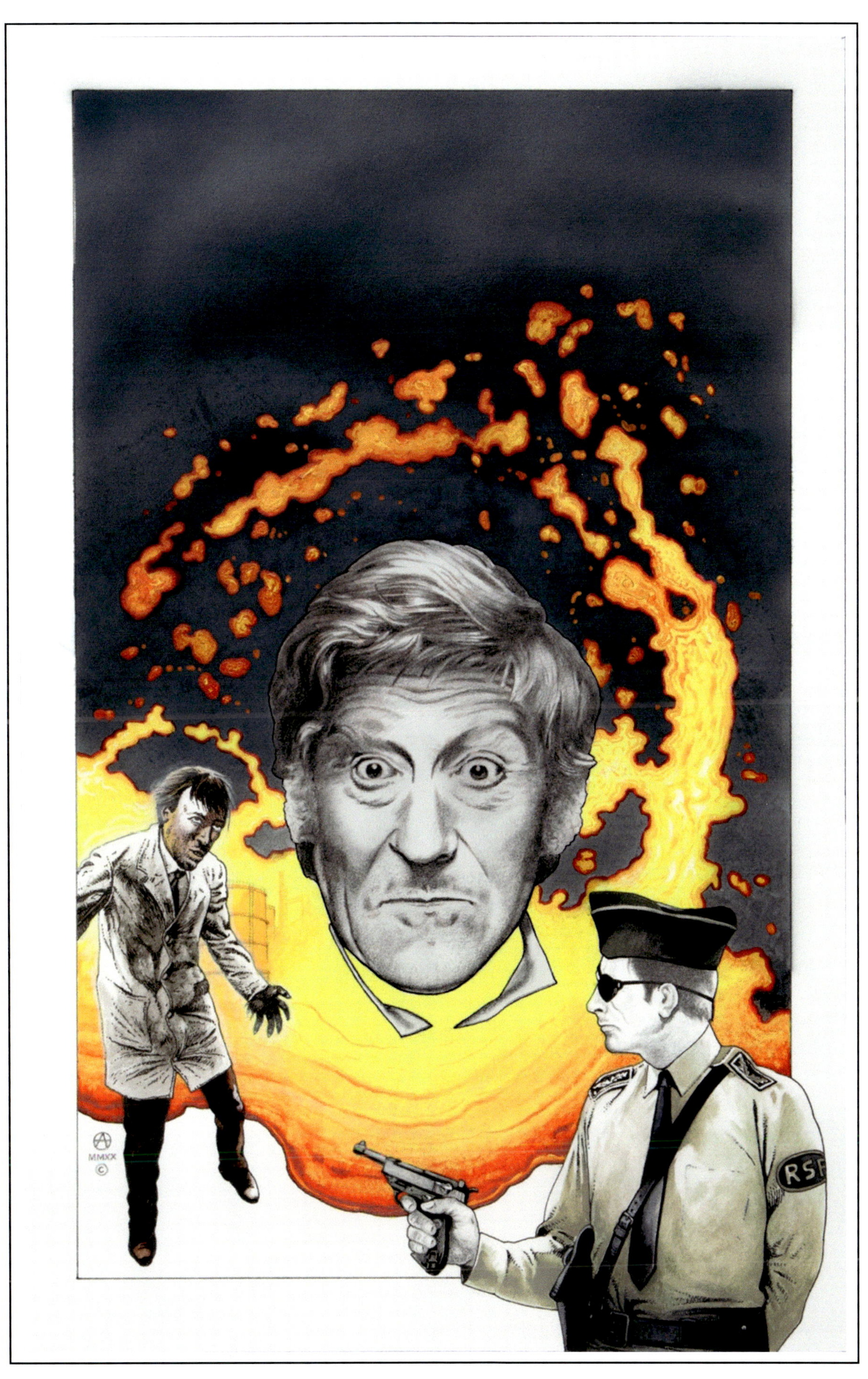

DOCTOR WHO AND THE GREEN DEATH

Writer: Malcolm Hulke **Doctor:** Third **Release date:** 21 August 1975 **Release order:** 15

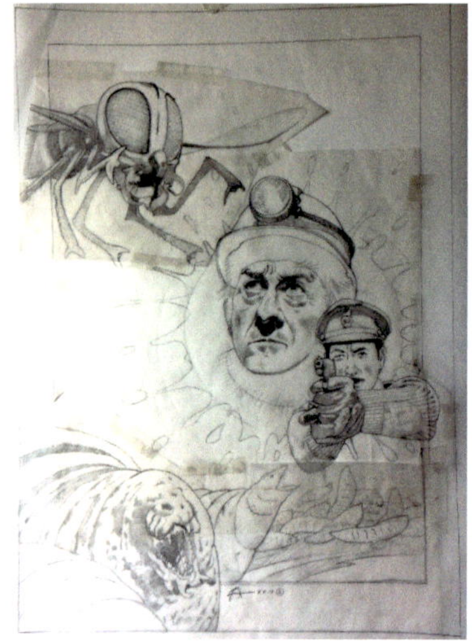

Original drawing for
The Green Death.

The Green Death begins slowly. In a small Welsh mining village a man emerges from the disused colliery covered in a green fungus. Minutes later he is dead. UNIT, Jo Grant and Doctor Who in tow, arrive on the scene to investigate, but strangely reluctant to assist their enquiries is Dr Stevens, director of the local refinery Panorama Chemicals.

Are they in time to destroy the mysterious power which threatens them all before the whole village, and even the world, is wiped out by a deadly swarm of green maggots?

"Two million light years away, the Doctor stood to catch his breath on a blue rock mountain. He was exhausted, having run to escape from the pecking blue birds and the blue unicorns.

'Wait till I tell the Time Lords about this,' he said to himself. 'It's the most unfriendly planet I've ever visited.'

Then he let out a cry as he felt something stick into his foot. Blue ants an inch long were swarming over his left foot, digging through the shoe to get at the human flesh beneath."

christos achilleos

❝ The original cover for *The Green Death* was drawn by Peter Brookes. I like to think that the kids back then would have loved my interpretation, with the giant red-eyed fly menacing the Doctor and the Brigadier, who in turn is firing his gun at the fat and viscous, teeth-baring maggots. ❞

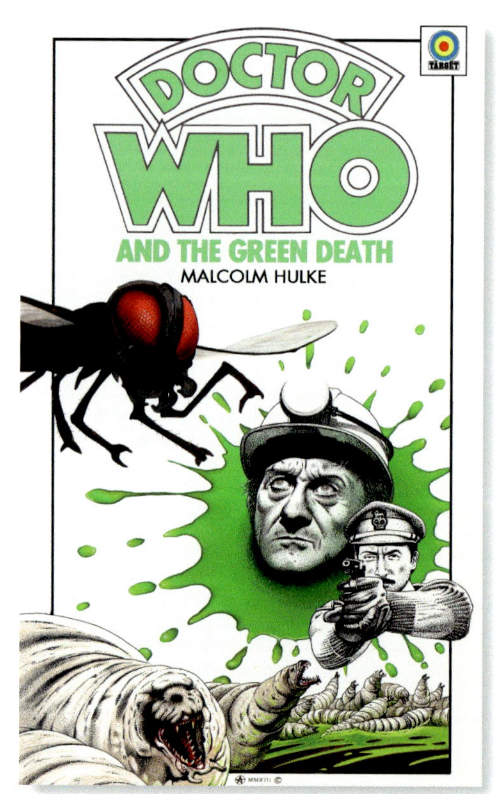

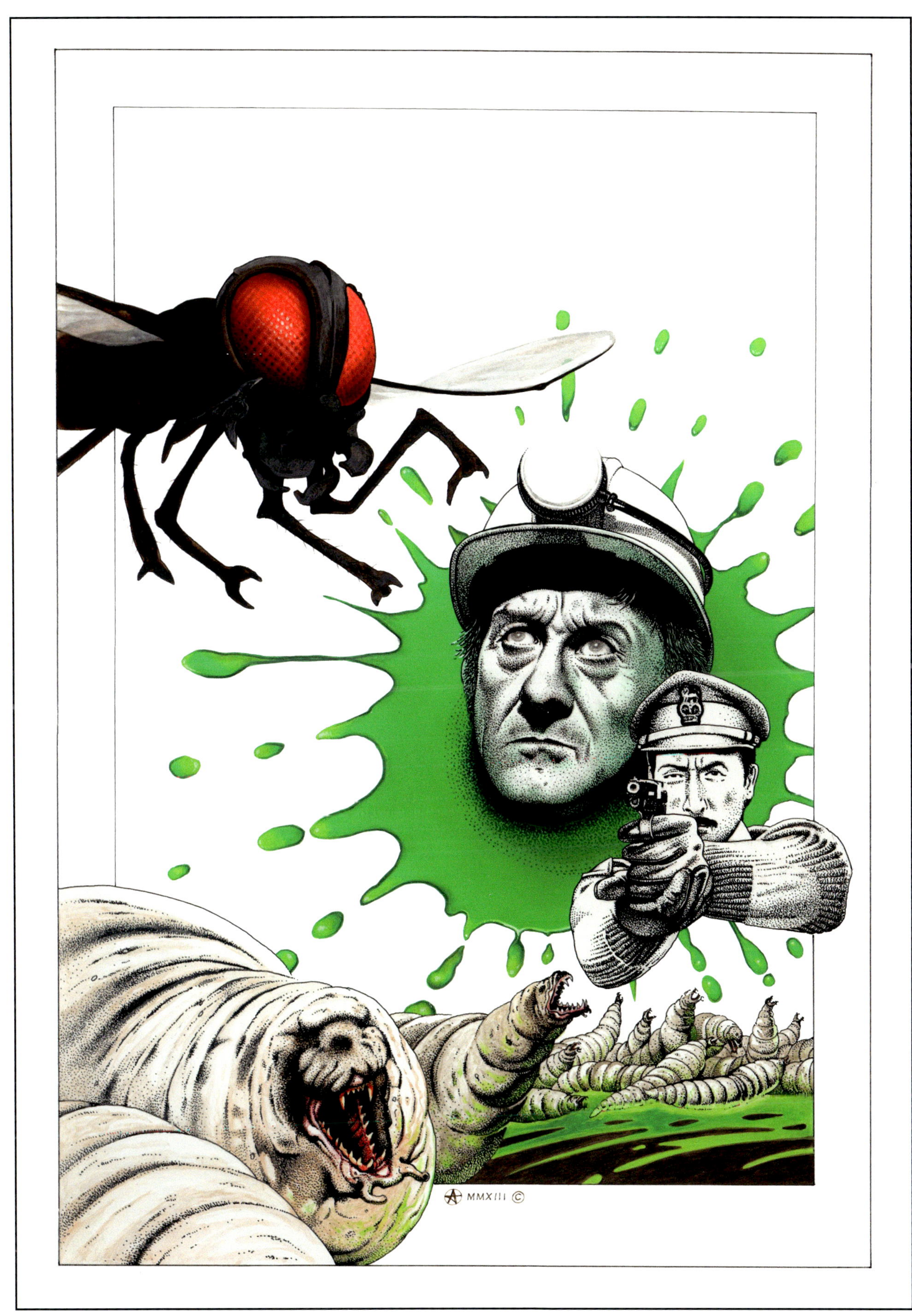

DOCTOR WHO AND THE BRAIN OF MORBIUS

Writer: Terrance Dicks **Doctor:** Fourth **Release date:** 23 June 1977 **Release order:** 33

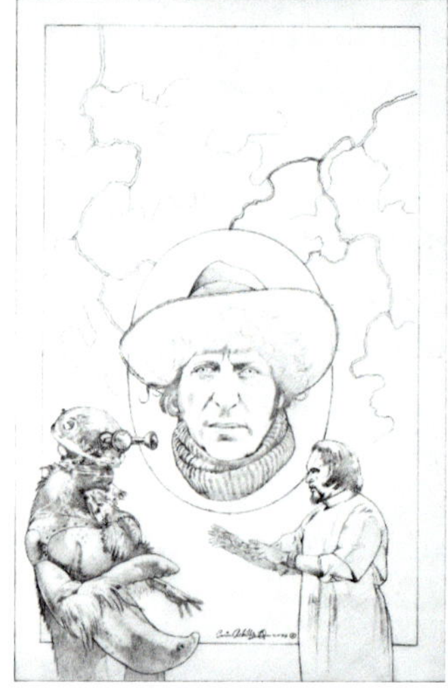

*Original drawing for
Brain of Morbius*

"Reluctantly, Sarah let the Doctor lead her across the rocky plain. Her fears were returning full force. It was bad enough being suddenly blind. But to be blind on an alien planet full of unknown horrors... And now the Doctor was leading them, by his own admission, straight towards the greatest danger of all..."

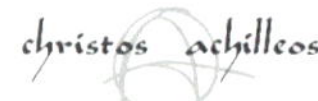

❝ This is the fourth of the my new images painted exclusively for this book. I really enjoyed doing this cover for *The Brain of Morbius*. In my opinion eye contact is very important, and this really works with Tom Baker's blue eyes staring right at you. With the story's references to Frankenstein it was obvious to include lightning bolts and electricity sparks. My instinct told me to use purple for the background and it works fine. I wanted Morbius and the creature to be right. This is another one that I like a lot. **❞**

Why do so many spaceships crash land on Karn, a bleak, lonely and seemingly deserted planet?

Are they doomed by the mysterious powers of the strange, black-robed Sisterhood, jealously guarding their secret of eternal life? Or does the mad Dr Solon, for some evil purpose of his own, need the bodies of the victims? And more especially, the body of Doctor Who ...

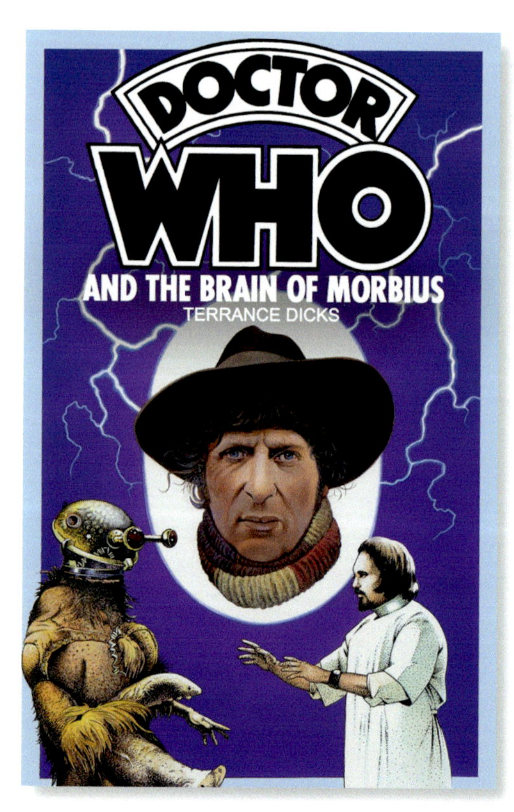

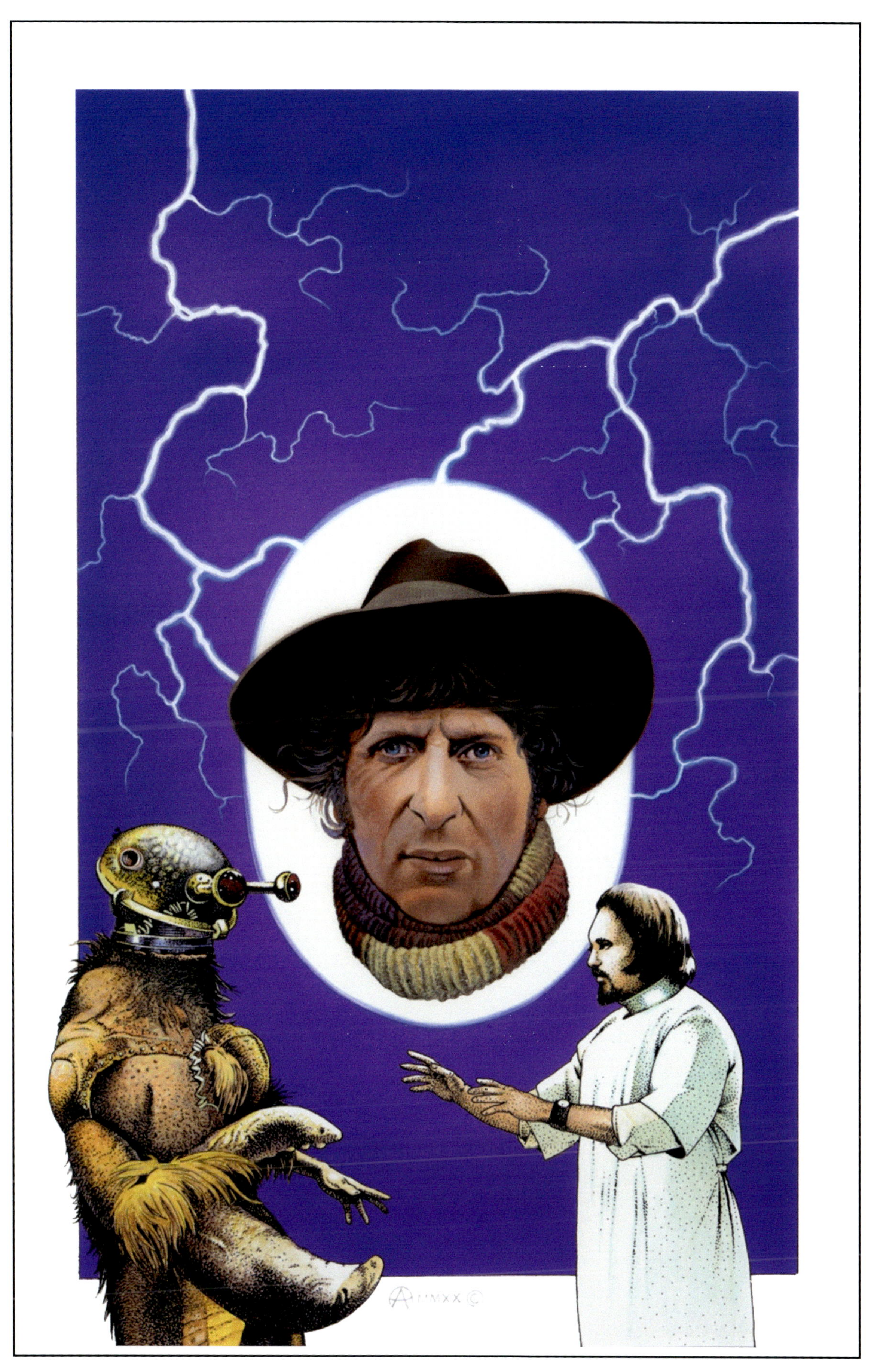

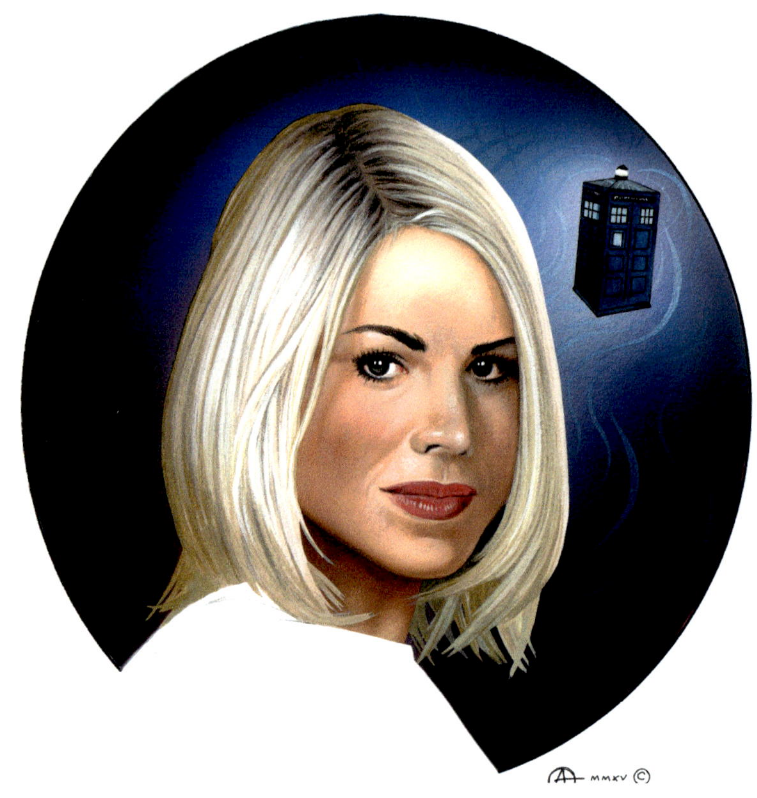

(top) Portrait of Billie Piper as Rose, painted in 2005. (bottom) Young David Tennant portrait.

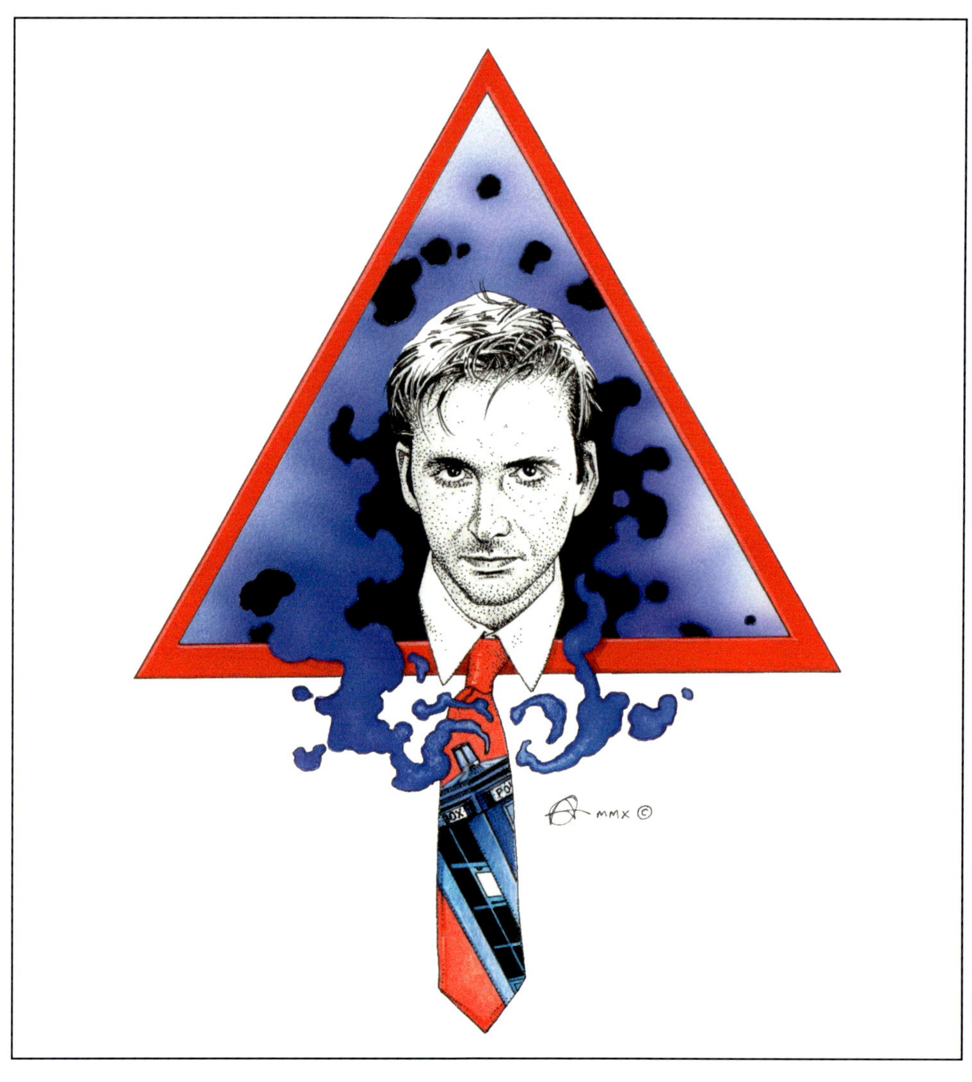

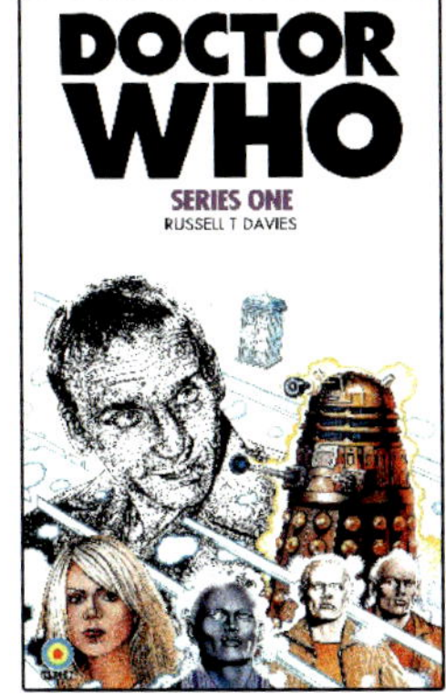

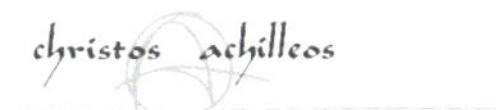

I did the next four illustrations for *SFX Magazine*. Previously they had kindly labelled me the UK's top fantasy artist. With *Doctor Who* returning to TV they asked me to do a cover. I only had basic images of Rose for reference, and I'm not really happy with my final drawing, but it was completed under difficult circumstances.

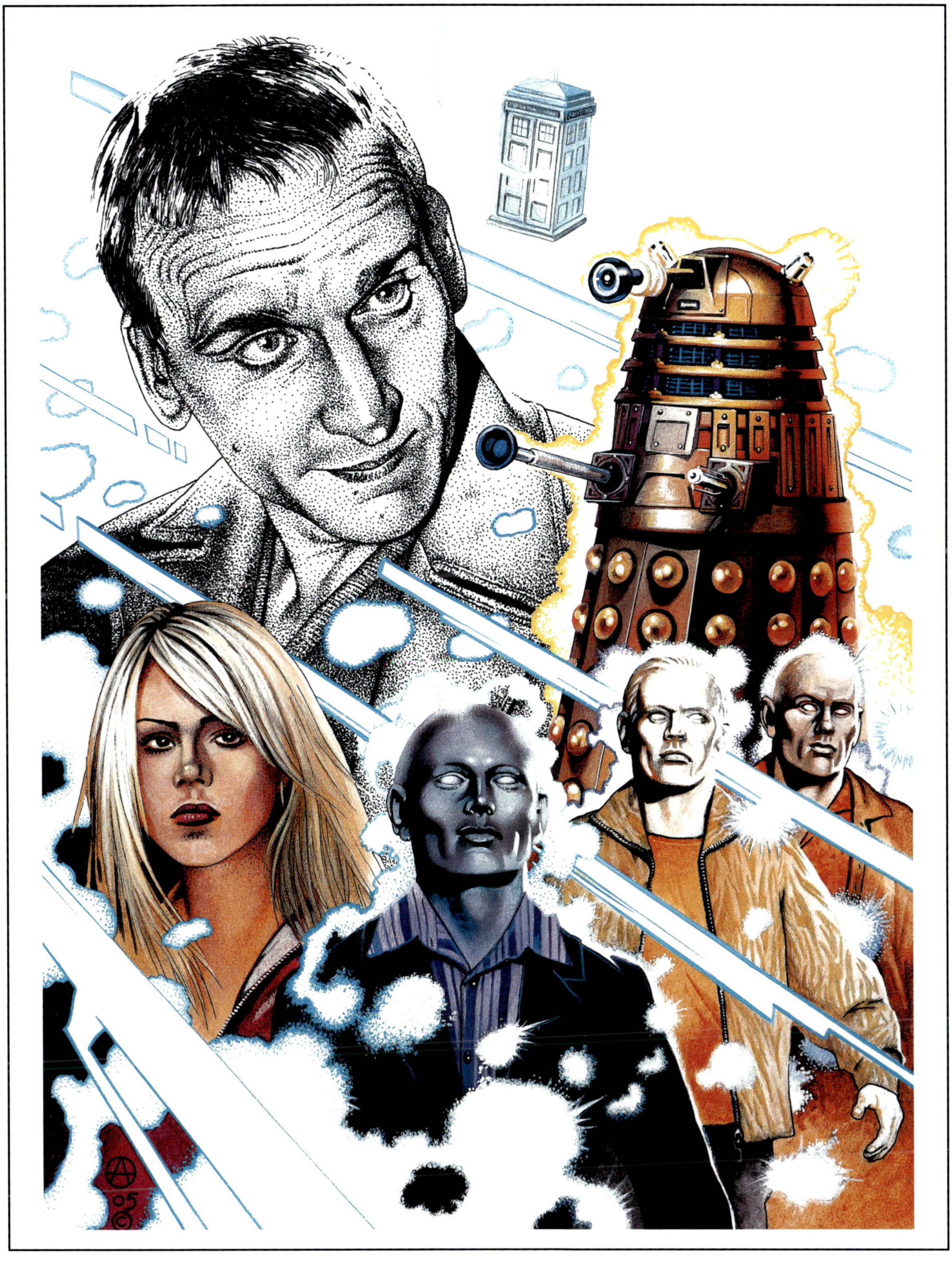

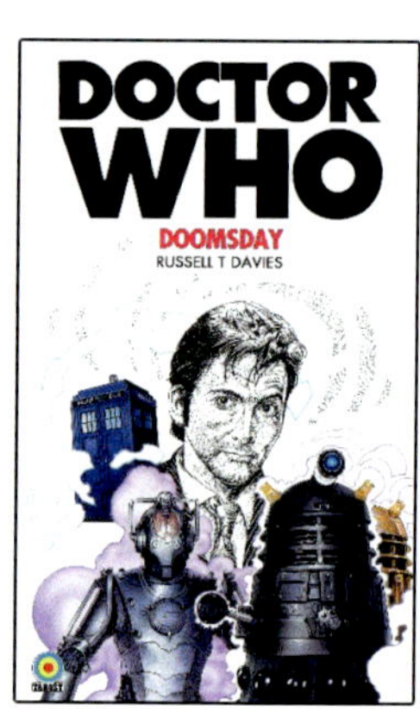

In *Doomsday* I had a young David Tennant to draw. I do find it difficult to draw young people. Often they don't have the wrinkles or definition that older people have. I'm not sure I captured his likeness. I do like the overall effect. This story has new Cybermen, and the design is much better.

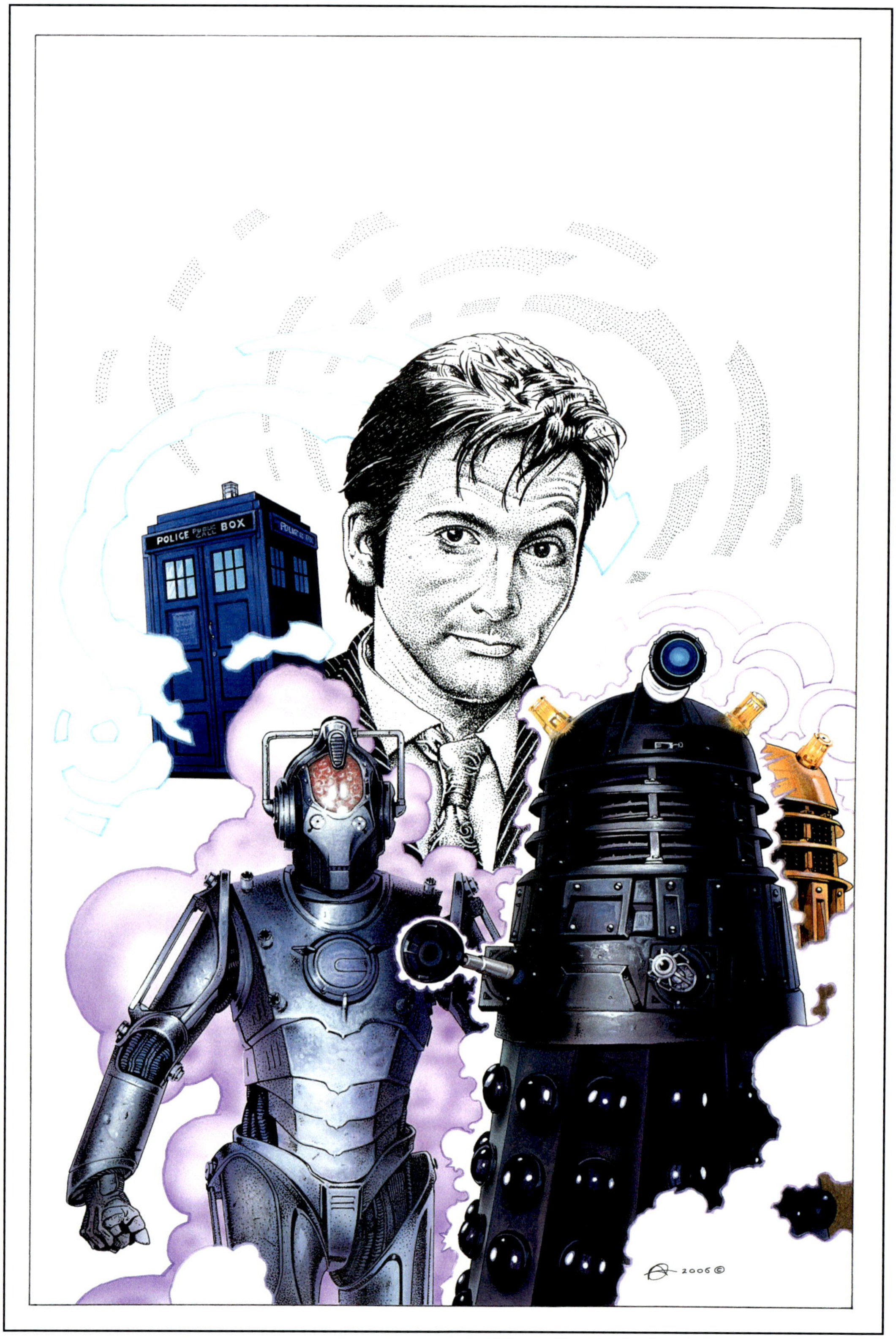

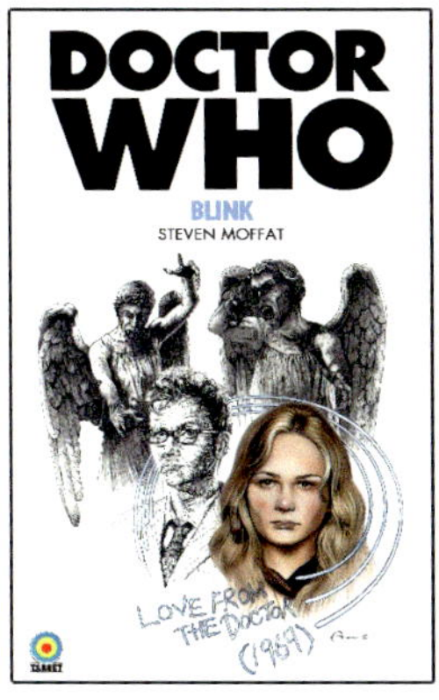

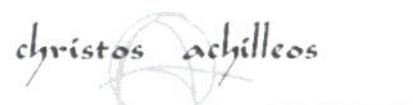

This was commissioned by Russell Lewin from *SFX Magazine*. I was aware of the popularity of *Blink*. I watched the episode and it's unlike anything I had seen before. I decided to include all the elements in my picture – the writing on the wall, references to 1969, Tennant in his glasses and the beautiful Carey Mulligan.

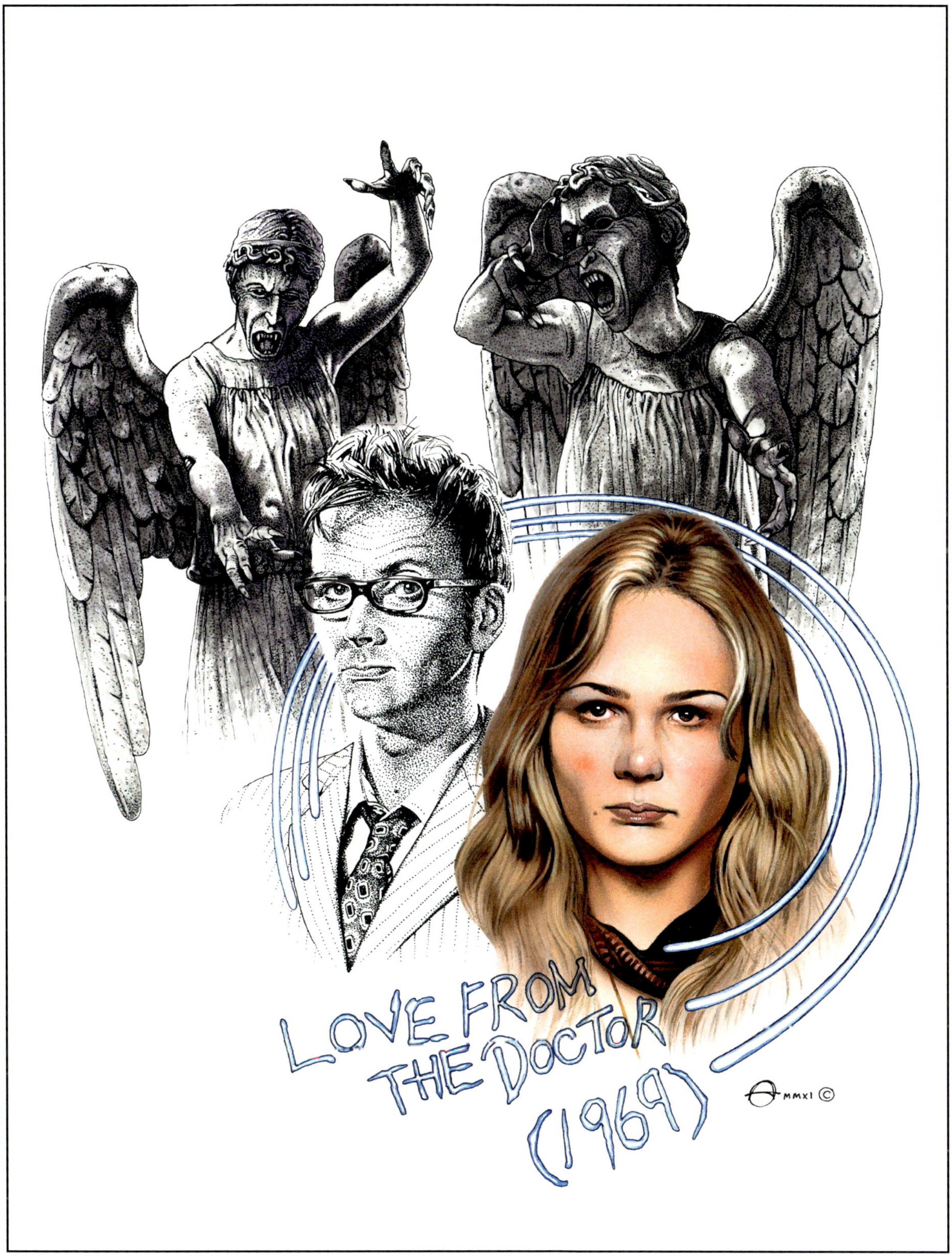

A GOOD MAN GOES TO WAR

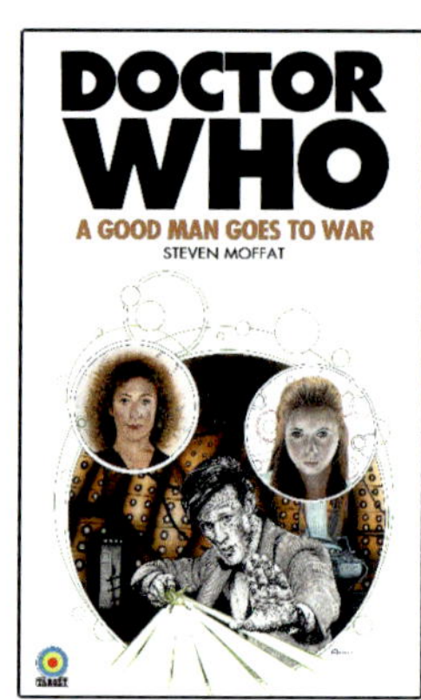

Matt Smith is an unusual looking young man so when I drew him it wasn't as difficult as I thought it might be. Also, the TV series now featured weird circles and rings when the TARDIS went through time. This, I think, added a different dimension to the cover. Strangely this is the first time I used the image of the sonic screwdriver.

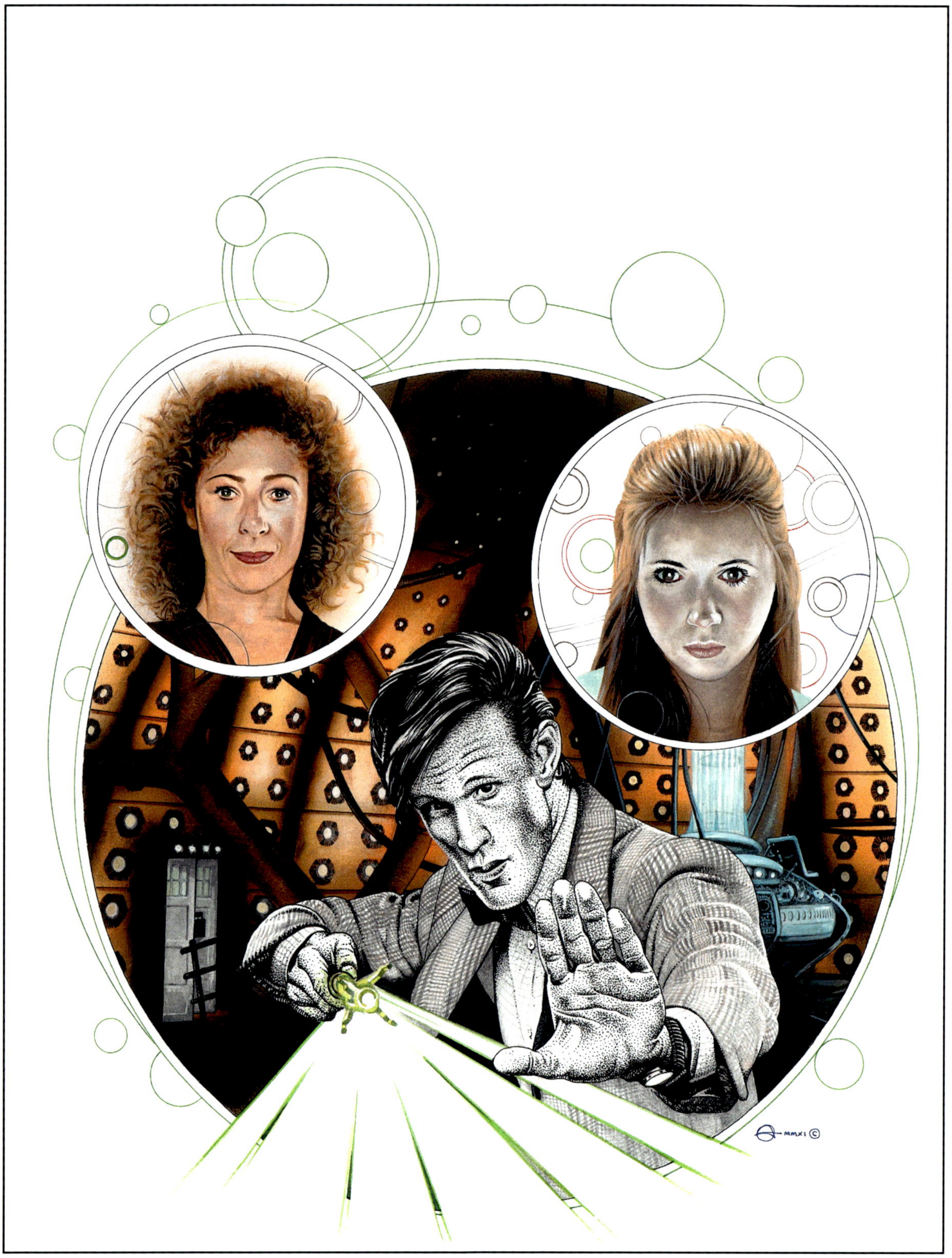

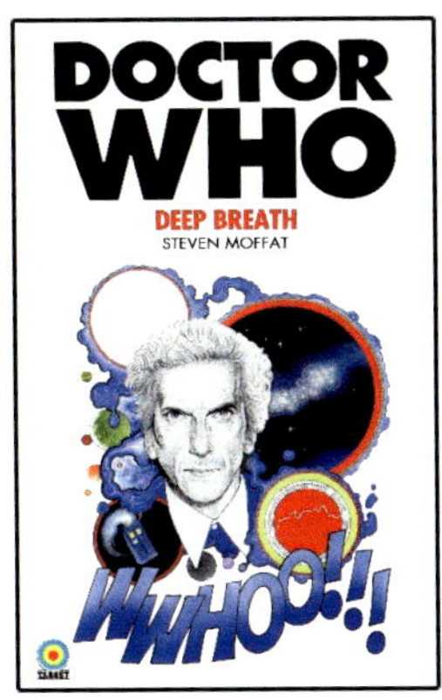

Natasha says, "Chris painted this image of Capaldi when they were both guests at the LFCC. Capaldi was one of my favourite doctors and we both liked his gruffness, and welcomed a return to an older version of the Doctor. Chris enjoyed painting his characteristics – his eyes being particularly a feature. Chris liked to draw interesting, older faces as "they were a more interesting subject" to paint. "Wwhoo!!!" was added as a visual reference to WHO and the composition reflected his space-like imagery of stars and planets. The composition was done as a personal project and not in reference to any commission or cover request."

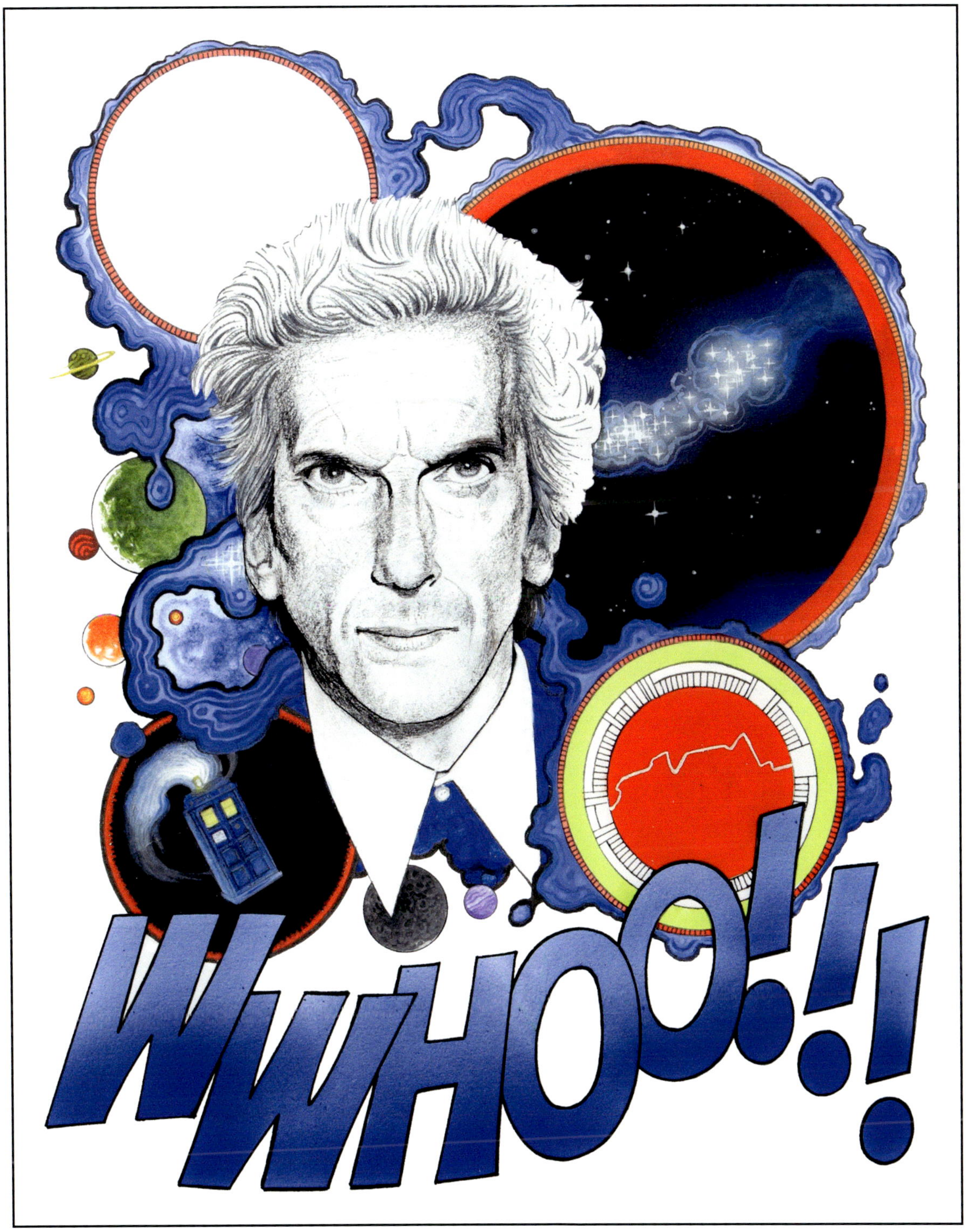

MUGS

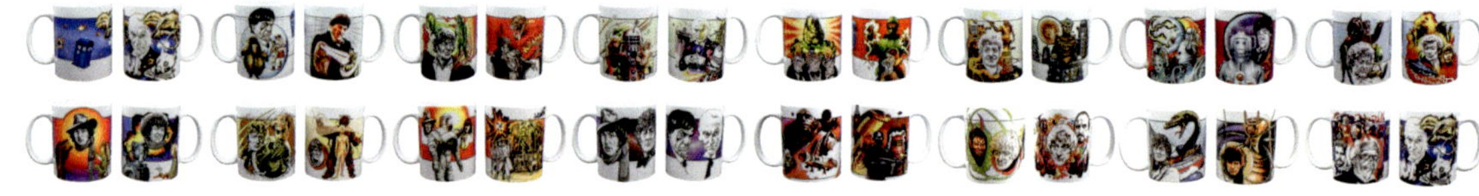

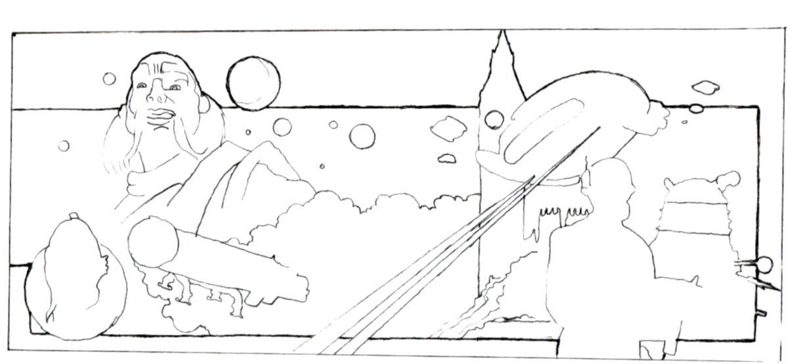

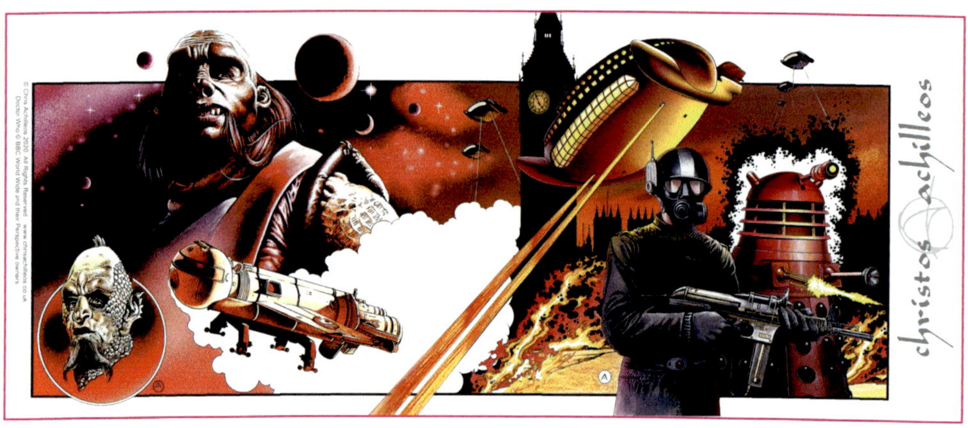

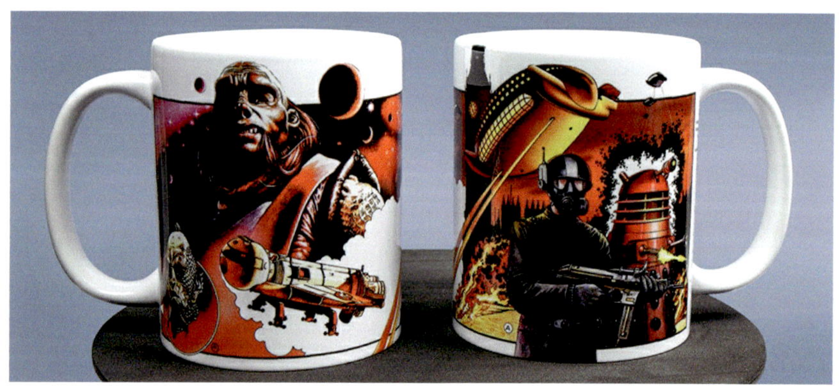

Mark Norman, the person behind all sixteen mug designs, was excited but slightly reticent about the responsibility of tackling the iconic images. He said, "Chris would email me a template sketch and I would send back a working proof. He would then apologise and say, 'I know I'm being fussy but could you move that bit over 2mm, and that bit shouldn't be there,' and so on. Thankfully, the interest in the mugs has been phenomenal. They have really put Chris' artwork back into people's minds."

The drawings shown below are the final layouts of the paintings. They are where the concepts of the designs take place. The reference material available from the story is assembled and carefully chosen to fit in and collectively, hopefully, encapsulate the story. Once done, then they are drawn up to the same size of the painting and traced on the art board. In effect, the drawings are where the concept is born.

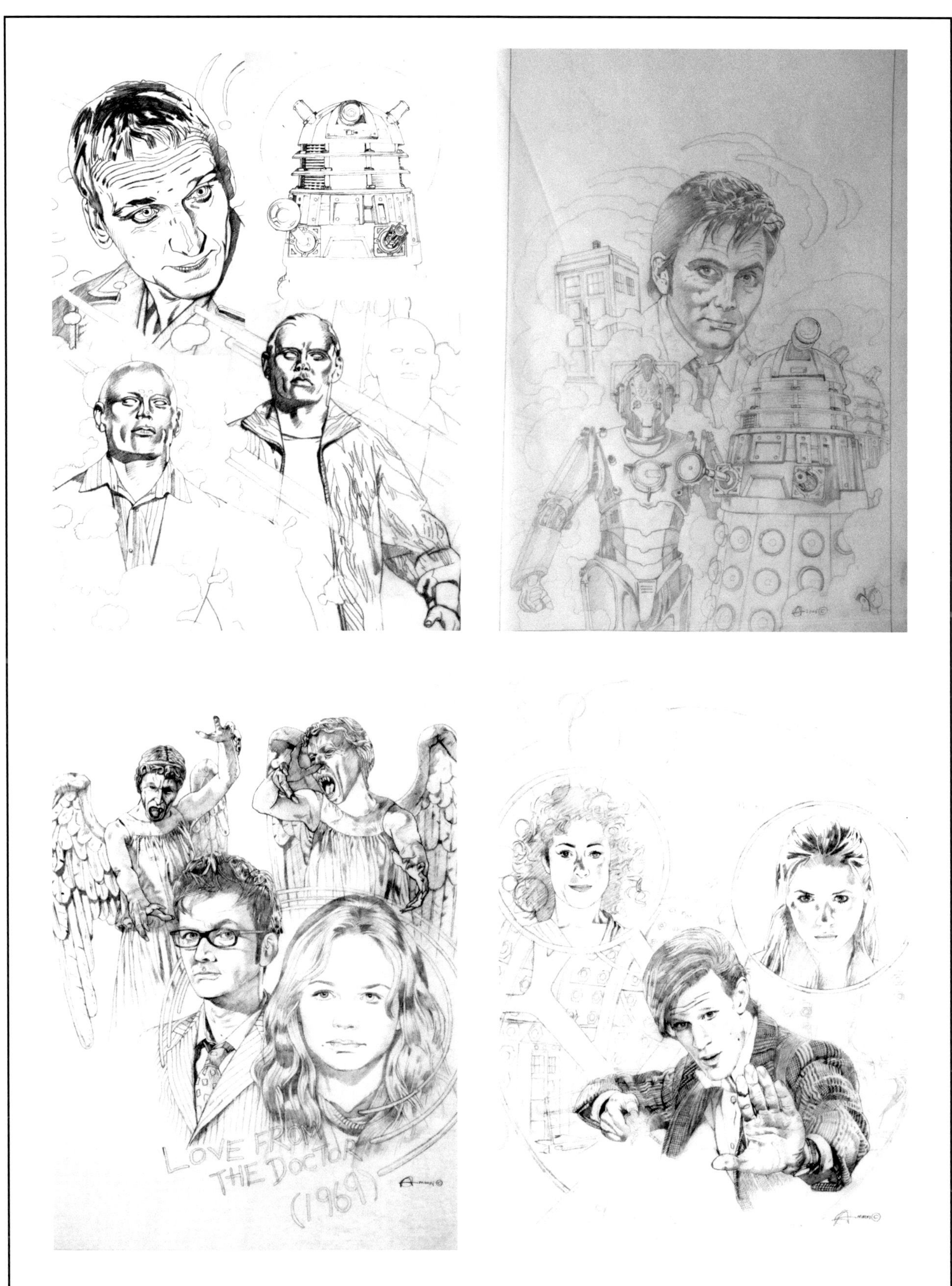

ESTHER ACHILLÉOS HARTSHORN

My dad, a Greek Cypriot, had a difficult start in life. Having lost his father to cancer at a young age, he was raised by his mother together with his three sisters. This was during the period of conflict in Famagusta. He grew up surrounded by soldiers, having to navigate his way through war-torn streets and houses. It was a tough life for a young boy without his father to guide him, I can only imagine.

In his own words, he wrote, "A rifle was levelled at me by a British soldier who, due to my hiding in a tree, had mistaken me for a sniper."

Dad moved to London in his teens. A young man in a new country, in a big city and a new school, having to learn a new language and culture. His strong mother leading a new future.

However, Dad had a special gift that would protect him on his journey. He found a way to channel his emotions through his artistic talent and his love for science fiction, Greek mythology, history, and beautiful, strong women.

He focused hard on his gift and found his purpose in life. His determination resulted in the creation of his iconic *Doctor Who* Target book covers. They were enjoyed by many and remain just as cool and respected today. My boys are so proud of the accomplishments of their grandad. They are proud to have his prints and artwork framed on their bedroom walls.

Dad had a unique talent. However, it was his focus and drive to keep learning that I consider to be the gift he has passed on to me, my husband, and our children.

Life is not fair or easy, but you can channel it to achieve greater happiness. In his words, "Nothing that is really great is ever achieved without labour or hardship." I looked at him with pride.

I so miss my father, my friend and grandfather to my two boys. I am so proud that his special gift will live on through these pages.

ANNA ACHILLÉOS

My father worked hard when I was young. Throughout the 1980s it was common to not see him for days at a time, as he worked to tight deadlines. However, the time I had with him was special. He opened my mind to a world of imagination, adventure, and nature.

One of his favourite pastimes was to spend hours on his latest Airfix kit. I would watch him as he carefully and painstakingly painted every tiny piece and glued it all together using tweezers. He would indulge my interest by helping me paint miniatures of goblins, dragons, and armoured knights ready for battle.

We would spend weekends visiting bird of prey sanctuaries and butterfly farms, or going to the British Museum, where we would draw what we had seen. He used to make my sister and I bows and arrows and kites out of sticks and bin liners, and then we would go over to the Chingford Plains to watch them fly!

One holiday he taught me how to fish on the rocks of a Greek island, and then we took our catch to a restaurant and asked the chef to cook them – much to my mother's embarrassment!

A favourite childhood memory of mine is when my dad brought me a German Omni robot back from a trip to a convention. Its wheels would get stuck on the carpet and I couldn't understand its deep German robotic voice, but I would spend so many hours of fun watching its eyes light up and it bumping into walls. I would give it pencils to hold in its claw-like hands, which would make my dad roar with laughter. I'm proud to say I still have that robot thirty-eight years later, and it is still the best present I have ever received! It will forever bring a smile to my face along with this wonderful memory of my daddy.

To me, he was my dad and I loved him very much, but it wasn't until my father's death, in December 2021, that I realised just how much his artwork had meant to so many. There was an outpouring of thousands of tributes on social media from people of all walks of life, sharing their mutual love for his art, and how his *Doctor Who* Target book covers brought the characters to life in the minds of so many young readers. It was such a heart-warming and comforting experience for my family and I to read at such a difficult time, for which we are truly grateful.

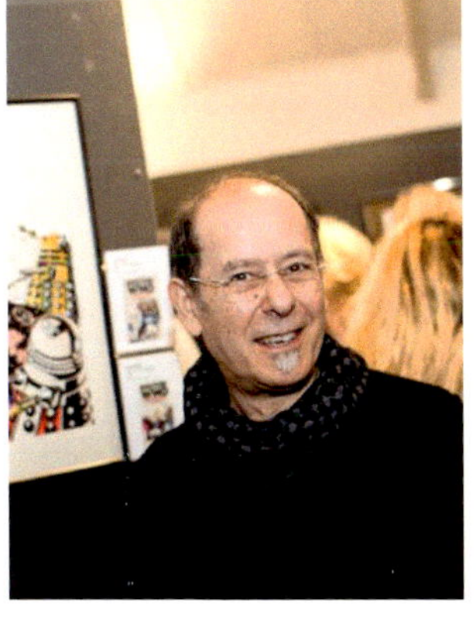

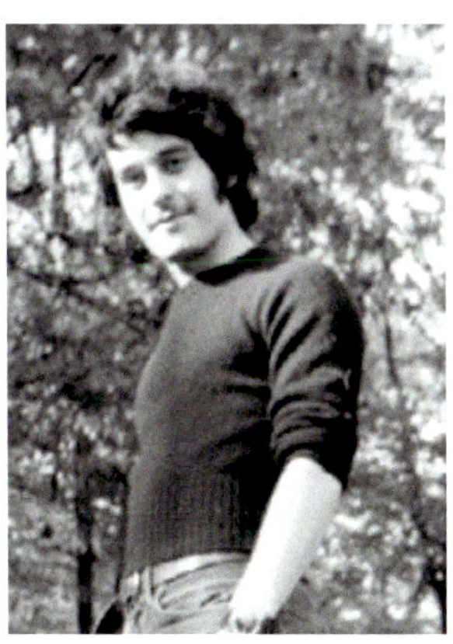

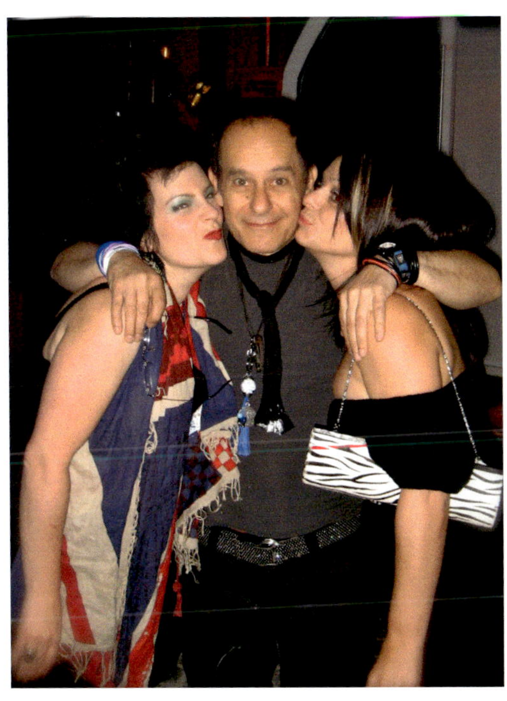

(left) Chris with Esther and Anna Achilléos.
(middle) Chris in 2018.
(right) Chris circa 1968.

THOMAS BLUNDEN

Uncle Chris had this downstairs loo like nothing you've seen before. Stepping in, you were met by a mural of 1950s sci-fi film posters in postcard size. Now some of the films were classics – *War of the Worlds*, *Forbidden Planet* and so on. But most were as obscure as you could wish for: *Disc Man from Mars*, *Attack of the Crab Monsters* and *The Brain from Planet Arous*. These and more merged with B-movie posters and pulp novel covers, so that *High School Hellcats* sat next to *H is for Heroin*, which sat next to *The Love Wanga*, whatever a wanga was.

Further across were magazine covers: *Real Men*, *Man's Action* and *Man's Epic*, all depicting women in various states of undress and terror; the (real) man would be battling Nazis, or a fierce tiger. Around the mirror were exploitation films of the '50s: *Problem Girls*, *Boys' Prison*, *Female Fiends* and *Jail Bait*.

It was a wall-to-wall world of absolute insanity and it was glorious. When I first saw it, my mind was made up; I would watch all the films on the walls of Chris' downstairs loo. 'The Loo Collection' had been born.

I lived with Chris for almost seven years, and after 'Conspiracy Sundays' we did 'Cult Sundays'. We would sit and watch one of the Loo Collection films that I had managed to buy (or he would dig out some of his old video tapes of equally obscure films). *Colossus: The Forbin Project* was a favourite of ours.

Quotable dialogue was very important to us – "Get up, you big tub a guts" a favourite from *One-Eyed Jacks*!

Over the years we watched a lot of movies together. Those that particularly come to mind are *Emperor of the North* with Lee Marvin and Ernest Borgnine and the amazing spaghetti western *The Great Silence* (I loved it, Chris hated it) particularly come to mind.

Chris would have his thimble of red wine, while mine was a slightly larger vessel. We would open the dark chocolate Brazil nuts and enjoy each other's company as we watched whatever peculiarity we had decided on. Great viewing and great times.

I still haven't seen all those movies in the Loo Collection, but I'm trying to. And I still miss my friend. See you on Planet Aruos, Chris.

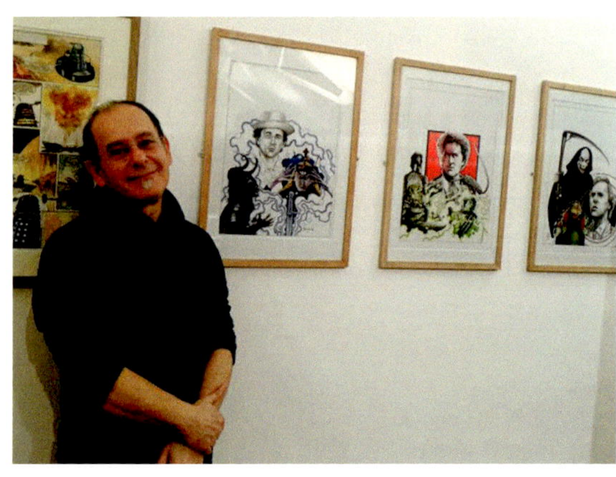

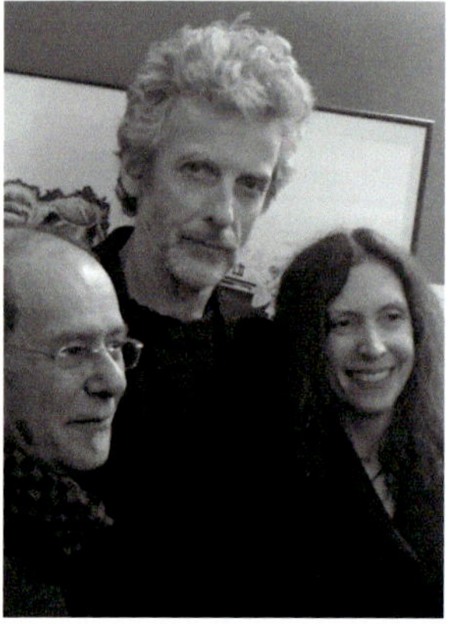

(left) Chris at the Cartoon Museum, 2016.
(right) Chris with Peter Capaldi and Natasha Achilléos.

NATASHA ACHILLÉOS

Over the years, I had the honour of assisting Chris at many occasions, conventions and events organised and run in the name of *Doctor Who*.

As I got to know the people, artists, event organisers and guests who regularly attended these shows, stories of how Chris' art had become an important part of their childhoods resonated with their developing relationship with Chris. So the idea of the testimonials was born, providing an important bridge between Chris, his art and their memories.

Chris met Shaun at a little event in Cardiff, and through his working relationship and friendship, the idea of *Klakk!* was formed, eventually reaching publication as both a softback edition and a hardback version in 2021. Chris thoroughly enjoyed working on the book, providing sketches and the creation of three more imagined *Doctor Who* book covers as part of its release. Sat at his drawing board, I watched them all come into fruition.

Klakk! has proved to be a final superb compendium of his *Doctor Who* artwork and a fitting tribute to his contributions to *Doctor Who*. I think all those who love and admire the world of *Doctor Who* understand the significance of the original Target *Klakk!* cover. A bit controversial at the time, the design has since become synonymous with and uniquely identifiable as Chris' work. It was itself an influence taken directly from his own love of comic book artists Frank Bellamy and Jack Kirby.

Over his career, Chris worked often with others to re-imagine his work, but his vision always remained at the heart of everything he did. He was a methodical craftsman and visionary artist.

Chris will be forever remembered as a major contributor to and iconic cultural figure in the world of *Doctor Who*, as well as a fantasy master in his own right. Through his incredible talent and hard work, he will continue to inspire others willing to take up the brush, and tributes to his life's work will always be part of the world he became so recognisable within.

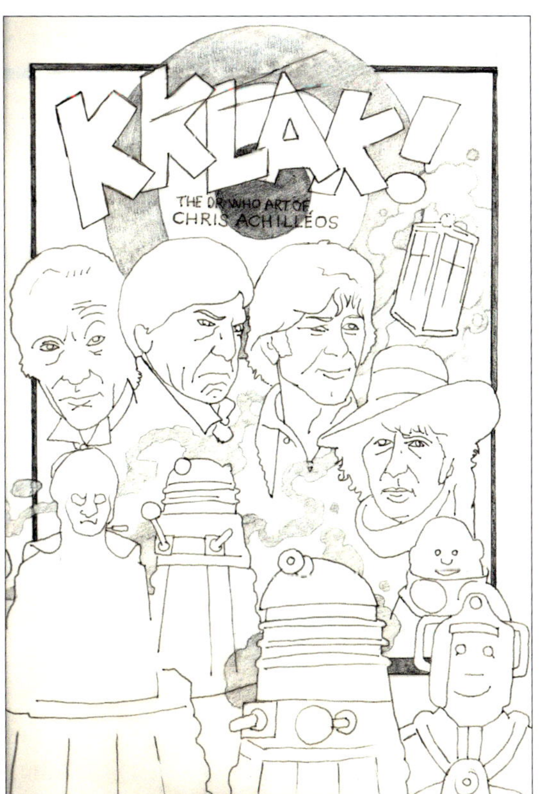

(Left) The original rough cover artwork for this book.

TREASURE HUNT BY SHAUN RUSSELL

In 2018 I went to a brand new *Doctor Who* convention and it had everything you'd expect to make it a success. The guests were wonderful, the venue excellent, the organisers were very friendly, so we booked a table to sell our Lethbridge-Stewart novels.

But sadly, on the day, very few people turned up. This happens. It's not anybody's fault; it's just how things go.

This meant we had longer than usual to chat to the other sellers. I spotted Chris Achilléos on the other side of the room. Like most *Doctor Who* fans I have followed his work from an early age, but as I approached him a long-forgotten memory pushed its way back into my mind.

In my early teens I remember cycling around Bristol, visiting libraries and secondhand bookshops looking for old Target novels. It was like a treasure hunt. Sometimes I was lucky. Sometimes I wasn't. We didn't have e-Bay back then, so this was my own way to build my collection. I remember one time visiting a bookshop in Staple Hill. It had recently opened and was quite a trailblazer. This wasn't just a bookshop, it was a café too!

I often visited the bookshops in Staple Hill and I remember the thrill of seeing this new one on the other side of the road. I hurriedly rode up to the traffic lights and rather dangerously zigzagged through the traffic to get to the other side. As I did so, my chain came off. The horror! I was so close. I pulled the chain back on, getting my hands filthy. I wasn't taking any chances. Rather than riding the last few metres, I gingerly pushed my bike towards the new bookshop, locking it as swiftly as I could.

I peered through the window, and at that moment I felt like Indiana Jones.

Doctor Who and the Cave-Monsters was sitting there on the shelf, inviting me in. Beside it were other pre-1975 books. I was so excited I pushed open the door without thinking. Then my heart stopped as I noticed a big oil hand print on the door. I felt ashamed, then worried. Would the shop assistant tell me off and, more importantly, how was I going to pick up the book and not ruin it?

I crept into the shop and, for some reason, pretended I was looking for something else. I then spotted *Doctor Who and the Auton Invasion* and *Doctor Who and the Curse of Peladon.* This was too good to be true. I looked at my oily hands and rubbed them on my jeans, but it just made things worse. I must have appeared ridiculous. My hands and clothes were filthy. I probably looked like a little urchin.

I guess I must have also looked suspicious. That's when the assistant spotted me. As far as I remember she was a nice-looking, bookish girl. She smiled at me and asked if she could help. I pointed at the books and held up my hands. 'I have the money,' I said, rummaging in my pockets. 'Please help me.' I squirmed. I felt so geeky, but I didn't care.

'Which ones?' she asked. I pointed at them, my heart beating fast. She delicately picked them up, dropping them into a paper bag. They were safe. I paid for them, quickly left, and cycled home very carefully.

Back in 2018, when I spotted Chris Achilléos, my heart skipped a beat. Not for long though. Chris is friendly and very welcoming and, as we chatted about his career, I suggested doing a book of his *Doctor Who* artwork. To my surprise, Chris was not against the idea.

And you are now reading the book we discussed. A cornucopia of Chris' artwork!

I would like to thank Chris for being so supportive, helpful and creative. It was also such a privilege to be the first person to see brand new Chris Achilléos artwork, to create Target-style covers, and see Chris produce his new innovations such as mugs and t-shirts.

I feel like Indiana Jones finding the lost ark, but this time, especially in 2021, I always wash my hands.

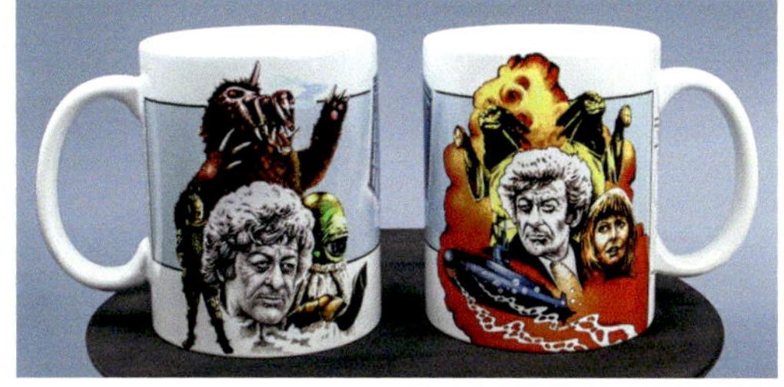

The Curse of Peladon *&* The Sea-Devils *mugs.*

A MASTER AMONG ARTISTS BY DAVID HOWE

I first met Chris in the early 1980s. My history with the Target *Doctor Who* novelisations goes back to around 1974, when I bought my first copy of *Doctor Who and the Curse of Peladon,* and I fell in love with the range. I quickly picked up those I had missed, and eagerly awaited each new book. I joined the Target Book Club and received news and advance covers of the books. And I adored them.

In 1977 I met Chris and we chatted and I took photos of several of his pieces of art to reproduce in the fanzine. It was at this time that I also asked Chris whether he might consider selling some of his *Doctor Who* art. To my pleasure he was agreeable, so we struck some deals, and I became the proud owner of several of his pieces of iconic *Doctor Who* art – including his first three *Doctor Who* covers.

What really impressed me were the colours: how rich and vibrant the original art was compared to the reproductions on the book covers... and with that a life-long love of original *Doctor Who* cover art was born.

There was an iconic immediacy about the simple black *Doctor Who* logo above Chris' glowing art, usually displayed against a white background. His galaxy swirls and explosions, which often peppered the backgrounds, suggested worlds of adventure, and the monsters and hardware, surrounding a black and white portrait of the Doctor, fired my imagination as I followed his covers into adventures with Autons, Sea Devils, Zygons, Mummies, Krynoids, Cybermen and more!

Chris handled them all with style and panache and earned himself a place in the hearts and minds of all those who saw and bought the books! He is truly a master among artists!

PICTURES OF WONDER BY GARY RUSSELL

It was a Saturday. I can't tell you the date but it was 1974, close to Easter. It was Woolworths in Maidenhead town centre.

And there, in one of those very seventies display racks that had the covers, not spines, facing forward, I saw the start of the obsession. *Doctor Who and the Day of the Daleks* and *Doctor Who and the Doomsday Weapon*. *Day of the Daleks* came home with me that day, *Doomsday Weapon* a few days later.

Putting aside the fact that these were *Doctor Who* novels, and began my lifelong love (fixation?) with all things Target, the thing that sold me on these books were the covers. These were clever mixes of what I remembered from the old *TV Century 21* Dalek stories my friend Steven used to show around school, plus that marvellous Frank Bellamy *Radio Times* front cover for, ironically, *The Day of the Daleks* two years earlier. Indeed, I assumed the covers *were* by Bellamy until about my fifth reading

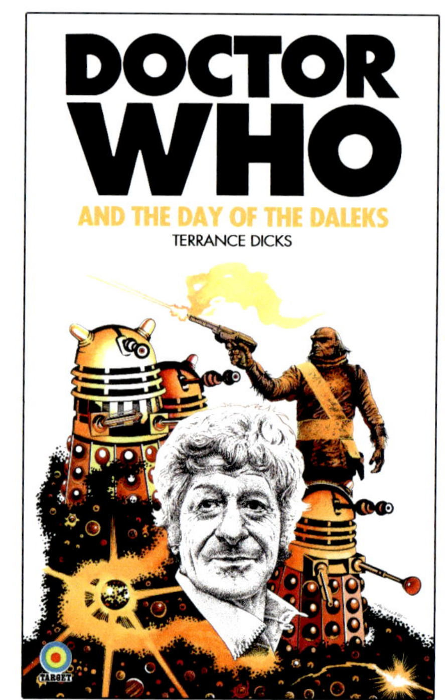

that weekend when I realised the word Achilléos was scrawled on the cover. I looked inside the book – in that boring copyright bit that no child really reads – and saw the name Chris Achilléos for the first time.

Until then, my love of book cover art (I have many books that are just page after page of '60s and '70s paperback book cover art) was restricted to the likes of Leslie Woods, Irene Williamson, Betty Maxey, Margaret Tempest and especially Robin Jacques, whose black and white stippling effects I had adored in the school library for years. Seeing that similar effect used for the Doctor's face on these two books (and a few weeks later when I found *Cave-Monsters*, *Auton Invasion* and the three Hartnell novels) drew me in, and I stared at those early Target covers for years. I loved the words inside but the pictures on the covers were equally important.

One of the teachers at my secondary school had access to a mythical beast known as "the photocopier" and she very kindly photocopied the book covers so myself and a couple of friends could have copies of Chris' work to put on the wall at home. I actually didn't pin them up; instead I stapled the sheets together so I had my own mini-flickbook of his art, albeit in black and white, to stare at endlessly, with new staples adding new pages every so often as books like *The Abominable Snowmen*, *The Curse of Peladon* and finally *The Cybermen* were added to the collection.

Then the shock of the new took hold. On the day I found *The Cybermen* in a shop, sitting next to it was *The Giant Robot*. Gone was Chris Achilléos' subtle and clever stippled faces set against beautifully painted backgrounds and "borrowed" Hal Foster squid monsters and in its place was a garish, colourful pop-art piece by Peter Brookes. And while I came to love the Brookes covers in time, the shock of it not being one of Chris' pieces was gut-wrenching.

But Target fans didn't have to wait long and, after a few months, Chris was back, but, abeit working in a slightly different style. The stippled monochrome Doctor was still there but the backgrounds were now more solid framed paintings (only *Revenge of the Cybermen* offered a true throwback to those early open cover designs of floating heads and Kirby crackle.

This second wave of covers provided us with even more masterpieces – *Carnival of Monsters*, *The Three Doctors*, *The Web of Fear* and the absolute highlight for me at least – the wonder that is *The Dinosaur Invasion*, or as it is affectionately known the world over – *Kklak!*

Eventually Chris would move away for good (well, okay, for forty-two years) and be supplanted by many other amazing artists: Cummings, Skilleter, Little, Geary, Knipe, Pearson, and many, many others. All superb illustrators and painters in their own right.

But for me nothing truly says Target Books, truly says *Doctor Who* in the seventies and truly says ground-breaking, scene-stealing, awe-inspiring and breath-taking like a Chris Achilléos Target cover.

Today I am lucky enough to have a number of Chris' original paintings framed on my wall. And pride of place, the ultimate expression of my love for Chris' work, is the original of *Kklak!* And every time I pass it by and look up at it, I never fail to say, "Thank you, Chris." You made my childhood that little bit better simply because you chose to paint these pictures of wonder.

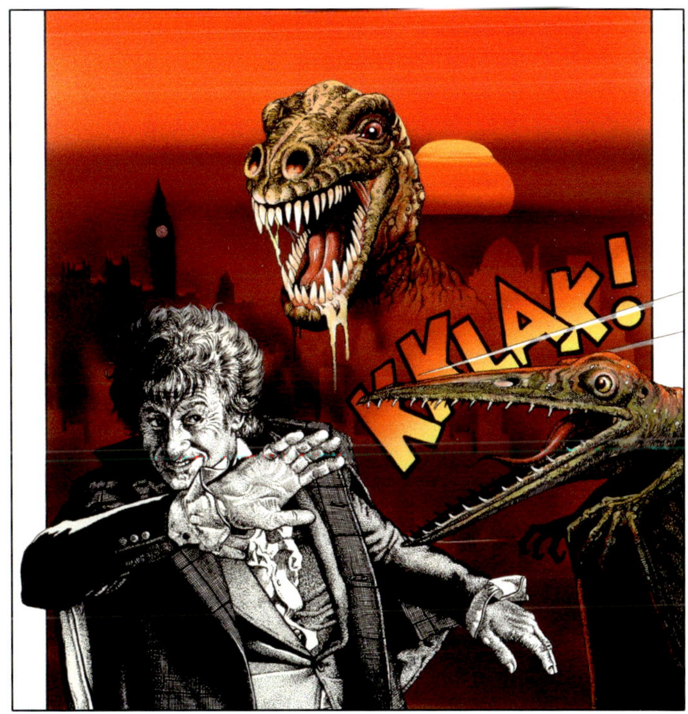

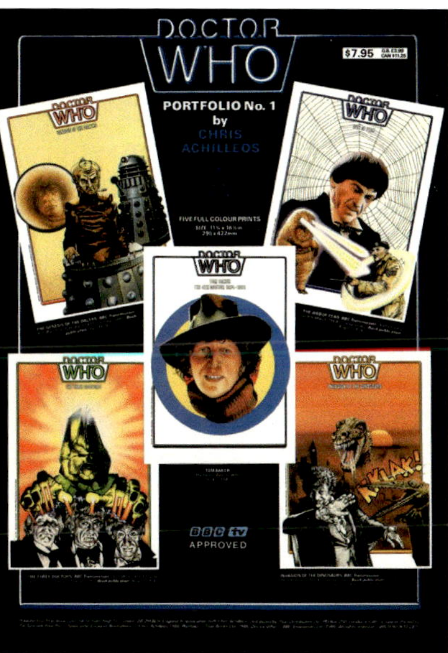

(left) Gary Russell owns the original print of of The Dinosaur Invasion. *(below) Forbidden Planet released some of Chris' prints in the 1980s*

MY IMPRESSION OF CHRIS BY JON CULSHAW

My very first memories of *Doctor Who* go back to around 1971. I'll never forget the sense of my three-year-old self being utterly transfixed by stories such as *The Dæmons*, *The Claws of Axos*, *Day of the Daleks* and endless more.

Jon Pertwee's Doctor was paternal, heroic and created a fantastic atmosphere of pace and adventure against the backdrop of psychological fear. All to be safely experienced while clutching the arm of your chair. It was absolutely irresistible stuff and formed the foundation for a lifetime ahead as an ardent *Doctor Who* fan.

Of course, the early 1970s was an era before iPlayer, catch up TV, YouTube and even video recorders. There was only one other way to get an extra fix of your favourite TV programme, and that was through the range of wonderful Target *Doctor Who* novelisations.

These fantastic books, the majority written by great Terrance Dicks, brought a feeling of joyful impatience to begin reading and keep your head locked into the story right to the very last page.

The first thing that springs to mind about the Target novelisations is the unique and striking manner in which those front covers captured and crystallised all the excitement of the *Doctor Who* adventures contained within. This is singularly thanks to the brilliance and instantly recognisable style created by their great artist, the one and only Chris Achilléos.

I can remember how the art of Chris Achilléos inspired and encouraged me to try to create similar pictures of my own. I have the fondest memories of being a seven-year-old lad in Lancashire with a sketch pad, a packet of felt tip pens and a Bic biro. There I would sit at the kitchen table for many contented hours, emulating that precise point, dot matrix style to build up my picture.

This was the equivalent of 'screen time' back in the 1970s and infinitely preferable in my view.

It was such a great pleasure to meet Chris back in 2017 at 'The Capitol' Convention. He's such a timeless and amiable fellow! There were long queues of fans keen to express in person their appreciation and long held admiration for Chris' art.

I was struck by his very gracious humility with the fans. He showed such warmth and generosity as they were delighted to meet him and share the memories of what his artwork meant to them.

I was there amongst them of course and I couldn't miss the golden opportunity to buy some prints of my favourite stories. Chris was kind enough to sign each one and now my walls are punctuated by *The Sea Devils*, *The Day of the Daleks*, *The Pyramids of Mars* and *Invasion of the Dinosaurs*.

The artwork of Chris Achilléos is simply mesmerising and totally unmistakable. His front cover creations have an explosive sense of movement and action. To me they are the illustrated equivalent in many ways of the *Doctor Who* theme music itself.

Over recent years it's been my honour and great pleasure to record the narrations for many Target novelizations including *The Ark in Space* and *Genesis of the Daleks*.

As I read the text, I always keep a snapshot of a Chris Achilléos cover in my mind's eye. It gives me a focus and I find this helps me to convey the action and urgency of the story as I go along. It helps me recreate the feeling I had all those years ago as I read these same stories when I was young. Just what you need when you're sat for hours on end in a Croydon voice booth. Chris' cover art generates all the tantalising anticipation you need for the impending adventure to come. They act as the perfect gateway to grab you and power you forward into the story. Each cover is a memorable classic in its own right. Chris Achilleos and all of his artworks, illustrations and covers fully deserve their reputation as iconic.

Here's to you, Chris! Kklak !

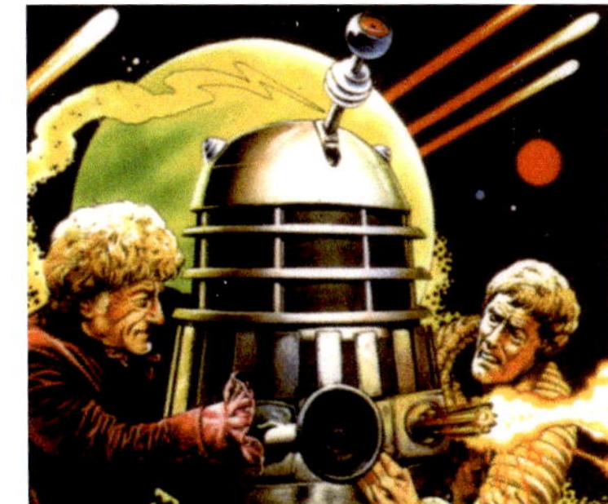

(above) Planet of the Daleks *artwork*
(below) Original Doctor Who
Monster Book *and poster.*

IT'S A FUNNY OLD WORLD BY STEVE PASQUE

My strongest memory of Chris Achilléos' artwork was when I was about seven or eight. A friend had a copy of the original *Doctor Who Monster Book*. I was desperate to get a copy, having missed it in my local John Menzies where I had been getting the novels. My friend wouldn't part with it, even writing his name on the top of the opening page to demonstrate this. No amount of baseball cards, *Star Wars* figures or assorted sweet combinations would prise it from him. I gave in.

Fast forward a few years and I'm looking in a shop in St Andrews, just up the coast from me. Tucked away in the corner is a menagerie of *Doctor Who* books. Most of them I had, but then I notice, on a little plinth, the original edition of the *Doctor Who Monster Book*. Fair condition, good asking price. Turn to the centre to find no poster! Nuts! Hell, I can live with it. I notice some annuals behind and buy a couple.

Getting home I am looking through my treasure trove, flicking through the Baker annual (the frustratingly different-sized one to all the rest) when I find the neatly folded poster from the *Monster Book* in pristine condition. Placing it back in its rightful place, I notice something slightly faded at the top of the opening page: "This book belongs to..." and the name of my old friend.

It's a funny old world!

INSPIRING THE FUTURE BY COLIN HOWARD

It's difficult to put into words just what Christos Achilléos means to me; he is certainly the artist who was most influential on me.

As a youngster in the 1970s I was an avid *Doctor Who* fan, and I would often badger my parents when we were out and about to buy me some of the early Target novelisations, which I would devour over and over again.

Back then there were no VHS tapes or DVDs and the only repeats of *Doctor Who* were few and far between, so those treasured novels were the only way you could re-live those stories or in some cases experience them for the first time!

I would spend hours sometimes just drinking in Chris' fantastic cover artworks, and as I grew older I started to attempt to recreate them in coloured pencils and felt tip pen! The covers for the Monster Books became my artistic bibles and his incredible art spurred me on to fulfil my artistic ambition – to become a *Doctor Who* cover artist.

As I grew older I wanted to explore more of Chris' astounding artwork, so his portfolios: *Beauty & the Beast, Sirens* and *Medusa* became my constant source of inspiration; his mastery of the human form and his love of detail and fantasy were also incredibly inspirational to me, and those impressive volumes were indispensable to me, and still are.

Last year (2019) was my first opportunity since I started freelancing in 1982 to meet Chris (and Tasha). Michelle and I journeyed to the Capitol-DWAS Convention in Crawley, basically just because Chris was due to be there. I was certainly not disappointed. Chris is a lovely human being, and was modest and humble about his achievements and his work.

The awesome Jeff Cummings was also in attendance to complete my line-up of most influential, warm and generous art-icons so this photo just had to be taken... KKLAK!

Thank you, Chris, for all you have done with your art.

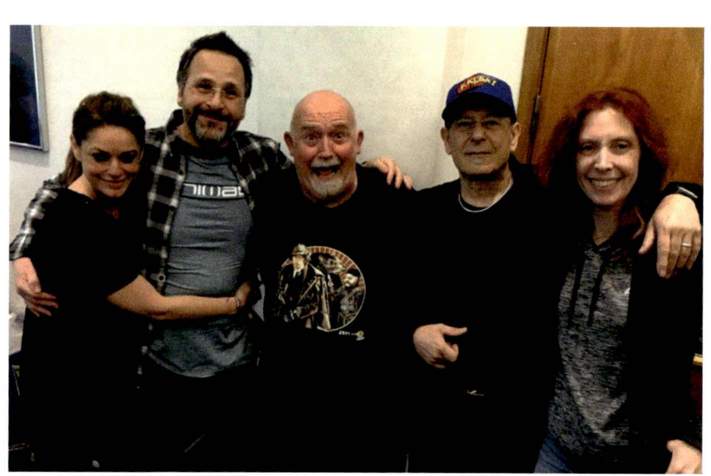

(right) Michelle, Colin, Jeff Cummins, Chris and Natasha.

THE COLOURS IN BETWEEN BY ANDREW CHALMERS

Jumping Jehoshaphat… 1975, what a time that was.

For anyone, now in their 40s (or past them, I type begrudgingly) it was a heck of a time. Saturday. BBC1… around half past five. *Basil Brush*, the English Division One football scores when our dad's sat on the end of their seat, church-like silence in the living room as they dreamed of winning a million on the "pools". Saturday. It was beautiful.

Then we jumped in the TARDIS and off we went. The highlight of the week. The Saturday episode of *Doctor Who*. Saturday night was spent in a blur of excitement as we marvelled about what we had just watched.

What would happen next? Sunday was spent thinking about the episode. Monday was spent talking about it at school.

But it wasn't enough… I wanted more.

My mum told me that there were other Doctors. What? Others? Not just Tom? My imagination fired up. I became a question machine, squeezing more info from my mum, who, let's face it, obviously possessed magical *Doctor Who* knowledge. And made really good chips.

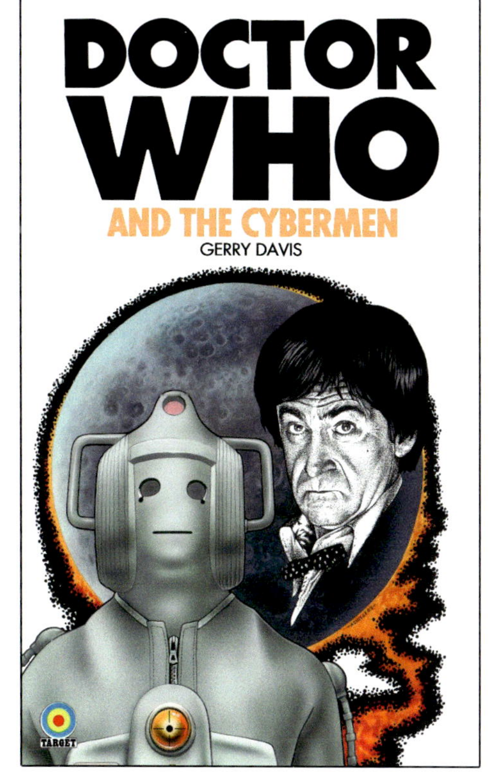

In 1975 I became financially independent. I was five. I was given one pound per week as pocket money. I gazed at this paper note, this wonderful windfall, and wondered what I was going to spend it on. Every Saturday my family went into Edinburgh. Princes Street to be exact. I would run up the stairs in John Menzies. I loved the place. Amazed, I spent an eternity standing in front of rows and rows of Target books. Other Doctors. Other adventures. I now had them. All within reach… unless they were on the top shelf. I was only a little lad.

Usually I did judge the book by its cover. It had to look brilliant. There was only one winner. I spent that pound on a dream. My first? *Doctor Who and the Cybermen* Target book. Great times indeed. I didn't know his name, but the man who illustrated my new *Doctor Who* book cover would be with me for the rest of my life. How did he make all these wee dots into such a galaxy of imagination? I sat there entranced, in the back of my dad's Volvo, reading the books, chewing cola bottles and being mesmerised by the artwork. The wise yet whimsical expression on the Second Doctor's face made me feel as though I knew him already. The cover spoke to me. And the illustration was magnificent.

Now I have Chris's prints on my office wall. I work as a counsellor helping people with disabilities find a job. When clients are having a tough time I often say, "Life isn't always black and white, it's often the colours in between. That's where you truly live, in those colourful moments."

As I say this I point to the artwork, showing the client black, white and then the colours in between. Great art takes you away, transports you – perhaps even protects you. I find that, at those moments, the clients are different – it's a hopeful distraction. I've lost count of the times that I've followed up with clients about their quest for 'the colourful moments'.

Chris made us hopeful and continues to do so. After all, here I am, writing this. With his uncanny ability to capture expression, every brush stroke expertly placed to create the story itself, he fired our imaginations. This imagination was a little flame burning bright in the past. Now, I remember and bring that imagination into the here and now, to inspire myself and people around me. Created and inspired by the sheer brilliance of a visionary artist. What a gift. Thank you, Mr Achilléos. For helping us realise that the hope of yesteryear always burns bright, and every time we see your work, we have the gift of imagination. The gift of hope. Your artistic vision inspired us. We remembered.

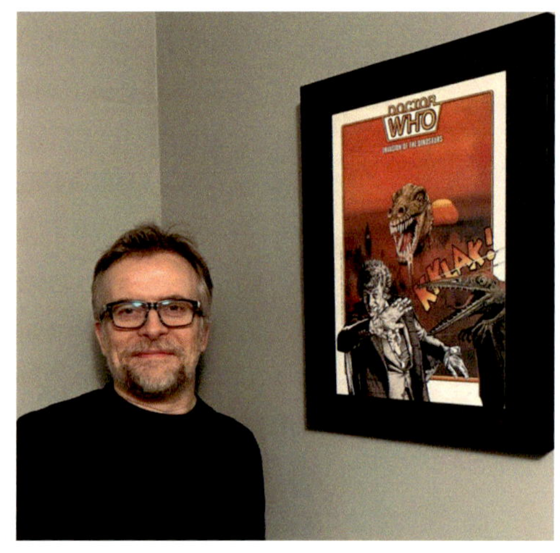

Andrew with the cover for The Dinosaur Invasion.

IF YOU COULD SEE ME NOW BY DAVID BICKERSTAFF

I can't stress how important the *Doctor Who* Target covers were to me all those years ago. I was from a working class family, with very little money coming into the house, so books were low on the priority list. However, my mum always managed to surprise me with one from time to time.

Enter the *Doctor Who Monster Book*. It was the cover that drew me in – a menagerie of the Doctor's enemies. But the icing on the cake (and a brilliant advertising strategy) was showing the covers of the other Target books available. I used to sit for hours (yes, literally!) looking at them, marvelling over the tiny artwork of *The Cybermen*, *The Doomsday Weapon*, *The Three Doctors*, and my favourite *The Abominable Snowmen*.

Around 1977 the book peddler came to Arkleston Primary in Renfrew. On the table was *The Ice Warriors*! I excitedly begged my mum to buy it, and eventually she gave in to my pleading.

It was mine!

As the years progressed, the Target books became my escape from reality, especially from a father whose only interests were alcohol and football. Arguments were frequent in my house, so I'd stay in my room drawing the covers. On days where it was just myself and mum in the house, I'd take the books out and lay them all down. I'd call Mum and ask her to choose her favourite cover. *Genesis of the Daleks* won. In primary 6, my school report said: 'David is a hard-working pupil but must curb his obsession with *Doctor Who* books'. Oh, Mrs Rule, if you could see me now. I owe so much to Chris Achilléos' work, even to this day. I have them all out on my bookcase in my lounge. I can't stress how important the *Doctor Who* Target covers are to me now. Follow your dreams, always. I did.

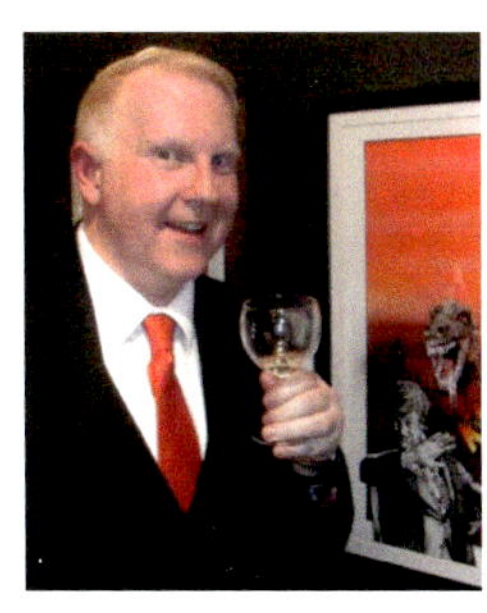

(above) David celebrating Chris' artwork at the Cartoon Museum exhibition 2018.

THANK YOU, CHRIS ACHILLÉOS BY JOHN WAUDBY

It was a Saturday morning sometime back in 1986. I had taken the bus to the long since gone Odyssey 7 bookstore in the Manchester University shopping precinct, off Oxford Road. Chris Achilléos and Nigel Suckling from Paper Tiger publications were there to sign copies of the newly released *Sirens*, the second Achilléos art book. I was sixteen at the time and already had aspirations to become an illustrator of some sort.

As he and Nigel signed and dated the black title page in gold ink, I wanted so much to tell Chris that it was his Target cover illustrations that had so inspired me as an eight-year-old to pick up my very first *Doctor Who* book, *The Cave Monsters*. Coupled with Terrance Dicks' sublime writing, that very book began a lifelong fascination with all things *Doctor Who* and illustration.

But, being a bit tongue-tied, I think I simply thanked him and slipped the still treasured book into a bag.

A whole universe of his work shone out from those pages of *Sirens* – the awesome DWAS poster of *The Five Doctors*, *Fighting Fantasy*, *Lord of the Rings*, *Supergirl*, pin ups and *Star Trek*. Each painted and drawn as vivid and eye-catching as the last.

Chris Achilléos inspired me massively to use varied techniques such as inking with Rotring pens, airbrushing, washes with inks, watercolour, gouache and in later years the digital arena. And I've loved every minute.

To me, Chris Achilléos is one of the greatest fantasy illustrators of all time, and an iconic part of everything that is visual in the *Doctor Who* universe.

I hope he knows how important his art has been to so many people, and it is so good to see that a new generation of fans have been as captivated by his work as I was all those years ago.

Thank you, Chris.

BIBLIOGRAPHY

The Making of Doctor Who, Piccolo, 1972. Reprinted 1976 by Target Books, W. H. Allen & Co Plc.

En De Zarbi's, En De Kruis-Varders, En De Invasie Van Automen, En De Holen-monsters, En De Dag Van De Daleks, En Net Dodelijke Wapen, En De Demen, 1974, RTV, Netherlands. *Doktor Kim: Ve Daleker, Ve Ontonlar, Ve Dalek Baskini, Ven Gizi Silah, Ve Korkunc Karadamlari, Ve Sibermenler*, 1975-76, Remzi Kitabevi, Turkey. *Doctor Who Und Das Komplott Der Daleks, Und Der Schöpper Der Daleks, Un Der Planet Der Daleks*, 1977, Goldman.

Photo of Tom Baker holding the *Doctor Who and the Genesis of the Daleks* novel. We have endeavoured to track down the original photographer but without any success. We have included this picture in good faith. Please contact us if you are the owner and we will make the appropriate amendments.

Quote, David Whitaker, *Doctor Who and the Daleks*, 1964, Frederick Muller Ltd. 1973 (Hardback) Allan Wingate Ltd, UK, (Paperback) Target/Universal Tandem Publishing Co Ltd, UK. ISBN: 0-426-10110-3.
Blurb from *Doctor Who and the Daleks*, 1973, Allan Wingate Ltd, Target/Universal Tandem Publishing.
The audio is available from BBC Audiobooks (7 March 2005) – 978-0563527299
The paperback is available from BBC Books (7 July 2011) – 978-1849901956

Quote, Bill Strutton, *Doctor Who and the Zarbi*, 1964, Frederick Muller Ltd. 1973, (Hardback) Allan Wingate Ltd, UK, (Paperback) Target/Universal Tandem Publishing Co Ltd, UK. ISBN: 0-426-10129-4.
Blurb from *Doctor Who and the Zarbi*, 1973, Allan Wingate Ltd, Target/Universal Tandem Publishing.
The audio is available from BBC Worldwide (7 March 2005) – 978-0563504245
The paperback is available from BBC Books (28 April 2016) – 978-1785940354

Quote, David Whitaker, *Doctor Who and the Crusaders*, 1964, Frederick Muller Ltd. 1973, (Hardback) Allan Wingate Ltd, UK, (Paperback) Target/Universal Tandem Publishing Co Ltd, UK. ISBN: 0-426-10137-5.
Blurb from *Doctor Who and the Crusaders*, 1973, Allan Wingate Ltd, Target/Universal Tandem Publishing.
The audio is available from Audible (16 October 2006) – B002SQFB12
The paperback is available from BBC Books (7 July 2011) – 978-1849901901

Quote, Terrance Dicks, *Doctor Who and the Auton Invasion*, 1974, (Hardback) Allan Wingate Ltd, UK, (Paperback) Target/Universal Tandem Publishing Co Ltd, UK. ISBN: 0-426-10313-0
Blurb from *Doctor Who and the Auton Invasion*, 1974, Allan Wingate Ltd, Target/Universal Tandem Publishing.
The audio is available from BBC Audiobooks (4 June 2008) – 978-1405687669
The paperback is available from BBC Books (7 July 2011) – 978-1849901932

Quote, Malcolm Hulke, *Doctor Who and the Cave-Monsters*, 1974, (Hardback) Allan Wingate Ltd, UK, (Paperback) Target/Universal Tandem Publishing Co Ltd, UK. ISBN: 0-426-10292-4
Blurb from *Doctor Who and the Cave-Monsters*, 1974, Allan Wingate Ltd, Target/Universal Tandem Publishing.
The audio is available from BBC Audiobooks (3 September 2007) – 978-1405677998
The paperback is available from BBC Books (7 July 2011) – 978-1849901949

Quote, Terrance Dicks, *Doctor Who and the Day of the Daleks*, 1974, (Hardback) Allan Wingate Ltd, UK, (Paperback) Target/Universal Tandem Publishing Co Ltd, UK. ISBN: 0-426-10380-7
Blurb from *Doctor Who and the Day of the Daleks*, 1974, Allan Wingate Ltd, Target/Universal Tandem Publishing.
The audio is available from BBC Audiobooks (10 November 2016) – 978-1785293535
The paperback is available from BBC Books (10 May 2012) – 978-1849904735

Quote, Malcolm Hulke, *Doctor Who and the Doomsday Weapon*, 1974, (Hardback) Allan Wingate Ltd, UK, (Paperback) Target/Universal Tandem Publishing Co Ltd, UK. ISBN: 0-426-10372-6
Blurb from *Doctor Who and the Doomsday Weapon*, 1974, Allan Wingate Ltd, Target/Universal Tandem Publishing.
The audio is available from BBC Audiobooks (6 September 2007) – 978-1483016504

Quote, Malcolm Hulke, *Doctor Who and the Dæmons*, 1974, (Hardback) Allan Wingate Ltd, UK, (Paperback) Target/Universal Tandem Publishing Co Ltd, UK. ISBN: 0-426-10444-7
Blurb from *Doctor Who and the Dæmons*, 1974, Allan Wingate Ltd, Target/Universal Tandem Publishing.
The audio is available from BBC Audiobooks (2008) – 978-1405657969
The paperback is available from BBC Books (7 July 2011) – 978-1849901949

Quote, Malcolm Hulke, *Doctor Who and the Sea-Devils*, 1974, (Hardback) Allan Wingate Ltd, UK, (Paperback) Target/Universal Tandem Publishing Co Ltd, UK. ISBN: 0-426-10516-8
Blurb from *Doctor Who and the Sea-Devils*, 1974, Allan Wingate Ltd, Target/Universal Tandem Publishing.
The audio is available from BBC Audiobooks (7 June 2012) – 978-1445824673

Quote, Terrance Dicks, *Doctor Who and the Abominable Snowmen*, 1974, (Hardback) Allan Wingate Ltd, UK, (Paperback) Target/Universal Tandem Publishing Co Ltd, UK. ISBN: 0-426-10583-4
Blurb from *Doctor Who and the Abominable Snowman*, 1974, Allan Wingate Ltd, Target/Universal Tandem Publishing.
The paperback is available from BBC Books (7 July 2011) – 978-1849901925
The audio is available from Audible (23 January 2009) – B00SLTDEDW

Quote, Brian Hayles, *Doctor Who and the Curse of Peladon*, 1975, (Hardback) Allan Wingate Ltd, UK, (Paperback) Target/Universal Tandem Publishing Co Ltd, UK. ISBN: 0-426-10452-8
Blurb from *Doctor Who and the Curse of Peladon*, 1975, Allan Wingate Ltd, Target/Universal Tandem Publishing.
The audio is available from BBC Audiobooks (2 May 2013) – 978-1445826257

Quote, Gerry Davis, *Doctor Who and the Cybermen*, 1975, (Hardback) Allan Wingate Ltd, UK, (Paperback) Target/Universal Tandem Publishing Co Ltd, UK. ISBN: 0-426-10575-3
Blurb from *Doctor Who and the Cybermen*, 1975, Allan Wingate Ltd, Target/Universal Tandem Publishing.
The audio is available from BBC Audiobooks (2008) – 978-1405657969
The paperback is available from BBC Books (7 July 2011) – 978-184990191

Quote, Terrance Dicks, *Doctor Who: The Three Doctors*, 1975, Allan Wingate Ltd, UK, (Paperback) Target/Universal Tandem Publishing Co Ltd, UK. ISBN: 0-426-10938-4
Blurb from *Doctor Who: The Three Doctors*, 1975, Allan Wingate Ltd, Target/Universal Tandem Publishing.
The audio is available from Audible (1 April 2010) – B003F1GPDW
The paperback is available from BBC Books (10 May 2012) – 978-1849904780

Quote, Terrance Dicks, *Doctor Who and the Loch Ness Monster*, 1976, Allan Wingate Ltd, UK, (Paperback) Target/Universal Tandem Publishing Co Ltd, UK. ISBN: 0-426-11041-2
Blurb from *Doctor Who and the Loch Ness Monster*, 1976, Allan Wingate Ltd, Target/Universal Tandem Publishing.
The audio is available from BBC Audiobooks (10 November 2016) – 978-1785293535
The paperback is available from BBC Books (10 May 2012) – 978-1849904759

Quote, Malcolm Hulke, *Doctor Who and the Dinosaur Invasion*, 1976, Allan Wingate Ltd, UK, (Paperback) Target/Universal Tandem Publishing Co Ltd, UK. ISBN: 0-426-10874-4
Blurb from *Doctor Who and the Dinosaur Invasion*, 1976, Allan Wingate Ltd, Target/Universal Tandem Publishing.
The audio is available from Audible (20 November 2007) – B002SQ94ZQ
The paperback is available from BBC Books (28 April 2016) – 978-1785940378

Quote, Gerry Davis, *Doctor Who and the Tenth Planet*, 1976, Allan Wingate Ltd, UK, (Paperback) Target/Universal Tandem Publishing Co Ltd, UK. ISBN: 0-426-11068-4
Blurb from *Doctor Who and the Tenth Planet*, 1976, Allan Wingate Ltd, Target/Universal Tandem Publishing.
The audio is available from BBC Audiobooks (7 December 2017) – 978-1785296567
The paperback is available from BBC Books (10 May 2012) – 978-1849904742

Quote, Brian Hayles, *Doctor Who and Ice Warriors*, 1976, Allan Wingate Ltd, UK, (Paperback) Target/Universal Tandem Publishing Co Ltd, UK. ISBN: 0-426-10866-3
Blurb from *Doctor Who and the Ice Warriors*, 1976, Allan Wingate Ltd, Target/Universal Tandem Publishing.
The audio is available from BBC Audiobooks (7 January 2010) – 978-1408426708
The paperback is available from BBC Books (10 May 2012) – 978-1849904773

Quote, Terrance Dicks, *Doctor Who: The Revenge of the Cybermen,* 1976, Allan Wingate Ltd, UK, (Paperback) Target/Universal Tandem Publishing Co Ltd, UK. ISBN: 0-426-110997-X
Blurb from *Doctor Who: The Revenge of the Cybermen*, 1976, Allan Wingate Ltd, Target/Universal Tandem Publishing.

Quote, Terrance Dicks, *Doctor Who and the Genesis of the Daleks*, 1976, Allan Wingate Ltd, UK, (Paperback) Target/Universal Tandem Publishing Co Ltd, UK. ISBN: 0-426-11260-1
Blurb from *Doctor Who and the Genesis of the Daleks*, 1976, Allan Wingate Ltd, Target/Universal Tandem Publishing.
The audio is available from BBC Audiobooks (5 October 2017) – 978-1785298073
The paperback is available from BBC Books (28 April 2016) – 978-1785940385

Quote, Terrance Dicks, *Doctor Who and the Web of Fear*, 1976, Allan Wingate Ltd, UK, (Paperback) Target/Universal Tandem Publishing Co Ltd, UK. ISBN: 0-426-11084-6
Blurb from *Doctor Who and the Web of Fear*, 1976, Allan Wingate Ltd, Target/Universal Tandem Publishing.
The audio is available from BBC Audiobooks (3 August 2017) – 978-1785296185
The paperback is available from BBC Books (28 April 2016) – 978-1785940361

Quote, Malcolm Hulke, *Doctor Who and the Space War*, 1976, Allan Wingate Ltd, UK, (Paperback) Target/Universal Tandem Publishing Co Ltd, UK. ISBN: 0-426-11033-1
Blurb from *Doctor Who and the Space War,* 1976, Allan Wingate Ltd, Target/Universal Tandem Publishing.
The audio is available from Audible (19 February 2008) – B002SQ6Y54

Quote, Terrance Dicks, *Doctor Who and the Planet of the Daleks*, 1976, Allan Wingate Ltd, UK, (Paperback) Target/Universal Tandem Publishing Co Ltd, UK
Blurb from *Doctor Who and the Planet of the Daleks*, 1976, Allan Wingate Ltd, Target/Universal Tandem Publishing.
The audio is available from BBC Audiobooks (1 June 2013) – 978-1471346569

Quote, Terrance Dicks, *Doctor Who and the Pyramids of Mars*, 1976, Allan Wingate Ltd, UK, (Paperback) Target/Universal Tandem Publishing Co Ltd, UK. ISBN: 0-426-11666-6
Blurb from *Doctor Who and the Pyramids of Mars*, 1976, Allan Wingate Ltd, Target/Universal Tandem Publishing.
The audio is available from BBC Audiobooks (5 January 2010) – 978-1602838239

KKLAK!: THE DOCTOR WHO ART OF CHRIS ACHILLÉOS

Quote, Terrance Dicks, *Doctor Who and the Carnival of Monsters*, 1977, Allan Wingate Ltd, UK, (Paperback) Target/Universal Tandem Publishing Co Ltd, UK. ISBN: 0-426-11025-0
Blurb from *Doctor Who and the Carnival of Monsters*, 1976, Allan Wingate Ltd, Target/Universal Tandem Publishing.
The audio is available from BBC Audiobooks (13 Nov 2014) – 978-1785290039

Quote, Philip Hinchcliffe, *Doctor Who and the Seeds of Doom*, 1977, Allan Wingate Ltd, UK, (Paperback) Target/Universal Tandem Publishing Co Ltd, UK. ISBN: 0-426-11658-5
Blurb from *Doctor Who and the Seeds of Doom*, 1977, Allan Wingate Ltd, Target/Universal Tandem Publishing.
The audio is available from BBC Audiobooks (5 September 2019) – 978-1787537729

Quote, Terrance Dicks, *Doctor Who and the Dalek Invasion of Earth*, 1977, Allan Wingate Ltd, UK, (Paperback) Target/Universal Tandem Publishing Co Ltd, UK. ISBN: 0-426-11244-X
Blurb from *Doctor Who and the Dalek Invasion of Earth*, 1977, Allan Wingate Ltd, Target/Universal Tandem Publishing.
The audio is available from BBC Audiobooks (5 November 2009) – 978-1408409923

Quote, Terrance Dicks, *Doctor Who and the Claws of Axos*, 1977, Allan Wingate Ltd, UK, (Paperback) Target/Universal Tandem Publishing Co Ltd, UK. ISBN: 0-426-11703-4
Blurb from *Doctor Who and the Claws of Axos*, 1977, Allan Wingate Ltd, Target/Universal Tandem Publishing.
The audio is available from BBC Audiobooks (2 June 2016) – 978-1785293191

Quote, Terrance Dicks, *Doctor Who and Ark in Space*, 1977, Allan Wingate Ltd, UK, (Paperback) Target/Universal Tandem Publishing Co Ltd, UK. ISBN: 0-426-11631-3
Blurb from *Doctor Who and the Ark in Space,* 1977, Allan Wingate Ltd, Target/Universal Tandem Publishing.
The audio is available from BBC Audiobooks (16 July 2015) – 978-1785291630
The paperback is available from BBC Books (10 May 2012) – 978-1849904766

The Amazing World of Doctor Who, 1976, World Distributors and Ty-Phoo Tea.
A PDF of this book can be found on the BBC DVD release of *The Face of Evil*.

Quote, Eric Saward, *Doctor Who and the Visitation*, 1982, BBC Books.
Blurb from *Doctor Who: The Visitation*, 2016, BBC Books
The audio is available from BBC Audiobooks (16 July 2015) – 978-1785291630
The paperback is available from BBC Books (28 April 2019) – 978-1785940392

Quote, Philip Martin, *Doctor Who: Vengeance on Varos*, 1988, BBC Books.
Blurb from *Doctor Who: Vengeance on Varos*, 2016, BBC Books.
The audio is available from BBC Audiobooks (7 November 2019) – 978-1787537774
The paperback is available from BBC Books (28 April 2019) – 978-1785940408

Quote, Marc Platt, *Doctor Who: Battlefield*, 1991, BBC Books.
Blurb from *Doctor Who: Battlefield*, 2016, BBC Books.
The audio is available from BBC Audiobooks (7 November 2019) – 978-1787537774
The paperback is available from BBC Books (28 April 2019) – 978-1785940415

Quote, Philip Hinchcliffe, *Doctor Who: The Keys of Marinus*, 1980, W. H. Allen & Co Plc.
Blurb from *Doctor Who: The Keys of Marinus*, 1980, W. H. Allen.

Quote, John Lucarotti, *Doctor Who: The Aztecs*, 1984, W. H. Allen & Co Plc.
Blurb from *Doctor Who: The Aztecs*, 1984, W. H. Allen & Co Plc.
The audio is available from BBC Audiobooks (2 August 2012) – 978-1445891781

Quote, John Peel, *Doctor Who and the Tomb of the Cybermen*, 1978, W. H. Allen & Co Plc.
Blurb from *Doctor Who and the Tomb of the Cybermen*, W. H. Allen & Co Plc.
The audio is available from Audible (1 March 2013) – B00BNDF16Q

Quote, John Peel, *Doctor Who: The Evil of the Daleks*, 1993, Virgin Books.
Blurb from *Doctor Who: The Evil of the Daleks*, 1993, Virgin Books.

Quote, Ian Marter, *Doctor Who: The Invasion*, 1985, W. H. Allen & Co Plc.
Blurb from *Doctor Who: The Invasion*, 1985, W. H. Allen & Co Plc.
The audio is available from BBC Audiobooks (9 January 2006) – 978-0563523277

Quote, Terrance Dicks, *Doctor Who: Inferno*, 1984, W. H. Allen & Co Plc.
Blurb from *Doctor Who: Inferno*, 1984, W. H. Allen & Co Plc.
The audio is available from Audible (2 May 2011) – B004YWGTT6

Quote, Barry Letts, *Doctor Who: The Green Death*, 1975, Allan Wingate Ltd.
Blurb from *Doctor Who: The Green Death*, 1975, Allan Wingate Ltd.
The audio is available from Audible (4 May 2008) – B002SQ6ZYY

Quote, Barry Letts, *Doctor Who: The Brain of Morbius*, 1976, Allan Wingate Ltd.
Blurb from *Doctor Who: The Brain of Morbius*, 1976, Allan Wingate Ltd.
The audio is available from Audible (19 February 2008) – B002SPXNNQ